# KNOW
# YOUR
# PLACE

# KNOW
# YOUR
# PLACE

How society sets us up to fail –
and what we can do about it

# DR FAIZA SHAHEEN

**SIMON &
SCHUSTER**

London · New York · Sydney · Toronto · New Delhi

First published in Great Britain by Simon & Schuster UK Ltd, 2023

Copyright © Faiza Shaheen, 2023

The right of Faiza Shaheen to be identified as the author of this work has been
asserted in accordance with the Copyright, Designs and Patents Act, 1988.

1 3 5 7 9 10 8 6 4 2

Simon & Schuster UK Ltd
1st Floor
222 Gray's Inn Road
London WC1X 8HB

www.simonandschuster.co.uk
www.simonandschuster.com.au
www.simonandschuster.co.in

Simon & Schuster Australia, Sydney
Simon & Schuster India, New Delhi

The author and publishers have made all reasonable efforts to contact
copyright-holders for permission, and apologise for any omissions or errors in the form
of credits given. Corrections may be made to future printings.

A CIP catalogue record for this book
is available from the British Library

Hardback ISBN: 978-1-3985-0537-7
eBook ISBN: 978-1-3985-0538-4

Typeset in Perpetua by M Rules
Printed and Bound in the UK using 100% Renewable Electricity
at CPI Group (UK) Ltd

MIX
Paper | Supporting
responsible forestry
FSC
www.fsc.org
FSC® C171272

# CONTENTS

# PROLOGUE

## TAKING ON THE MAN IN THE MANSION AND LOSING

'Terrorist sympathiser,' they shouted, 'you can't win!' It felt like a grenade had gone off. I had been standing outside the polling station, happy and hopeful under my umbrella, smiling for the camera. Now, two middle-aged men were moving towards me, arms swinging, veins throbbing in their very red faces. My smile fell, panic filled my lungs and I ran into the polling station. As I looked back out of the window, I could see them still standing there, screaming at me. The polling agent immediately called the police, but I still needed to do what I had come here to do. As I crossed the box for 'Faiza Shaheen', I was shaking. It felt like a bad omen, and it was.

The bell had rung on general election day, 12 December 2019. I was standing for Labour in my home constituency of Chingford and Woodford Green in the first winter general election since 1923. It was intense and exciting – and very, very cold. We had worked hard to build a campaign that might finally dispatch the Tory grandee, Iain Duncan Smith. It had been a campaign of major highs. Breaking records on the number of doors knocked, huge US-style rallies and Stormzy – the grime artist whose lyrics had prompted me and a hundred thousand other people to scream 'Fuck Boris' at Glastonbury – retweeting my campaign video. Even the still-ridiculously charming Hugh Grant turned out to support me at a campaign rally. Watching him take questions from local journalists in the Tesco car park in Highams Park was one of the most surreal experiences of my life. It was like a weird political romcom – with hundreds turning up chanting my name, local women falling over themselves to meet Hugh Grant, cutting a 'Faiza and Hugh' rally cake made by a local baker as if it was an engagement party and my husband getting more than slightly jealous.

Even without big draws like Hugh Grant, we had crowds of people coming to support the cause day after day. We would ask at the beginning of every session who was new to campaigning and dozens would put up their hands. People were stopping me in the street to wish me well, some hugging me, others crying and one even buying me flowers. With this much enthusiasm it felt like I really might win.

For a large part of election day it was raining hard. Not one of those average wet days, where drizzle ruins your hair, but a full-on deluge where even your best raincoat struggles. Yet, hundreds of volunteers still turned up, demonstrating their resolve and commitment by knocking on doors to remind those that had said they would vote for me to venture out in the cold to their nearest polling station. Soaking wet and freezing, they would go out time and time again to ensure we got as many people to vote as possible. They truly believed in what we stood for: kindness, equality, addressing the climate emergency, investing in public services and stopping a hard Brexit.

I started the morning at my old bus stop on Chingford Mount, in front of the beautician's where I used to get my eyebrows threaded and across the road from the Greggs I'd spent my teenage years working in. Commuters greeted me with surprised faces. 'This was your bus stop?' 'Yes, I lived down that road' — I pointed to a road with a fish and chip shop on the corner.

It was an unlikely scenario. The daughter of a Fijian car mechanic, someone who had grown up doing the newspaper round and going to the local state schools versus a wealthy man who lives in a mansion and is married to the daughter of a baron. It was the sort of clash that we love to watch in movies.

And for me, it was personal. My mother was one of the thousands of sick and disabled people who had been on the receiving end of Smith's cruel welfare reforms. She had been harassed by benefits assessment officers knocking on her door and putting her through a series of questions about her health that made her feel like she was a criminal. 'I want to work, but I can't' were the sincere words she kept repeating. It still makes my heart hurt when I think about the stress and humiliation she endured.

My mother had heart failure and struggled with her health for many years. After a heart transplant in 2016 my family thought our hopes of a better life for her would finally be realised. We talked about fulfilling her dream to visit Rome, and she told me she couldn't wait to be well enough to attend my speaking events. But three months later we were back in an overcrowded, underfunded NHS A&E, and a few weeks later she was dead.

When cleaning out my mum's house I found files bursting with letters to the benefits office pleading her case and to the council begging for more social care support. Sewn into her lines were her fears, all dignity lost. I cried for hours packing up the house, not just because I missed her, but because she'd suffered more than she needed to as a result of ill-conceived policies designed by people who have very little empathy for those struggling.

This election was also personal because this was the neighbourhood in which I'd grown up, where I'd been born in the local – now crumbling – hospital, where my primary-school teacher hadn't had a pay rise for ten years, where knife crime was on the rise and where my old high street had an increasing number of closed shutters and charity shops. These were the streets where my dad had punched racist skinheads to protect my pregnant mother. If I could win here it would mark a sea change locally.

Iain Duncan Smith had supported the policies that had gutted my local community over the last decade, that had decimated the public services that had lifted me up and given me support when I'd needed it. His policies had directly made my mum's last years of life a misery and the added stress had likely contributed to her early demise. This was more than a political battle, it was a fight for justice for me, my family and all those who found themselves stung by Tory austerity.

Early on in the campaign I was told that the odds were against me. Various betting companies had sided with the Conservative incumbent. This was not a surprise. After all, as someone completely new to politics, I was doing something audacious – taking on the ex-leader of the Conservative Party. And in Chingford and Woodford Green of all places! This seat had been Conservative since the dawn of time; it was once the seat of Winston Churchill, as well as Norman Tebbit. And here I was, a Muslim brown female, the type that Churchill had termed 'beastly' and Tebbit, aka the 'Chingford skinhead', had never wanted here. And to top it all off, the Tories had so much more money to spend on their campaign than we did. It was a classic David versus Goliath scenario, with the added dimension that Goliath had tormented David's dying mum.

But the odds didn't bother me. In front of a crowd of supporters I arrogantly proclaimed that I had beaten the odds my whole lifetime: my school grades, my entry to the University of Oxford, my PhD and professional positions. 'My mum called me Faiza because it means winner in Arabic,' I said at one Saturday rally to loud applause. 'The betting odds mean nothing.' I had done everything that those from privileged backgrounds had done; I wasn't going to let statistics stop me now. Yes, going up against the machine that entrenches power and inequality was daunting, but surely after playing and winning the game for so long, I'd earned my place.

And then came election night.

'Things are looking good.' My campaign manager Mick called me at 1 a.m. from the count. 'Start making your way here.' My heart skipped a beat. How was it possible that it was looking good for me when the exit poll showed things were dire for the Labour Party?

As I walked into the count at Waltham Forest town hall, I could feel the tension. I hadn't been in this high-ceilinged, oak-panelled hall since coming to a colourful Pakistani wedding twenty years ago. I took a deep breath and stood up tall. Stacks of voting ballots lay on the different desks. The officials, who had been there for over five hours counting the ballots, looked tired. There was a breathless silence as everyone turned to look at me. Several smiled, betraying their political allegiance. No one was sure what the result would be.

'Iain Duncan Smith, Conservative Party, 23,481.'

'Geoff Seeff, Liberal Democrats, 2,744.'

'Faiza Shaheen, Labour Party, 22,219.'

*There is no justice*, I remember saying over and over again in my head as I watched Iain Duncan Smith go to the podium to give his victory speech.

As I came off the stage, I hugged my sister. 'What about Mum?' I whispered.

The next few days, as I nursed a broken heart and tried to make sense of what happened, feelings of foolishness crept in. Who did I think I was to beat all the odds? Statistics are my profession, my career! In 2016 I was employed to calculate the chances of a Black working-class person ever becoming politically successful for the BBC documentary *Will Britain Ever Have a Black Prime Minister?* (at odds of 1 in 17 million). I should have known better. I'm not Black, but as a working-class Pakistani-Fijian the odds weren't much better than the 1 in 10 million chance of a Black person going to the University of Oxford and becoming an MP, at least five times higher than the odds of being hit by lightning.[1]

Had I drunk the Kool-Aid and accepted the propaganda, believing that as long as you worked hard you could be anything you wanted to be? Had I bought into Hollywood notions of good triumphing over adversity? Or was it simply that I hadn't worked hard enough or employed the right election strategy? Or maybe, all of the above? Elections are shaped by various factors, many of them out of the control of the candidate, but the promise of social mobility, of meritocracy and the rewards of hard work, suggests that the person who had gone from a local state school to the University of Oxford should win, rather than the person who had lied on his CV.[2] But that was my naivety.

I sank into a malaise. Of course, some of that was ego, but there was also an intense feeling that I had let people down. As the months passed, I found myself looking at the bigger picture and going over calculations I had done for the BBC documentary – finding that while the odds of me going from my household to Oxford and then on to becoming an MP were 1 in 10 million, they were 1 in 10,000 for David Cameron and Boris Johnson. I asked myself – *Why should anyone have to work a thousand times harder than anyone else to do exactly the same thing?* Yes, I had failed, but I had failed within a system that had made it near impossible to get to the point where I could legitimately run to be an MP. The underdog winning makes for a heart-warming, tear-jerking story, but what about all the underdogs that lose? What do their stories teach us?

Some are no doubt reading this and wanting me to say something positive here, to highlight a bright note and talk about the swing to Labour in the constituency. Or perhaps to offer excuses in the form of context: that it wasn't about me but about Brexit, for example. Or to recite warm, fuzzy platitudes that you should never give up on your dreams. That may be so, but as Oscar Wilde supposedly said, 'They've promised that dreams can come true – but forgot to mention that nightmares are dreams, too.' *This book is going to get real. The thing about trying to defy the odds is that most of the time, you lose.*

And this isn't just about politics. Look at almost any industry and you will see the same social mobility tropes trotted out – the one working-class Black person who became a judge, a Hollywood director, a university lecturer – each time with a shallow story of beating the odds, of what made them special, what made them winners. But these exceptions do nothing to shift the odds for the millions of others like them – if anything they create the illusion that anyone can follow the same path.

A society which holds up the examples of those that do beat the odds – by definition the few lucky ones – provides a powerful mythology that ultimately ends up leaving most people in their place and feeling like failures. This is not about giving up or being defeatist – there is far too much at stake to do that. Indeed, I am putting myself up to run as an MP again in Chingford and Woodford Green, exactly because I haven't given up. But we can't keep accepting a game stacked against most of us. *It is time we change the game*, and our first step on this journey is understanding how and why the game is rigged.

# I

# THE EXCEPTION THAT
# PROVES THE RULE

When I was four years old, my mum told me that I would beat the odds. I don't remember much from that age, but the moment she told me my future while she washed me in the bath is still crystal clear. It was as if she had a vision: all of a sudden joy and excitement filled my mum's face, and she told me in Urdu, 'One day, you'll go to the University of Oxford – the best university in the world.' I had never heard of this place before, but in that one sentence she had planted an idea firmly in my head.

Statistically speaking, her belief was misplaced. I was the daughter of a car mechanic with no wealth. Our family of five – me, my two siblings and parents – lived in a two-bedroom house, which we didn't own. My dad was dodgy. Dodgy with money, dodgy with women and dodgy with his fists. The police and debt collectors were not strangers to the doors of the various houses we lived in during my childhood. He had met my mum in Pakistan while on the run from the police, lied to her about what he was doing in the country and stolen her heart. (I'll come back to my father later.)

There was no obvious pathway for a working-class brown girl to make it to an elite university, certainly not through my secondary school – that David Beckham once attended – which, when I started, saw less than 1 in 5 of the pupils achieve 5 A–C grades at GCSE level. Yet fourteen years later, when I got into the University of Oxford, my mum showed no surprise, just delight. She explained that she'd always known, that it was written in the stars. Destiny.

Many books contain these clichéd stories, stories that tell you that anything is possible if you dream big and work hard. People always ask me how I made it given my background, trying to glean how they may also follow that same route, or encourage their children to. It started years ago, when two young, working-class fathers asked me in the Harrods (where I worked during my Christmas holidays as a student) staff canteen. They couldn't believe that I was studying at Oxford and wanted to know how they could get their kids to do the same. Catering for the rich every day, seeing their lives of luxury and buying habits is bound to make you want to be rich too. After a moment of thinking about it, I spoke about my mother and her encouragement and belief in me. I still find myself saying something about this and my luck of being born to her. Yet, the true story of my entry into a British elite university is far from this simplistic. If I tell only this sweet story of a mother's love I would be omitting the community and public investment – including welfare benefits – that I received; the encounters with supportive teachers along the way; and the pure luck of having a race expert in the room when I was interviewed at the University of Oxford.

And, if I go deeper, I need to talk about my journey being in part the product of fear and pain. I grew up in fear: fear of my dad, fear of my dad hitting my mum, fear of being kicked out of our house, fear of my dad leaving and never coming back. I knew the thing I had was my academic talent, and I knew from a young age that this was my ticket out. From my early teens I used to count the stars I could see from the back garden and beg them to let me escape. It was an intense wish, a prayer I repeated dozens of times a day. I then used all the public resources that existed around me, some of which have since been eradicated by successive Conservative governments. My story isn't a nice story, it is one of desperation. It is not something I would want others to go through.

Most importantly, my story, as positive and aspirational as it may seem, is merely the exception that proves the rule. Someone like me getting into the University of Oxford being *unusual* only confirms that it is *usual* for the rich to attend. There are always a handful of outliers – but these outliers are precisely that – outside of the general pattern. In fact, when you look at the statistical likelihood of making this journey, there is under a 0.3 per cent chance that someone similar to me would make it to the University of Oxford, or a 99.7 per cent chance that they wouldn't.[1]

These cookie-cutter and almost impossible to obtain mantels of success are not unique to the UK. In the US, it looks like Oprah Winfrey's and Serena Williams's stories of poverty to mega-rich status, commonly used to show that the American Dream is alive and kicking. Wherever you find extreme inequalities, you find urban legends and wishful movie-esque storylines about the people who 'make it'. And who can blame us for wanting to believe that these rags-to-riches stories can happen to any one of us; after all, without hope in the future what do we have left? There is so much raw talent and a wealth of skills in our working-class neighbourhoods and our council estates – of course the world should allow that talent to blossom.

Yet the world is not that way. It is not just that these exceptions wrongly convey that there is some sort of meritocracy in who gets to 'make it' – that where you end up in society is directly correlated to how many hours you put in. It is a story that points at individual people and their individual efforts, stripping out the role of society, the economy and policymakers. When we focus on the exceptions at the top, we ignore the declining conditions for those left at the bottom and indeed anyone in the middle too. While we tell children that 'anyone can make it as long as they work hard enough', we ignore the fact that if they happen to be working class or part of a marginalised ethnic or racial group, the barriers to success are getting ever higher and the 'hard work' required is becoming ever more unrealistic. And, crucially, while we doggedly focus on being at the top of the ladder, we reinforce an ugly hierarchy of human worth, casting judgement not just on those at the very margins of society but the lowest-paid people who are often critical workers for society – the carers, the cleaners, the rubbish collectors. The idea that going to the University of Oxford, a place that instils a sense of superiority and, at least in my time, taught economics in a way that favours the rich, constitutes 'making it' doesn't say much for the type of society we are celebrating.

While we cling to these falsehoods and seek to reinforce these hierarchies, the rich are retaining their privileges, using their networks to get the top jobs – such as those in finance or property development that often cause harm to society and make things more unequal – and creating loopholes so that they can avoid taxes and get richer. While the majority of us have to 'dream big' and reject our communities in order to 'make it', the rich only need to embrace their reality and stay on the escalator they were put on from birth.

My Oxford education and the privileged spaces I've been allowed into thereafter have given me a peek into this world of the elite. It has brought me up close and personal with the lack of social mobility in society. I've seen that those at the top are often not the most hard-working nor the most talented and I've seen the damage the social mobility lie does to societal progress. I have been around people with generations of wealth and silver spoons. I have sat on panels with high-profile politicians and leading businesspeople. I have been in the houses of ambassadors, where the only other people that looked like me were serving the food. I have been privy to conversations where the 'educated elite' proclaimed Black and Pakistani migrants 'obsolete'. And, on Budget day, while in a BBC green room preparing to talk about the impact of public-spending cuts, heard my fellow panellists flippantly complain about rich Indians taking all their children's places at top private schools.

Think of me as a mole. Someone who has been part of two diametrically opposed universes at the extremes of society. In one life, growing up fighting the cold by sleeping in the same single bed as my sister under a tower of blankets, only to wake up to slimy snail trials on the floor of a house not fit for human habitation in Walthamstow, East London (this was before gentrification, long before Pret turned up). And in another, my adult life, surrounded by gold-leaf wallpaper, cheese platters and sparkling cutlery for every course.

I'm someone that was never meant to be in these rooms. The elite had often forgotten I was there when they said offensive things or told the truth about the favours called in to allow them to progress in life. Or they may well have believed that now I too was in those rooms with them that I had reneged on my working-class roots and socialist values. These experiences have exposed me to just how privileged the privileged are; how power and control work; the extent to which the elite believe they deserve to be at the top while you don't; and how they maintain the status quo through the stories they tell the rest of us and themselves. These encounters are retold in these pages in the hope that they puncture the belief that the rich are at the top because they deserve it, or that they are the smartest of us all, or that notions of the 'top' are helpful at all.

## MISUNDERSTANDING MOBILITY AND MERIT

*'The Britain of the elite is over. The new Britain is a meritocracy.'*

Tony Blair, Commonwealth Heads of Government
Meeting, October 1997[2]

The idea that anyone can make it if they work hard enough, and the use of this belief as an organising principle for society is nothing new and neither are efforts to point out the flaws in this argument. A schoolbook from the 1800s first posed the question 'Why can a man not lift himself by pulling up on his bootstraps?' as a physics problem,[3] accidentally coining a phrase which was used to capture the impossibility of climbing the socio-economic ladder without any outside support. But the biggest twist was that a century later people were using this term to actually tell people to 'pull themselves up by their bootstraps', implying they should achieve through only their own means. How this reversal in meaning happened is anyone's guess, but that it stuck tells us a lot about the political power of the idea. Margaret Thatcher and other right-wing politicians over the years have used 'pull yourself up by your bootstraps' as an individualist vote-winning phrase, but it's based on physical impossibility. Other derivatives of the term have emerged over the years, including from another Conservative MP of Chingford, Norman Tebbit. His famous 1981 speech told people that if they couldn't get a job, they should do what his unemployed dad did, who in the 1930s apparently 'got on his bike and looked for work' — as if it was that easy for the miners who were watching their livelihoods being destroyed around them.[4]

When people talk about the type of society they want, they often refer to social mobility's sister term — meritocracy. A world where the people at the top of society are there purely because of merit, no matter their gender, race, ethnicity or disability. However, rather than being cooked up to show us the way forward, the term meritocracy comes from a satirical book. *The Rise of the Meritocracy, 1870–2033* by socialist Michael Young[5] was written in 1958 as a caution to governments not to pursue the cruel world in which people are left impoverished because their skills don't fit the needs of the economy or what we define as 'making it'. For example, physical strength would have put you at the top of society in medieval times, whereas now knowing how to code gets you ahead. Born at the wrong time, you and your skills could therefore be seen as worthless by the economy. The book describes a world where merit is equated to intelligence plus effort and where government intervenes to identify those with this merit at an early age, selecting them for intensive education, shaped by an obsession with quantification, test-scoring and qualifications. It is a world of intense inequalities between those deemed to have merit and those not, causing polarisation and grievances between groups. It is a dystopian warning rather than a blueprint for equality. Yet, while the book was meant as a warning *not* to follow this route, its effect was the exact opposite.

Young wrote a *Guardian* comment piece in 2001, expressing his dismay that his warning instead became the foundation of New Labour's approach in the 1990s and a term used worldwide to define a litmus test for society.[6] It was a clear sign that the ministers in charge at the time had not read the book, but adopted an idea that sounds good in theory but has very damaging effects in reality.

Then there is the added problem of how we define merit. The Nobel Prize-winning economist Amartya Sen[7] argues that the idea of meritocracy and the very concept of merit itself depend on the lens through which we see a good society and the criteria we invoke to assess its successes and failures. He points out that meritocracy often attaches the label of merit to people rather than *actions*. Therefore, a person with the 'talents', however defined in a particular time and context, is more important than what they use the 'talents' to do – even if what they do has bad consequences for society. What would happen if we considered meritocracy as less about the individual and more about positive collective impact? The difference would be huge – instead of applauding the rich, well-educated property developer, we would focus on the people doing good for society like the carers and teachers who work unpaid overtime to support those struggling.

All over the world, these narratives of merit, success and 'get on your bike' British conservatism or derivatives of the American Dream are used as a stick to beat us and a method for the wool to be pulled over our eyes. It is a social religion that has a stranglehold on equality and human progress. Even if you go back to the advent of the term the 'American Dream', analysis has found that the original meaning was about broader societal well-being, rather than individualism.[8] It's a theory of society that, despite being shown to be wrong repeatedly, persists. The failed ideology of 'anyone can make it as long as they work hard enough', a belief that sits so deeply in so many of our psyches, so deep that many of us no longer question it, is long overdue a reckoning.

But where do we start? While explaining the need to change the rules rather than focusing on being the exception to a group of eager low-income students on an online Zoom seminar a couple of years ago, I was confronted by a bereft fellow speaker who disagreed vehemently. 'We can all be the exceptions,' she asserted. One of the quick-witted students replied on the chat, 'That is statistically impossible.' He took the words out of my mouth. Let's start with the facts.

## SOCIAL IMMOBILITY: HOW BAD IS IT?

The issue of inequality and elitism came alive on my first night at Oxford University. I had spent my summer break working in a mobile-phone shop in Camden Town, which was a dream job for a teenager. At that time, you were instantly more popular when you had the newest phone or could get your mates a phone charger for a fiver. It was also convenient given that I loved shopping for bargain secondhand clothes in Camden Market. That first night I wore some of these purchases: red trousers and a black sleeveless top with a South Asian-style sparkly trimming. It was the perfectly balanced outfit that brought all my loud and ethnic vibes together. But as I walked with others to our freshers' night festivities, I quickly realised that I was a bit too loud and ethnic for this crowd. Looking at the admission statistics to the University of Oxford from 2000, there were only 7 British Pakistani students out of the total 2,928 British residents accepted, which is 0.2 per cent.[9] The 2001 census showed that Pakistanis made up almost 2 per cent of the UK population.[10] There were only 24 Black British students accepted and a total of 2 British Bangladeshis. British Indians at Oxford, who in my experience tended to have gone to private school, were a tiny bit more visible, at 2.5 per cent of the British applicants accepted. Considering I had just left a further education college in Walthamstow where 85 per cent of the students were people of colour, it was a culture shock.

The bar was in a dark and dingy basement and was full of nervous 18- and 19-year-olds. Having come from East London and worked in retail, I was full of chat, which was a huge contrast to some of the more reserved people in the room who looked extremely uncomfortable in a bar setting. Still, whether I was speaking to the awkward ones or the posh drunk ones, everyone seemed to open with the same question.

'What school did you go to?'

I was confused by this. Why would they know my sixth-form further-education college Monoux in Walthamstow? After a couple of hours of watching this conversation play out, it dawned on me that many were replying Eton, Westminster, Winchester, St Paul's, King Edward's and a handful of other schools, most of which I'd never heard of, but all of which turned out to be costly private schools. Students were asking each other this question to categorise people into social groups – the 'in' crowd who did go to these schools versus those of us who didn't even get the premise of the question, let alone understand the culture and ways of being associated with attending those schools.

Later I would come to understand that many of these students' parents had gone to Oxford. Indeed, several of their parents had met there. What I was experiencing in my freshers' week was the echo of generations of wealth and privilege sprouting yet more wealth and privilege.

In 2014, a study by academics at the London School of Economics and the University of California explored the correlation between surnames and social mobility in the UK between the years 1170 and 2012.[11] It found that while the intergenerational correlation for height is 0.64, for Oxbridge attendance there is an intergenerational correlation of between 0.7 and 0.9 – very close to a perfect correlation of 1. In other words, if your parents went to Oxford or Cambridge universities, your chances of going there too are greatly increased – even more likely than you being their height. Your education is your birthright. So how can those of us from less educated backgrounds gain an equal shot at getting in?

The same research, which focused on a range of social markers rather than just income, found that surname status differences can persist for as many as twenty to thirty generations and that this stickiness has not changed for centuries. The authors conclude: 'Even more remarkable is the lack of a sign of any decline in status persistence across major institutional changes, such as the Industrial Revolution of the eighteenth century, the spread of universal schooling in the late nineteenth century, or the rise of the social democratic state in the twentieth century. Status persistence measured by education status is just as strong now as in the preindustrial era.'

What is more, when they examined and compared surnames in a diverse set of countries, the study found that fate is determined by ancestry in almost all societies. Countries as different as the United States, China, the United Kingdom and Japan all have similarly low social mobility rates.

In a book published on the data in 2015, *The Son Also Rises*, the author Gregory Clark claims[12] that this lack of mobility is 'a universal constant'; over time, we thrive or not according to a 'social law of motion', a 'social physics of intergenerational mobility'. And to make matters worse, the universal speed at which families and groups change their social position is slow – a lot slower than everyone thinks based on previous research. In 2018, the Organisation for Economic Co-operation and

Development (OECD, a think tank for rich countries) found that on average it took 4.5 generations across the 24 countries they surveyed for those born in low-income families, defined as the bottom 10 per cent of households, to earn the mean income for that society. For the UK it was 5 generations. Taking a measurement of a generation of 25 years, it would be your great-great-grandad who was working class! In South Africa, with their recent history of racial apartheid, it was 9 generations. Even in Norway, one of the most equal countries in the world, it was 2.[13]

Research by academics at the University of Oxford and the London School of Economics examining 120 years of data from the UK's anthology of the rich, *Who's Who*, mapped the changing relationship between Britain's most elite private schools – the nine 'Clarendon schools' (Eton, Harrow, Winchester, Rugby, Westminster, Charterhouse, Shrewsbury, Merchant Taylors' and St Paul's) – and recruitment into the *Who's Who* list. Old boys who attended Clarendon schools are 94 times more likely to enter *Who's Who* than those attending any other school.[14]

My parents had always told me that I needed to work twice as hard to overcome the race and income barriers ahead of me, warning me that this would be the only way I'd get anywhere. 'You have to be so good that they can't function without you,' is what my dad used to tell me. But even though this is already a lot of pressure to put on a child, the numbers demonstrate that working twice as hard is not enough. Our current system demands that we have to work multiple times harder to play catch-up but how can someone make up for centuries of privilege in just one lifetime?

If you strip out all the wider markers of social status and just look at general income mobility while ignoring the extremes at the very top and dividing the income spectrum into five quintiles, the picture is dire. Analysis by Lee Elliot Major and Stephen Machin[15] charts how Britain has become less mobile over generations since 1958, although there is a lively debate about this shift.[16] In 1958, 25 per cent of sons born in the most impoverished homes remained among those on the lowest incomes as adults, while 32 per cent of those born into the richest families stayed among the top earners when they grew up. Twelve years later, in 1970, this had increased to 33 per cent of sons from the poorest backgrounds remaining among those on the lowest earnings as adults and over 40 per cent of those born into the richest 20 per cent of society remained there as adults. By 2020, a survey across the UK found that nearly half feel they have a worse standard of living than the previous generation and only 29 per cent felt they had better job security.[17]

Unless there is an expansion of middle-level jobs, like well-paid non-graduate jobs insulating homes, the movement at the top and bottom is directly related. If the rich don't move downwards, how can the poor move upwards? The world of social mobility is zero-sum – one person's gain depends on another moving down. Given the stakes of being at the top, it's no surprise that the system is rigged to protect the status quo.

In short, while the narrative is that anyone can be rich if they work hard enough, the truth is it is a big help to be rich in the first place. In the UK in 2019, our top actors were 6 times more likely to have attended a private school than the general population.[18] Sixty-one per cent of doctors went to private school, just over half of print journalists, 71 per cent of barristers and almost three-quarters (74 per cent) of those in judiciary positions, even though only 7 per cent of the population actually attended private school.[19] Again, these ratios have either stalled or got worse in recent years, because the underlying drivers of social immobility – including wealth accumulation, opportunities for well-paid jobs, investment in state education and public services – have worsened.[20] Anyone would look across the most coveted industries and think the only people with talent in this country are those with rich parents. Meanwhile, the very same politicians who have overseen the society and economy that has delivered this hierarchy of life changes tell us they are focused on increasing opportunities. Social mobility is more a game of musical statues than musical chairs.

When you look across high-income countries, the USA and the UK top the charts for the lowest levels of intergenerational social mobility measuring the association between parent-to-child income associations. Meanwhile, countries like Sweden and Norway have higher income mobility levels.[21, 22] As has been said before, if you want the American Dream, move to Sweden.[23] Sweden, though, has higher wages, a smaller gap between the rich and poor and a low-cost, high-quality universal childcare system, which is a hint at what needs to happen to truly deliver a society with more social mobility. This is the type of real and concrete change we should be focusing our efforts on.

## THE FLAW IN THE SOCIAL MOBILITY ARGUMENT: THERE'S NOT ENOUGH ROOM AT THE TOP

*'The reason they call it the American Dream is because you have to be asleep to believe it.'*

George Carlin, *Brain Droppings* (1997)[24]

Given the stickiness of the social hierarchy, what would it take for you to be the exception to make it? Entry to the universities of Oxford and Cambridge (in elite lingo, Oxbridge) has come to dominate our definition of success in the British education system, but how many can be deemed to be successful under this metric? Only 1 per cent of the population will attend these universities and even now after decades of pressure and improvement, different measures across the universities put the proportion of those from low-income backgrounds at just 7 per cent.[25, 26] Before recent improvements in figures, it was the norm for the universities of Oxford and Cambridge to be the subject of headlines such as 'Oxford university under fire after admitting only one Black Caribbean student'[27] and for them to have only a handful of students from the north of the country versus hundreds from just one London borough.[28] However, even if the chances were equal among socio-economic groups, only a thousand or so young people from poor households would enter these two elite educational institutions, simply because there are so few places. This is an elitist model of success, hence the majority will always be excluded.

Conversely, in this system 'failure' is inevitable for a large proportion of the population. A 2017 survey in the United States found that 20 per cent of young people want to be athletes, actors or singers: taking those in professional roles and on IMDB, this at most only adds up to 1 per cent of the population in the US. Some 15 per cent of respondents said they would like a job as a doctor, nurse, veterinarian, pharmacist and/or dentist: only 6 per cent get to do these jobs. Meanwhile, 0 per cent wanted to be in office or administrative roles, yet this is where 15 per cent of the American workforce currently work[29] – that is a lot of disappointment waiting on the horizon.

Here in the UK there are similar gaps between expectations and reality. The Office for National Statistics (ONS) captured the top five jobs chosen as what 16- to 21-year-olds wanted to do, versus what they were actually doing five years later in 2017. Again, jobs that would make one famous were at the top, with almost 12 per cent wanting to be in the artistic, literary or media industry: five years later less than 2 per cent were working in these jobs. For those that wanted to be health professionals, the gap was smaller, with over 8 per cent saying they wanted these jobs and just under 2 per cent actually working in them five years later. So 3 in 4 young people ended up unable to fulfil their career aspirations.[30] But before you say these young people should have worked harder, remember this – there are not an endless number of medical schools, news articles being written or films being made. *There is only so much room at the top.*

Kevin Courtney, the joint general secretary of the biggest UK teaching union, the National Education Union, explained the rationing system within education in an online event I helped convene in 2020. Kevin is a gentle giant at six foot seven and full to the brim with wisdom. A former physics teacher, his years of experience in keeping teenagers engaged means he knows how to pack a punch when giving speeches. 'Success is rationed,' he explained, 'every year thirty per cent of students have to get a poor or failing grade in English – the native language of the UK!' Ofqual (Office of Qualifications and Examinations Regulation) sets the grade boundaries depending on the scores, so the mark you need to get a passing grade changes every year.

So in a 'high-achieving' year, the 30 per cent boundary might mean including a pupil who had scored 60 per cent in an exam and certainly had not failed in any real sense – and yet they would achieve a failing grade. Far from grade inflation, which is often touted by older generations who insist that young people have it easier these days, after forty years in education Kevin has found that 'no matter how hard the pupils and teachers work, there will always be roughly thirty per cent who will fail.'

This rationing of success continues throughout life – who gets the coveted internships, the top jobs and the biggest houses. Not everyone can be winners or the exceptions, but should, at the end of all this rationing, so many people be deemed losers? It begs the question: why would we design society in such a way as to ration success? And with the stakes so high, who gets to win? You can probably guess.

## THE CASE OF PRIME MINISTER SUNAK: NOT THE EXCEPTION, BUT THE RULE

*'People want me to be proud of a brown politician who voted against extending free school meals simply because I also have brown skin . . . until my dying breath it'll be a no.'*

Poorna Bell, tweet, October 2022[31]

As the third Conservative Party leadership contest in six years kicked off in July 2022, I was inundated with journalists asking me to comment on the diversity of the contenders. The questions were all very skewed towards seeing this diversity as a triumph. What does it say about progress in the UK? Modern Britain? About who can be successful in Tory Britain and the opportunities available to women and people of colour within the Conservative Party? I had to burst the bubble. Yes, Liz Truss is female, but what's to celebrate when her platform is about making the rich richer? Suella Braverman may be the child of immigrants, but she is committed to the immoral and inhumane policy of deporting those people claiming asylum in the UK to Rwanda. Later, when Kwasi Kwarteng became chancellor, I had to remind people that he is another Etonian – but even if he wasn't, what use is having the first Black chancellor when his first mini-budget in the midst of rising energy costs handed a top banker earning £2.5 million a tax cut of £117,000, while a teacher on a starting salary of £25,700 would see a tax rise of £121 per year?[32] This is *not* progress and this is *not* good for social mobility.

This line of enquiry and blind enthusiasm ramped up when Liz Truss's disastrous forty-five days as prime minister left Rishi Sunak as the only viable candidate to take on the premiership. Rishi Sunak – the richest MP to ever set foot in Parliament and listed in the *Sunday Times* Rich List 2022, a database of the thousand richest individuals in the UK – is the first prime minister from a minority ethnic community in the UK. This is a first, but his journey is not a shining example of social mobility. Rather, his trajectory emulates the majority of the prime ministers that have come before him.

Rishi Sunak was born to a doctor and a pharmacist, a strong middle-class background but not the kind of elite family history of David Cameron.[33] However, it did mean he was able to have an elite education. He first attended Stroud School, a preparatory school in Romsey, followed by one of the most elite schools in the country, and part of the Clarendon club of schools, Winchester College. From there he went on to the University of Oxford. Top elite private school, to Oxbridge, into Parliament and then to PM is actually a very standard route – more than half of all our prime ministers have taken this path. He also stopped in at the City, specifically at Goldman Sachs, on his way to becoming a politician, again strengthening his establishment pedigree.

The other problem with using Sunak as an example of

social mobility is that he hasn't won a general election; he barely won a Conservative leadership race. Sunak did not win against Liz Truss in the July–September 2022 leadership election. He was unable to command the faith of the majority of the less than 142,000 Conservative members who voted. In October 2022, MPs had to race to block the shameless Boris Johnson from running again because if the vote had gone to the Conservative Party members instead of just the party MPs there was a strong sense that Johnson would have beaten Sunak. Those that were using Sunak to say that we are now a country that sees beyond race and ethnicity[34] were conveniently leaving out that only a few hundred Conservative MPs were able to choose him to become prime minister; no one else had a say.

Sunak's elite schools, his time working in finance and his very rich wife, Akshata Murthy, the daughter of the Indian billionaire businessman who co-founded Infosys, meant he also had a rich pool of people to fund his leadership campaign. He received half a million pounds in donations for his first leadership bid, more than Liz Truss, as well as a gifted office space and had a private jet at his disposal.[35] Donors included Michael Farmer, hedge-fund boss and metals-trading multimillionaire, property investor Nick Leslau and a number of people with strong links and investment in the oil and gas industry.[36]

Far from being a sign that the UK is a country where anyone can make it to the top, Rishi Sunak becoming prime minister only further demonstrates the reality that a very small club of people, educated in our most elite institutions, with the most lucrative connections, can reach the most coveted positions in society. It is telling that someone who is an actual exception in politics – the deputy leader of the Labour Party Angela Rayner, who was formerly a care worker – has found herself subject to flagrant class prejudice from the Conservatives and mainstream press.[37]

## THE INCONVENIENT TRUTH

In 2021, Elon Musk, the entrepreneur, industrial designer and prolific businessman, famous for electric cars, getting high with Joe Rogan on his podcast, space travel and later undermining Twitter, was crowned the richest man in the world. To mark the occasion, the BBC published an article 'Elon Musk's six secrets to business success', the six secrets being: '1. It isn't about the money, 2. Pursue your passions, 3. Don't be afraid to think big, 4. Be ready to take risks, 5. Ignore the criticism, 6. Enjoy yourself.'[38] It was a classic example of the way in which we treat the rich. Instead of thinking about the privileges or luck he had, or the way he conducts his businesses, it sought to hold him up as a shining example of humankind, someone that any of us could and should want to be.

Nowhere in this list was there the most obvious factor – the pure luck and privilege of being born white in apartheid South Africa. He was born into a society at a time where literally everything was set up for him to succeed, a society that told him he was superior, while ensuring Black people were denigrated and held back. All the opportunities were reserved strictly for people of his skin colour; Musk didn't need to compete with the majority of the population. They had also missed that his dad was well-off enough to buy him a computer and send him to an early computer conference in South Africa in the 1980s;[39] the $5 billion in grants he has received from the US government (aka US taxpayers) for Tesla and SpaceX;[40] and the various serious reports of low wages and mistreatment of workers in his various factories.[41,42]

How does it change the picture when we bring in these factors too? This is what we will explore throughout this book, and the short answer is, *a lot.*

## THE ELEPHANT IN THE ROOM

*'I was icily determined — more determined, really, than I then knew — never to make my peace with the ghetto but to die and go to Hell before I would let any white man spit on me, before I would accept my "place" in this republic.'*

James Baldwin, *The Fire Next Time* (1963)[43]

*'If your dream only includes you, it's too small.'*

Ava DuVernay, tweet, February 2015[44]

Let me be clear: I'm not saying that we shouldn't dream big or that we shouldn't work hard. So many of the people we admire most in the world are those that beat the odds. My mum instilled a sense of possibility that meant I could make the most of the resources available to me and the luck that came my way. We need to feel like we can control things in our lives, otherwise we might as well give up. It is hard to puncture the notion of 'you can be whatever you want to be' even after all the work I've done that has shown that this is almost always true for the rich and seldom true for the poorest. But it is vital.

There are things we *can* control, but also so much we *can't*. It is important to grasp that the things that we can't control as individuals, and that make our lives more difficult, are getting worse. The two key drivers of low social mobility – economic and educational inequality – are on the rise. Over thirteen years of spending cuts and the trashing of all our public services – from the NHS to our energy system – means that even the middle class will struggle to live good lives and certainly will see their children's standard of life decline – and that is without considering the climate emergency. A global survey in 2023 found that only 23 per cent of the UK population felt that their family would be better off in five years' time. That is a lot of pessimism about the future.[45]

There are no quick fixes to inequality. While symbolism and representation can be powerful, they are not – on their own – transformative change. Social mobility *is* a fairy tale. In simple statistical terms, *it is a lie*. It is a lie now, it was a lie twenty years ago and a lie two hundred years ago. The promise of making it one day may be the pick-me-up that helps many get through the day, but it is also a false hope for many of us. The inconvenient and often unmentioned truth is that for a few to climb the ladder most must remain on the lower rungs, living in increasingly desperate conditions. The politics of social mobility keep most of us in our place and do not give people the chance of a happy and fulfilling life. That's not acceptable.

# 2

# 'ASPIRATION NATION': THE POLITICS OF SOCIAL MOBILITY AND OPPORTUNITY

*'This is personal for me. Every opportunity I've had in life began with the education I was so fortunate to receive. And it's the single most important reason why I came into politics: to give every child the highest possible standard of education.'*

Rishi Sunak, speech, January 2023[1]

*'We will transform Britain into an aspiration nation ... with high-paying jobs, safe streets and where everyone everywhere has the opportunities they deserve.'*

Liz Truss, first statement as PM, September 2022[2]

*'Indeed the best way to level up and to expand opportunity is to give every kid in the country a superb education, so that is why we are levelling up education funding across the country.'*

Boris Johnson, Conservative Party Conference, October 2019[3]

*'I want Britain to be the world's great meritocracy – a country where everyone has a fair chance to go as far as their talent and their hard work will allow.'*

Theresa May, speech, September 2016[4]

*'We are the party of the want-to-be-better-off, those who strive to make a better life for themselves and their families – and we should never, ever be ashamed of saying so . . . Line one, rule one of being a Conservative is that it's not where you've come from that counts, it's where you are going.'*

David Cameron, Conservative Party Conference, October 2012[5]

*'Let us affirm that in return for opportunity for all that we expect and demand responsibility from all: to learn English, to contribute to and respect the culture we have built together.'*

Gordon Brown, special Labour Party Conference, June 2007[6]

*'I want to see social mobility, as it did for the decades after the war, rising once again.'*

Tony Blair, speech, October 2004[7]

Can you imagine being asked to play a game of Monopoly where of the ten players (yes, I know you can only actually have up to eight, but bear with me), one player has been given four times the amount of money you have and can take the first three rolls of the dice? What would you do? Most would refuse to play and demand things are made fairer – yet this is the equivalent to how we live in society. In 2022, the top 10 per cent of UK earners received 4 times more than the bottom 10 per cent, when including earnings from work, benefits and investment income, with taxes deducted.[8] This gap gets even more pronounced when you consider wealth, where those individuals in the top 10 per cent have average wealth hundreds of times bigger than those even in the bottom 20 or 30 per cent. In fact, those in the bottom 10 per cent have next to nothing once insecure credit-card debt and short-term loans are taken into account.[9] The top 10 per cent have half of all wealth in Great Britain, whereas those in the bottom 50 per cent have just 5 per cent of the wealth in total![10] Despite the huge odds in their favour, when the privileged player inevitably wins the game, we celebrate them as if the playing field is equal.

This injustice is how the myth of social mobility works – and every prime minister in the UK for the past forty years has perpetuated the lie. The language of social mobility, meritocracy, opportunity and aspiration is the common currency among our political leaders, with each one promising to deliver the fabled 'aspiration nation'.

Meanwhile, as I will chart in this book, it has become more expensive to be educated to degree level, harder to buy a house and more difficult to earn a decent wage. Despite the rhetoric, politician after politician has avoided taking the decisions that would genuinely address privilege and elitism, which keeps wealth in the same families, while increasingly painting those who are struggling as lazy. The situation has become so absurd, that short-lived prime minister Liz Truss talked about an 'aspiration nation' and tax cuts for the rich in the same speeches. The language of opportunity has become a political calling card, justifying a country of winners and losers.

So why would our leading politicians want to dupe us into thinking that our hardship is primarily because of our own lack of effort or hard work? Simple: because then they don't have to do anything to change the system that ensured their own success.

## THE SOCIAL MOBILITY SCORECARD

To be fair, between 1997 and 2010, the New Labour government did put some money behind their rhetoric of social mobility. However, they forgot, or perhaps wilfully ignored, that in the hierarchical and zero-sum nature of social mobility, if they want the poor to move up, the rich must move down. Under Tony Blair and Gordon Brown, spending increased quickly, especially on schools with the poorest kids, and was complemented by multiple regeneration and investment programmes in the most deprived areas as well as more generous benefits for low-income families.[11] While child poverty decreased dramatically, this investment did not result in greater social mobility, with one study concluding that a child born in 2000 had roughly the same life chances as a child born in 1970.[12]

Why did all this spending fail to achieve its desired effects? During this same period, private school fees doubled, bankers' bonuses more than trebled[13] and CEO pay for the top bosses ballooned.[14] These outcomes were not accidents. Tony Blair's chief strategist, Peter Mandelson, famously proclaimed, 'We are intensely relaxed about people getting filthy rich as long as they pay their taxes.'[15] Tony Blair and his government hadn't done the maths – with the rich richer than ever, there was still no place for the middle class, let alone the working class, to find their way to the top. The rich were increasingly blocking the cogs of social mobility.

The New Labour approach was akin to giving more money to the poor players at the beginning of the Monopoly game, while failing to notice that the rich had gained even more. The richest 1 per cent had seen their share of income increase from just under 7 per cent to almost 9 per cent, an increase of 25 per cent.[16]

While Blair and Brown tried and failed, David Cameron and Theresa May didn't even try. Both prime ministers presided over real-term cuts in funding to education and welfare.[17] The wages of low- and middle-income earners stagnated.[18] The 2010s saw the closure of thousands of Sure Start centres for children growing up in deprived areas and reductions in regeneration and community funding, with the poorest communities most affected.[19]

Some might chalk this up to bad policy but this wasn't just about misguided mistakes. By 2010, and after the experiments of the Blair years, there was ample evidence to show tackling low social mobility requires addressing overall levels of income and wealth inequality.[20] Yet under David Cameron there were tax cuts for the richest and — as it later emerged — he had benefitted from loopholes which allowed him to avoid paying any tax on the £300,000 he inherited from his father.[21] In the decade after the financial crisis of 2008, while the number of food parcels handed out at food banks rose from the thousands to over a million,[22] the *Sunday Times* Rich List recorded a doubling in the wealth for the richest thousand individuals.[23]

Policies were so contrary to delivering on promises of a meritocratic society that the Social Mobility Commission's entire board quit dramatically in December 2017. Its chair, ex-Labour minister Alan Milburn, claimed there was 'little hope' of the then prime minister Theresa May translating her rhetoric on social justice into real, meaningful change.[24] Within a year, a new set of social mobility commissioners were found, the work continued as if nothing ever happened, with a notable absence of direct criticism of the government.[25]

And so the social-mobility circus continued. Under Boris Johnson, in its manifesto in 2019[26] the Conservative Party said it would be 'levelling up every part of the UK', providing a few vague bullet points on how it would invest more in towns, cities and rural and coastal areas outside of London, and provide more funding for apprenticeships. Later, in a 2020 White Paper, they provided a few more details, opening up applications for a £4.8 billion 'levelling-up fund', which promised to invest in infrastructure such as town centres and local transport, as well as freeports – special areas within the UK's borders where different economic regulations apply, including lower taxes – to supposedly help deprived communities.

You might look at this list and say job done. After years of people like me arguing that inequality is a major issue in the UK, there seems to be a political consensus that regional inequalities need to be addressed. A government that puts levelling up at the heart of its policy agenda may sound like the right match. But from a policy standpoint the agenda is flawed in design.

Take freeports: previous freeports in the UK have too often resulted in jobs being moved from one place to another, rather than creating all new jobs,[27, 28] so companies can avoid tax! In other areas, such as skills investment, the money they are putting in doesn't even take us back to 2010 levels. The budgets for public services – and indeed many of the services important for social mobility – have been completely decimated. One billion pounds was cut from youth services in England and Wales, a cut of 70 per cent in real terms resulting in the loss of 750 youth centres and more than 4,500 youth workers.[29] A third of all libraries have closed amid a 44 per cent reduction in spending since 2010.[30] All English local authorities had reduced spending on such provision since 2010, but the extent of this varied from a 5 per cent cut in East Sussex to 69 per cent in Barking and Dagenham.[31]

Then there are all the contradictions between the words and actions of the Tories since the policy was introduced in 2020. Spouting 'levelling up' while condemning footballers wanting to fight for racial justice,[32] cutting Universal Credit,[33] using the cover of Covid-19 and suspended rules of procurement to give rich friends and relatives contracts worth billions of pounds[34] and showing blatant disregard for political leaders in cities across the Midlands and the North when planning responses to Covid-19 lockdowns.[35] The government has contradicted their levelling-up agenda again and again. At the time of the local elections in May 2022, researchers at the University of West London found that 61 per cent of England's most deprived areas had not been allocated any money from the £4.8 billion levelling-up fund.[36] It was revealed that the government scheme designed to replace targeted funding from the EU would leave the regions of England almost £80 million a year worse off.[37]

Prime Minister Rishi Sunak actually seems to be proud of changing the formula of funding to advantage already affluent areas, boasting in one of his leadership campaign events about taking money that would have gone to 'deprived urban areas' and putting it into wealthy towns like Tunbridge Wells in Kent, which has a sizable Conservative majority.[38] Indeed, it later emerged that his own constituency, in wealthy rural Yorkshire, would receive £19.1 million from a £2.1 billion 'levelling-up' fund released in 2023.[39]

The already weak infrastructure of social mobility has been systematically dismantled with tokenistic attempts to repair the damage. It is extremely frustrating that the Conservatives can get away with lighting the fire and then be applauded for putting out part of the fire. In reality, they have been *levelling down* the UK for the past thirteen years.

In total, the agenda is a facade. Since first used by Boris Johnson in July 2019, the stated headline aim of levelling up is largely used as a rhetorical instrument. As a political tool, it has been used to erase and delegitimise other types of inequality, most notably gender and race. It is now a part of the lexicon of a culture war that pits working-class groups in the North and South against each other, distracting us from growing wealth concentrations at the top of society. Perhaps someone should have asked him what he wanted to level up to? Was it to Etonian standards of education? Eton costs over £46,000 a year,[40] whereas a state school education is £6,970 a year[41] – that is a gap I can't imagine we will fill.

In 2022, for Liz Truss, the fourth Conservative prime minister in six years, taxes were a symbol of 'anti-aspiration' and her ill-fated mini-budget moved to reduce taxes on the rich and remove the cap on bankers' bonuses. Truss and her chancellor, Kwasi Kwarteng, reheated ideas that not only linked back to Peter Mandelson's dismissal of the need to think about how much richer the rich are getting, but to the Thatcher and Reagan era economics of the 1980s. This full embrace of 'trickle-down economics', where the wealth of the richest flows down to the rest of us, was thankfully met by widespread condemnation. As the markets tanked, and Kwarteng and Truss were swiftly deposed, the Conservatives walked back some of the tax cuts but decided to stick with the move to enrich bankers through allowing higher bonuses.

A short, potted policy history of social mobility proves that the problem goes much deeper than politicians would like us to believe. We need a fundamental reset on how we define winning and losing in society. So far, policies have actually been designed to keep us in our place rather than give us all a fair chance.

## THE OTHER SIDE OF THE OPPORTUNITY AND SOCIAL MOBILITY RHETORIC

Politicians like to portray themselves as champions of opportunity and social mobility, but they also actively push a story of failure. This may seem contradictory, but by establishing the 'winners' as those that get to the top of the income spectrum, proponents of the social mobility concept also set up a narrative of 'losers'. Over the years, politicians have developed a formal 'failure' narrative, one sophisticated enough to draw different gradations of 'losing'. One prominent definition used by policymakers to describe the types of people not wanted in the economy is the term 'low-skilled'. In February 2020, the then home secretary, Priti Patel, announced what the immigration system rules would be in a post-Brexit Britain, setting an income threshold of £25,000, deeming all jobs under this figure low-skilled and therefore the holders of such jobs would not be eligible for British visas.[42] Who earns less than £25k? Carers, nurses in bands 1–4, essential NHS support workers like phlebotomists who take blood samples from patients, construction workers, hospitality workers and cleaners, to name a few. Far from being low-skilled, most of these jobs are merely low-paid.

A day after this announcement, I talked with a cousin, a construction worker, who brought up Priti Patel's speech. (I find that many of my friends and family save having their political conversations for me.) I could tell from his tone that he had been thinking a lot about it. 'I suppose I've failed in life, right?

Because I'm what the government would term "low-skilled".'
He looked down at the floor, and I could see his sense of shame.
It was heart-breaking. Living in such a stratified society inevitably impacts our mental health. This gets to the crux of one of
the reasons the myth of social mobility is so toxic. It sets up the
majority of people to feel like failures. Surely, if we considered
'failure' in the context of societal barriers, the mental health
impacts would lessen.

Unfortunately, we live in societies where politicians have
purposely cultivated narratives that let them off the hook and
firmly blame individuals. This approach is visible in the language used about people out of work.

A manufactured contempt for those of working age needing
state support was all the rage in the UK between 2010 and
2015. The speeches of politicians were filled with a sense of
moral panic targeted at 'skivers' and 'shirkers' too lazy to
work and claiming 'hard-working taxpayers'' money through
benefits. These speeches were backed by the tabloid media
and so-called documentaries such as *Benefits Street* (2014),[43]
with endless stories of 'feckless' single mums with seven
kids living in a big house, individuals pretending to be sick or
cheating the system by claiming under different names. This
language of 'workers' versus 'shirkers' is a straight lift from
the mid-Victorian moralism of the deserving and undeserving poor and meant the return of 'character' as the critical
determinant of poverty.

In 2012, the then chancellor George Osborne was making
a case for an extra £10 billion of cuts in addition to the £18
billion worth of measures that had already been implemented.
Osborne, the son of a baronet multimillionaire, went from
a prestigious private school, St Paul's, to the University of
Oxford to political speechwriter to Parliament. Now, he

stood at the Conservative Party Conference and made his case: 'Where is the fairness, we ask, for the shift worker, leaving home in the dark hours of the early morning, who looks up at the closed blinds of their next door neighbour sleeping off a life on benefits? We speak for that worker. We speak for all those who want to work hard and get on. This is the mission of the modern Conservative Party.'[44]

The chancellor and his colleague, the secretary of state for work and pensions at the time, none other than Iain Duncan Smith, could often be found using this divisive rhetoric to justify cuts to the welfare budget. In essence, pitting those on low incomes against those on even lower incomes. A United Nations (UN) special rapporteur on extreme poverty and human rights, Professor Philip Alston, visited the UK in 2018 to interview people across the country to track the consequences of these cuts. His conclusions were direct and seething. He wrote, 'The bottom line is that much of the glue that has held British society together since the Second World War has been deliberately removed and replaced with a harsh and uncaring ethos.' He added that some observers might conclude that the Department for Work and Pensions (DWP) had been tasked with 'designing a digital and sanitised version of the nineteeth-century workhouse, made infamous by Charles Dickens.'[45]

But the increased poverty, marked by an exponential growth in the number of people using food banks and a trebling in the number of homeless people, did not lose the Conservatives votes. The combination of targeted cuts aimed at a group demonised in their rhetoric and in the press meant that despite the economic fallacy and cruelty of the austerity programme, the Conservatives won a bigger majority in 2015.[46] They had succeeded in individualising hardship and breaking the empathy fellow citizens had for those struggling.

Perhaps the harshest of the cuts were reserved for the sick and disabled. The consequences were deadly. Between 2013 and 2019, more than 17,000 people died while waiting to hear whether their claim for disability benefit had been success-ful[47] and one study found 69 suicides associated with welfare changes.[48] One of the many heart-breaking stories was that of Errol Graham, a 57-year-old man with a history of depression who died of starvation when the DWP stopped his benefit payments. He weighed just 28.5 kilograms when his body was found by bailiffs who broke into his Nottingham council flat to evict him. In his flat, his family found a letter pleading with welfare officials to 'judge me fairly' because he was over-whelmed by depression.[49] Not so different from the letters I found in my own mum's house.

As the economic consequences of the Covid-19 pandemic took hold in the UK, and unemployment and hardship started to rise, stigmatising tropes about those out of work and the poor were concretised into further damaging policies. The ruling Conservative Party voted against feeding children below the poverty line during school holidays. One Tory MP, Ben Bradley, linked free school meal vouchers to spending in 'crack dens' and 'brothels'[50] – further demonising the poor by conveniently forgetting that vouchers could only be spent on food. Lo and behold, just weeks later, vouchers were replaced with food provisions distributed by private companies. Photos appeared on Twitter from desperate mothers showing a week's provision of food – images of half a carrot, a potato, some tuna in a coin bag and a handful of other ingredients, supposedly meant to add up to £30 of shopping. If this food was a symbol of human worth, it sent all the wrong signals to the children growing up in poverty. This point was laid bare by pictures of meals organised by the same company for private school canteens – the contrast was hard to stomach.

Had it not been for Marcus Rashford, a 25-year-old football player who has bravely decided to use his platform to champion the needs of hungry children,[51] this grotesque treatment of the poor would not have been reversed.

These stories may seem far from the fault of policies focused on conveying a meritocratic society where the hardest-working and most intelligent people get the top jobs, but they are two sides of the same coin. In concocting a story about winners, you also must build one about losers. This story doesn't have to tell the truth – between 2018 and 2021, seven in ten people with disabilities who saw their benefits cut won at tribunal,[52] showing their claims were legitimate – but as long as lies are given the space to be said again and again, they get lodged in the public psyche.

## SOCIAL IMMOBILITY MAKES POLITICAL SENSE

When you strip out the socio-economic context from the mobility myth, you strip out that wages are falling, that further-education colleges are closing and that there are few decent jobs in large swathes of the country. You erase systemic racism and any difficult childhood experiences like abuse and poverty. In other words, you divorce people's circumstances from the world in which they grew up and reside in. For some politicians, this is precisely the end goal because when you strip out all of the above, you let the state off the hook; you don't question their management of public services, the economy or society because all blame is situated firmly with the individuals being failed by these services. In this world, losing is all your fault. No wonder we have a crisis of well-being with 1 in 6 people experiencing depression or anxiety.[53]

It is a foolproof system, perfectly designed for us to believe it rather than question it. And it is so ingrained that apparently nothing, not even a global pandemic, can shake it. Less than a month after the then home secretary Priti Patel announced her new rules deeming millions of workers low-skilled, the government announced measures to combat the now raging global Covid-19 pandemic. Overnight many of these low-skilled workers became 'key workers' and 'essential workers' – fundamental to us getting through the pandemic. Suddenly the delivery driver, the supermarket shelf stacker, the street cleaner and the carer were no longer people we didn't value. Society couldn't function without them. While the rest of us hunkered down in our houses, safe from the pandemic, it was these people who were still getting the bus to work every day and serving our needs while heroically risking their lives.

Every Thursday at 8 p.m., millions of Brits went outside to clap for key workers. Judging by the sounds of banging pots, beeping horns and applause, there was indeed a vast amount of public appreciation for their efforts and sacrifices. Yet, at the time of writing, nothing has changed for these workers. One year after the first lockdown, a third of key workers got paid less than £10 an hour, just as they were at the beginning of the pandemic.[54] By December 2022, many of these workers, from transport workers to nurses, had to go on strike to get pay rises in line with the cost of living. Shamelessly, Conservative MPs, including Defence Secretary Ben Wallace,[55] accused trade unions of holding the country to ransom because of strike action. Somehow these essential workers had gone from heroes to villains! While the category 'low-skilled' is manufactured, the corresponding treatment of this group is very real.

Politicians of all stripes acknowledge the unfairness of life chances and continue to parrot social mobility propaganda, yet are unwilling to do what it takes to address systemic issues. There is, of course, very little incentive for those making the decisions to genuinely prioritise social mobility. After all, social *immobility* got them where they are today – in power. Our political landscape is dominated by the elite. Boris Johnson was the UK's twentieth Etonian prime minister, meaning over a third of all British prime ministers attended this one relatively small, elite school. In the House of Lords, there are currently 4 dukes, 1 marquess, 24 earls, 16 viscounts and 44 barons among the 92 hereditary peers.[56] A whopping 70 per cent of those in the House of Lords were privately educated, compared to 7 per cent of the British population.[57] It is also over 70 per cent male.[58] This is not just symbolically bad; the House of Lords plays a significant role in the legislative process.

Simply put, as elites are more likely to become politicians because of low social mobility, they are incentivised to protect elitism for their children and those around them. This is partly why studies consistently find that societies with lower levels of social mobility have higher levels of corruption[59] and this is as true for high-income countries like the UK and the USA as it is for low-income ones.

So how does this work? Well, there is the obvious direct route via networks and getting jobs through who you know. For instance, as prime minister, Boris Johnson promoted his brother to the House of Lords[60] and awarded contracts to private companies with close ties to Cabinet ministers[61] with no real consequence. A report by the *New York Times* found that of the roughly 1,200 central government Covid-19 related contracts that have been made public, together worth nearly $22 billion, 'about $11 billion went to companies either run by friends and associates of politicians in the Conservative

Party, or with no prior experience or a history of contro-
versy. Meanwhile, smaller firms without political clout got
nowhere.'[62]

It goes without saying that when institutions, in particular
governmental ones, over-represent one part of the population,
these institutions, and their policies and procedures, are less
likely to serve the population equally. This came to the fore
during the pandemic, for example when grouse shooting was
excluded from the UK government's coronavirus 'rule of six'
curbs, meaning that no more than six people could meet. On
a weekend when the UK's Test and Trace programme was in
free fall, with thousands reporting difficulty getting a Covid-
19 test, a meeting with a single agenda item – 'Exemption:
hunting and shooting' – was scheduled by the Cabinet Office's
special Covid-19 Operations ministerial committee, only to be
cancelled at the last minute.'[63] The 'outdoor activity' wording
was inserted into the regulations without the meeting, opening
the way for an exemption for so-called 'country sports' such
as grouse and pheasant shooting and hunting. Apparently, the
entire issue – affecting a tiny percentage of the country's population – held up the publication of the regulations until shortly
before the new law was due to kick in at midnight on Sunday.[64]

There are dozens of such incidents in just the last few years
alone. Kwasi Kwarteng, who took up the position of chancellor very briefly during Liz Truss's premiership, happened to
have a private lunch with his old boss, hedge fund manager
Crispin Odey, during Liz Truss's campaign to become the new
prime minister. A few weeks later, when Chancellor Kwarteng
announced a series of tax cuts for the rich which spooked the
markets, the very same Crispin Odey made a fortune by betting
on the pound falling.[65] Of course, Kwarteng might not have
told him about his plans, but it pays to be close to power to

get a sense of what is to come. Odey obviously thinks so, after all he has given more than £75,000 to the Tories in donations since 2017.[66]

These actions have consequences for levels of trust. In his best-selling book *Capital in the Twenty-First Century* (2013), French economist Thomas Piketty declared that Western society is returning to what he terms the 'patrimonial capitalism' of the nineteenth century, where an entrenched class of wealth owners, rentiers (those earning their income from properties or investment) and high-income labourers enjoy an unassailable position at the top of society.[67] Whether you look at the *Sunday Times* Rich List, the labour market or the class make-up of our Parliament, you can see how this conclusion fits the UK's situation. The consequences are far-reaching. Too many political leaders work against us in order to work for their friends and family.

## THE SOCIAL MOBILITY INDUSTRY

Social mobility and opportunity being used as a rug to sweep all of the realities of society under does not stop with politics. Perhaps an example of the industry of social mobility that annoyed me most was when I was judging a competition set up by an organisation that is focused on promoting innovation. There were many applications, from those creating new apps for people to be able to better understand the benefits they are entitled to, to short online courses to learn coding skills.

One of the ideas I originally thought stood out was an online tool that linked students and recent university or college graduates with employers who needed people for 'micro-internships'. As an employer myself I thought this was a great idea. I was intrigued by its mission statement: 'We champion social mobility and equal opportunity ... We rebalance intern opportunities regardless of background or network.' I wondered how the company would deliver on this aim, so I championed the company in the first stages of the competition to develop the idea.

Imagine my disappointment when it came to the final stage to find that the company had collected absolutely no data about the income background of those involved. They had some headline figures about the paid micro-internships that had been created, and how the majority of the interns had found more paid employment afterwards, but nothing about whether these were privately educated students who would have found jobs anyway, and no geographical data on where young people were finding the job matches. When a couple of us on the judging panel pushed back to remind them of their stated aim to increase social mobility, they simply stared back on Zoom and said that more women than men had got internships. They didn't even know what social mobility meant! And guess what – despite my protests – they won! Just like Hollywood propaganda, it's a form of false advertising, but it works because we all wanted to believe that social mobility is easy.

## THE ASPIRATION LIE

From politicians to PR agencies, the lexicon of aspiration and opportunity is used to hide efforts to achieve the exact opposite. It seems to me that in the UK, while we pretend 'anyone can make it as long as they work hard enough', we conversely celebrate our elitism. Just look at our biggest British TV and film exports. I would cringe every time my family in the US would want to talk to me about *Downton Abbey*. Years back an American professor told me he loved the royal family because they represented British values. I fought his assertion, saying our values were not summed up by a family with inherited status and wealth. Over time I realised he was right, but of course this is nothing to celebrate. One way I can make sense of why we keep voting for people who have no experience of struggle is that we have deep and ingrained deference to the old monied elite. We think they are better than us. As we will discuss further in this book, social mobility relies not only on us buying into a myth that anyone can make it, and a narrow idea of success, it is also psychological – getting us to value ourselves and others on the basis of social hierarchy.

Famously, the activist Dr Martin Luther King used the language of dreams to inspire the civil rights movement. But what is significant about Dr King is that he dreamed of a different society – he wanted to change the rules. Finding hope must be about disrupting the system and building one that offers a positive reality for all, not just the lucky few.

I read a great tweet once that summarised this point about societal versus individual aspirations: 'Nobody is trying to fix the problems we have in this country. Everyone is trying to make enough money so the problems don't apply to them anymore.'[68] Can you imagine if we stood up together and rejected the 'low-skilled' tag? If we had a society that understood we have a collective responsibility to each other? We would have so much power to change things if we didn't buy into the idea that a few poor people making it to the top was enough. We would build stronger public services, safety nets; we wouldn't accept people sleeping on the street; we would join trade unions and support everyone in their battles to secure decent pay and working conditions. This book is not about staying in your place, it is about *collective fighting* to break down this idea of hierarchy altogether.

When I started writing the book, I thought that having this conversation — a conversation ultimately about circumventing our ideas of human worth and success — would become easier. After all, millions of essential workers, usually (and unacceptably) defined as 'losers', are what kept society going through the Covid-19 pandemic. I think it is happening to an extent, with people joining picket lines and demanding higher wages, fighting back against a government that is delivering only for the few at the top. People are waking up and are willing to push back against a system that keeps us locked into an ugly hierarchy. Chapters 3–8 talk through what really defines life chances — where you are born, how rich your parents are, your class, race, the school you went to and what you do for a living. Once you look at the realities, I'm sure you will feel as angry as me. These times call out for a reimagining, for breaking out of the ways we have been told things should be and reinventing them how we *want* them to be.

# 3

## THE LOTTERY OF BIRTH

When I was at primary school, my class teacher Mrs Woffington pulled out a map at the front of the class and pointed at where Fiji is, where Pakistan is and then where England is. 'How did your parents meet and end up here Faiza?' I can't remember exactly how this became the topic of conversation, but I do remember the class, a sea of mostly white faces, staring at me inquisitively.

This was not the first time my apparently weird combination of parents had come up. We didn't know many people like us and because it was an odd occurrence on both my Pakistani and Fijian sides of the family, my parents' coupling was a family legend. So, despite being only seven, I felt ready to answer this question. I spoke about my dad visiting his sister who worked as a nurse in a hospital in Pakistan, how he met my mum there and how they liked each other so got married before coming to the UK. She looked fairly satisfied with the answer, and the pressure was off.

While I was factually correct, the real story was far more complicated. As I learned in my teen years, my dad was in Pakistan because he was on the run from the police, hiding out with his sister in Karachi. His sister, my aunt, had befriended my mum, who spent a lot of time on her hospital ward visiting her sick mother, and my aunt hatched a plan to introduce my unsuspecting mother to her wayward brother.

While my mum had told us the story of our origin many times, on the last day we spent together before she died she told me what happened in rich detail. The incredible charm of my dad, being captivated by his dark skin and light eyes, and the thought of a better life. The lies he and my aunt told her about why he was there. That her family was initially against the marriage because they'd never heard of Fiji and dubbed my dad 'a man from the jungle' and because he had already been married, to a white woman no less, and had a son. But they were a simple and trusting family, and my mum was headstrong and drawn to adventure. In the end, they relented and agreed to the marriage.

My mum thought she was going to move to Canada, but as she waited for her visa the plan changed. My dad insisted he had to come back to the UK urgently so she should meet him there. He didn't tell her that it was because the police had finally caught up with him. He had stolen his son from his first wife, taken him after their divorce in a barbaric act that had left a mother without her 4-year-old son for two long years. Of course, my mum had no idea. She had been told that the boy's mother had run away and had thought my dad was a good person for looking after his son on his own. How wrong she was. She turned up in the UK to be told by one of my dad's family members that her husband was in the newspapers. But there was no turning back, she was already pregnant with my sister, without money and thousands of miles away from any familial support.

As we sat on the sofa in those final hours that she would spend in our family home, my mum was replaying it all in her mind. We didn't know it was the last day we would spend together, we thought the heart transplant had worked and she was on the mend. Maybe it was her sixth sense that meant she wanted to tell me the story again, or that the trauma of her heart transplant operation had brought it all back to her. It wasn't just the injustice of what happened to her that she wanted to convey, but the serendipity of how my life, and our life in London, came into being. That destiny would have it that my grandmother was sick on that particular ward at that particular time; that she met my aunt on a hot summer's day, so my mum took up the offer to visit her house close to the hospital to get a cold drink; or even that my aunt was there in the first place, a journey made possible because of the Commonwealth and the links of both countries to the British Empire. For my mum, all these unlikely events coming together meant that it was written in her kismet – the will of Allah, just like me getting into the University of Oxford years later.

Destiny plays a hand in all our fates, but I often think about the sequence of events that meant I ended up being born in London. If my mum had found out the truth and married someone in Pakistan, or indeed if my dad had stayed in Fiji, my life would have been so different, with the probability of me attending an elite university, running to be an MP or writing this book all diminishing further. This is a reminder that the biggest factors that define your life outcomes are the parents you are born to and which country you are born in – two things none of us have any control over. Ultimately giving every child a fair chance in life is what we should be aiming for, but luck is currently more important than hard work.

What is your story? I love to ask people that question. It doesn't take long to work out that factors beyond your control are some of the most important in your life, but unless people are immigrants or have an immigrant history, the country you are born in often doesn't feature in these conversations. Yet none of us have a choice where our mother gives birth to us and indeed because of barriers to migration most mothers do not have a choice about where they give birth to their children.

There are 195 countries in the world, with only a minority deemed 'high-income'.[1] Fifteen per cent of the global population is born into one of these high-income countries,[2] but what if you happen to be born in the other 85 per cent? For this 85 per cent, in particular those not part of the very rich elite groups, which accounts for the majority of the world, any amount of hard work and effort could not lift them to being rich because the avenues are simply non-existent. Malala Yousafzai, for example, the young Pakistani woman who was shot in the head on the way to school by the Taliban in her village, who later became the youngest ever Nobel Prize winner at age seventeen and who graduated from the University of Oxford, may come to mind as one of the exceptions to this rule. I don't need to tell you how improbable her story is and how undesirable it would be for others to follow the same route.

Looking at life chances around the world is a sobering reminder that long before you get the chance to 'work hard', your destiny is already in motion. We are told that what we achieve in life is more personal curation than chance, but we are all in a lottery of life. It is a game with very few winners, but with huge pay-outs. There are some countries in the world where it is less about luck, including Finland and Norway, and the common factor in these countries is high-quality, universally accessible health and education services that give children more equal starts in life.

It is both wrong and unfair to apply the logic of 'making it' when the odds are so dramatically different depending on where you are born. So much of the mythology of hard work is negated by just this one factor. We have created a marathon race where we are letting some people start not just steps ahead, but miles ahead, and the key contributor, which you personally have no control over, is where you begin your race.

I start with the issues of global inequalities not only because where you are born in the world is the single most important factor in determining your life outcomes, but because country differences are perhaps the most obvious way in which to illustrate how much context and societal factors matter. Key factors like whether the country you live in is rich or poor, or even in conflict, are not in a baby's control. Once you realise the folly of assuming anyone can dig themselves out of any situation, it immediately changes the framing of so many arguments – from our welfare system in the UK, to our overseas development aid, immigration system and the arms we are willing to sell governments all around the world.

There is a deeper point here not just about your individual destiny, but the direction of the world. Just as our domestic systems are built to keep most of us 'in our place', so are those that govern the international order. It is not just people that are kept in their place within rigid class systems, but, as we will see in this chapter, whole countries. Opportunities are currently conceived as a zero-sum game. For someone to work in a car plant here, we need to make sure the jobs aren't moved to China. This leads us to build a system that puts certain already rich countries at an advantage. For instance, given their population size, already rich countries have a disproportional say on the rules of trade, the global tax regime and intellectual property rights, including on life-saving medicines. These key determining factors in the global geography of opportunity mean that it is very hard for low- and middle-income countries to break out of their relative positions.

Shifting away from the social mobility paradigm could not

just free us as individuals, but help build empathy and solidarity with those struggling here and abroad. It shifts blame from the individual to the people setting the rules, exactly what they don't want, and points to a very different set of solutions than those advocated by politicians of the last thirty years.

## THE BIG PICTURE: WHERE YOU WERE BORN

When the world's seven billionth baby was born in 2011, the UN secretary-general at the time, Ban Ki-moon, gave a speech in which he encouraged the world 'to recognise the moral and pragmatic obligation to do the right thing for him, or her'. He pointed to the 'terrible contradictions' where 'there is plenty of food on the planet, but one billion people go hungry; there are lavish lifestyles for a few, but poverty for too many others; huge advances in medicine while mothers die every day in childbirth; and billions spent on weapons to kill people instead of keeping them safe'.[3] In 2020, there were 2.4 million babies that didn't make it past their first month of life[4] and where they were born was the single most important determining factor. In the 1980s, if I had been born in Pakistan rather than the UK, I would have been 12 times more likely to die in my first month of life.[5] Whether or not you survive your first day is only the first question in a lifetime defined by where you are born in the world.

In 2015, the world-renowned economist Branko Milanovic devised a way to capture just how much where you are born matters to your life chances. Collecting data from household surveys in 117 countries, he looked at the country of residence and the distribution of income in that country to calculate a 'citizen premium' or 'citizen penalty', basically to quantify how much difference the colour of your passport makes to your life outcomes.[6] As you can guess, it matters a lot. According to Milanovic's findings, we can explain more than two-thirds of where you end up in terms of your global income percentile by only one variable – the country where you were born.[7] When you consider the vast majority of people – 97 per cent of the world's population – live in the country where they were born,[8] and that they have no control over their place of birth, this one statistic completely turns the current narrative of social mobility on its head.

Milanovic then created 'citizen premiums' for each country, a system to measure just how much better off you are if you are born or grow up in one country over another. The system works by comparing two countries and calculating the premium using a percentage for being in the richer country. So, taking the Democratic Republic of the Congo (DRC), one of the poorest countries in the world, as zero, the premium for the US was 355 per cent, and for Sweden it was 329 per cent. This means, on average, if you are born in the same income decile in Sweden rather that the DRC, you have 329 times more income. Before you even bring in personal effort, just by the pure accident of being born in the USA or Sweden rather the DRC, you are far more likely to end up at the top of the global income spectrum.[9]

Let's look at the DRC in more detail. The DRC is a war-torn country which has experienced violence, disease and extreme poverty over the last three decades. The country's timeline shows atrocity after atrocity. In 1994, for instance, genocide in neighbouring Rwanda meant hundreds of thousands of Hutus fled to the DRC (which was known as Zaire from 1971–97). This led to a cholera outbreak in and around overcrowded refugee camps in which hundreds of thousands of people died.[10] By 1996, the DRC was invaded by Rwanda to root out rebel groups taking refuge there, sparking the First Congo War. This drew in neighbouring countries such as Uganda and Angola, as well as other armed groups. A second war – known as the Great African War – in 1998 brought another wave of death, with estimates ranging from one to five million killed.[11]

A peace agreement was achieved in 2003, but the wars' deadly legacy continues to be felt in continuing violence by armed groups, instability, poor health outcomes and extreme poverty. The DRC has the highest number of people displaced by conflict on the African continent.[12] At the time of writing, over 25 million people face acute hunger and 3.4 million children are suffering from severe acute malnutrition.[13] The majority of people do not have access to clean water and in 2021 the country endured one of the world's worst recorded cholera outbreaks in a decade.[14] Meanwhile, the mineral resources of the country – including cobalt, which is used in batteries – have been exploited by Western and Chinese corporations, with the natural wealth of the country being captured by the already rich outside of the country.[15]

Many of the children born in the DRC will fail to make it to the top of today's success hierarchy. Is it the fault of these children? Obviously not. The law of 'you can make it as long as you work hard enough' is redundant due to the context these children are born into. And it is not as if they can escape. The Passport Index – billed as a 'leading global mobility intelligence platform' compiles data for 193 different passports around the world and ranks them according to which country passport affords you the greatest ability to move around the world through ease of access to visas. At the top of the list come the United Arab Emirates, Germany, the UK and most other Western nations. Scroll all the way down and you find the DRC close to the bottom, with Afghanistan receiving the very lowest ranking in 2022.[16] People literally have no other option but to stay in a country where 'making it' isn't an option.

## IT IS A MATTER OF LIFE AND DEATH

I love visiting Pakistan. It is not the fundamentalist and dangerous country that much of the Western media would lead you to believe. People, especially women, dress in colourful clothes with bold patterns and intricate embroidery. The aroma of spices is always in the air. Families love to get together, to eat, drink tea, laugh and show each other love. Through the years though, I've seen very little change for the better. The electricity fails at least once a day; the rich have automatic generators, but others must wait until it is back on to turn the light on, iron their clothes and get on with their daily business. Whenever I watch the fan slowing in rotation, I get a sinking feeling. Sitting in the Pakistani heat praying for 'the light to come back on' as Pakistanis say, is a common pastime.

In more recent years I've noticed a new problem: a water shortage. The first place we go to on reaching Karachi, my mum's place of birth in Pakistan, is her sister's flat. My auntie, lovingly named Phool, which means flower in Urdu, always greets us at her door with tears in her eyes, she is so genuinely pleased to see us. Her husband, a wonderful man with a big heart who loved to cook biryani, died a decade ago. Another story of not being able to afford proper healthcare. Now, as a widow with three children, my aunt must watch her budget. But in the past decade, due to water shortages in part caused by climate change, she finds herself having to pay for water twice over. As water in her building runs short, men selling water turn up, often the employees of the gangsters who have found a quick way to make money by stealing from the low water reserves and selling them back to the poor. The matter is made worse because the water these gangsters sell isn't even clean. There have been several times I've called to find my aunt and cousins all sick. Being on a low income in a poor country is a constant battle. Pakistan comes at the bottom of the list on the Passport Index too, even lower than the DRC.

In low-income countries, the average life expectancy is 62.7, while in high-income countries it is 80.8.[17] A child born in Chad can expect to live for 53 years while a child born in Japan can expect to live 85 years. That's a 32-year difference.[18] Being born in Pakistan would have reduced my life expectancy by more than a decade. I saw this statistic play out in my mum's life because of her genetic heart condition. Her siblings, who had the same condition, but who lived in Pakistan, died in their forties and early fifties. Even after a serious decline in her health in her mid-fifties, the NHS gave my mother an extra decade so that she died at sixty-four. Watching my family die before their time in Pakistan is both painful and infuriating, it seems so unjust that they pay the cost of global inequalities with their health. This is the reality of the lottery of birth.

One of the family illnesses that stressed me out most was my that of my little cousin – a sweet, intelligent and loving young man who dreamed of being a medical doctor. Instead, after a diagnosis of Hodgkin lymphoma at the age of fifteen, he spent years battling to be treated for recurring cancer. When I saw him a few months before his first diagnosis, he had a notable lump growing from his throat. I asked if he'd gone to the doctor and he replied that they had said it was nothing to worry about. With no free healthcare, the poorer members of my family tend to take the cheapest option and on this occasion the incompetence of the 'doctor' cost him dearly. Six months later, now with lumps in different parts of his young body, he finally got a proper diagnosis. By this time, it had spread. My uncle, a low-wage worker, did not have the money for his treatment, so the family network, including us in the UK, pitched in to help. He recovered. But, at nineteen the cancer returned and without the money for the recommended bone marrow transplant – a treatment he would have received automatically if Pakistan had anything akin to the NHS – he had to opt for a second bout of radiation treatment. But of course, this wasn't enough.

At twenty-one the cancer hit for the third time. By this time, my mum had died and my cousin reached out to me and my siblings. I had no idea what to do but a friend who had also had Hodgkin lymphoma in his early twenties told me that the only thing that would work was a bone marrow transplant. Pakistan's medical services are not as advanced as the UK's, but I asked a friend – from a wealthy family living in Karachi – if they could ask around for me. She came back saying that one hospital in Karachi did occasionally provide free bone marrow transplants. I sent my cousin there and to our relief they offered him the treatment, with only the cost of some drugs and post-treatment tests to pay.

The only reason my cousin is alive today is because he had family in the West who had connections to the Pakistani elite. He lived in the same city as these people, just a few miles away, but it was easier for me sitting in London to find out information on possible treatment. There is a lot of evidence out there about the importance of networks and who you know,[19] but this seems particularly egregious when it is the difference between life and death. It shouldn't be about the luck of knowing the right person. No matter how hard my cousin worked he would never have had the networks that resulted in his free cancer treatment.

These stories of hardship, of a lack of basic resources, can be found all over the Global South. About 80 per cent of non-communicable diseases (NCDs), such as cancer, diabetes and heart disease, are in low- and middle-income countries. In low-resource settings, healthcare costs for NCDs can quickly drain household resources, driving families into poverty.[20]

My cousin got lucky. But giving one person a way out is not going to solve this. What is needed is a societal change. Finland, now joint second in the Global Social Mobility Index[21] was once poor with high levels of child mortality. Two centuries later they are one of the healthiest and richest places on the planet. What's their story? They invested in public health and education systems for everyone – not simply giving more people a boat but calming the seas so it is easier for all. As Max Roser, the economist and founder of Our World in Data – a website cataloguing global social and economic data over time – has written: 'What gives people the chance for a good life is when the entire society and economy around them changes for the better.'[22] This is as much true for Pakistan as it is for us.

## THE DECISIONS THAT SHAPE THE GLOBAL GEOGRAPHY OF OPPORTUNITY AND MOBILITY

Global inequality involves the concentration of resources in certain nations which significantly affects the opportunities of individuals in poorer and less powerful countries. This inequality is also not just about incomes and wealth, but about the power that nations have to set the rules, including on trade and tax. The political and economic systems within the UK are designed to keep people in their place, and this is true on a global scale too. The financial system and ways of putting financial restraints on other countries is perhaps the most obvious example of how this happens.

In recent years there has been increasing exposure of tax havens. Leaks from the Panama Papers in 2016 and the Paradise Papers in 2017 exposed hundreds of politicians, royals and prominent businesspeople as tax avoiders.[23] The world's richest individuals and biggest corporations use tax havens and elaborate loopholes to retain their riches. Tax avoidance, as opposed to tax evasion, is not illegal, but it is immoral. It is estimated that the world's wealthiest keep $21–32 trillion of personal assets in offshore tax havens.[24] The Tax Justice Network found that collectively $427 billion (£321 billion) is lost to tax avoidance globally every year, money that could be used for hospitals, nurses, schools and other public services.[25] It is an issue that affects us too. While HM Revenue & Customs admits it is not sure of the exact figure, it does estimate that £570 billion of UK residents' wealth is in tax havens.[26] However, unlike the public losing out in most other countries, we are also culpable because it is the governments in rich countries that are setting the rules that allow this theft to occur. It is estimated that UK territories, like Jersey, that have become home to these elaborate tax avoidance schemes are responsible for a third of the amount lost globally. The same study found that lower-income countries' tax losses are equivalent to nearly 52 per cent of their combined public health budgets.[27]

Then there is how the global debt system works, which has put low- and middle-income countries, often the same countries the UK and other imperial countries extracted many resources from during their colonial rule,[28] in deep and inescapable levels of debt. To give you a scale of what that debt is, in Cameroon, health expenditures constituted just 3.9 per cent of revenue in 2019, while debt payments consumed 23.8 per cent of the budget. In fact, at least 64 countries spend more on debt repayments than they do on their healthcare.[29]

The situation worsened under Covid-19, which in part delivered a food and energy crisis, which was made a lot worse by Russia's invasion of Ukraine.[30] In May 2020, as the reality of the Covid-19 pandemic was unfolding, some debt relief measures were announced, but these suspended payments were added to debt, to be paid within five years. In addition, this debt 'relief' only applied to interest owed to governments, not what countries owed private lenders. What does all this mean in terms of who gets opportunities in the global economy and who doesn't? Well, while countries like the UK could respond to the pandemic by increasing stimulus spending, low- and middle-income governments were squeezed, with many even having to cut public spending during a pandemic.[31]

The climate crisis is an area where joining the dots between rich and poor countries is most salient. In 2022, Pakistan experienced it's biggest and most devastating floods with a third of the country under water and millions left homeless.[32] As small islands, Fiji and its Pacific neighbours are also particularly vulnerable to rising temperatures and sea levels; the hurricane season has intensified in the region and the impacts are already more severe on the poorest groups.[33] Pakistan and Fiji, just like so much of the Global South, are paying the price of a climate crisis instigated by rich nations who industrialised first and account for the lion's share of the carbon footprint. The UK should be atoning for their share in the crisis through increased resources for Fiji, Pakistan and other high-risk countries to mitigate the impact of climate change through the global Green Climate Fund and easing debt repayments rather than cutting overseas development assistance.

At the time Branko Milanovic conducted his research on

'citizen premiums', Yemen was rated slightly higher than the DRC. This was before the war, before Saudi Arabia and its allies, which include the UK who sold Saudi Arabia and others extensive weapons, started bombing the country. The UK's role as the world's second biggest arms exporter is key to this crisis.[34] While the UK courts ruled that the UK had to stop selling arms to Saudi Arabia after a public campaign in 2019, this was only temporary and sales started again in 2020.[35] In total they have sent millions of pounds' worth of arms and trained thousands over the past ten years.[36] In 2021, Yemen was one of the largest humanitarian crises in the world, UNICEF reporting that more than 24 million people – some 80 per cent of its population – were in need of humanitarian assistance, including more than 12 million children. They added that 'sanitation and clean water are in short supply. Only half the country's health facilities are functioning and many that remain operational lack basic equipment like masks and gloves.'[37] Of course, the typical way in which the defence industry is protected is on the grounds of how many jobs it creates, the rationale being that it is okay to kill people elsewhere as long as it makes us rich here.

To point out the arms sales from the West to the East, and the consequences, is not to say there are no other reasons poor countries are poor. But so many other reasons, like being landlocked or the climate, are also not the 'fault' of countries – they are not the 'fault' of any one person. In so many ways the simple truth is that we are rich because they are poor; we are privileged because they suffer.

The extent to which the actions of high-income countries impact upon the situations of low-income countries became starkly apparent through the unequal geographical distribution of Covid-19 vaccines that emerged in 2021. The Duke Global

Health Innovation Center found that the richest countries had reserved nearly five billion doses as the hunt for vaccines started. The European Union, Britain and Canada each entered into multiple bilateral deals, with the potential of securing enough doses to cover their populations more than three, five and nine times over respectively.[38] Meanwhile, poorer countries either had to wait and rely on the goodwill of rich countries or the handouts of the Chinese or Russians, whose vaccines have been found to be less effective than those derived from the US and Europe.[39] With fewer vaccines available, low- and middle-income countries were more vulnerable to further Covid-19 waves, so it was riskier for them to reduce Covid-19 restrictions. Those living in these countries have no control over these global inequalities and yet they affect their everyday lives considerably.

## COLONIAL LEGACIES

During 2017, when I regularly watched the BBC's *Question Time*, I noticed a recurrent angry intervention from audience members. The gist was, 'We should stop sending money abroad and spend it on our own population.' The problems that other countries face are seen by so many as 'their problem', of their own making, the result of corrupt leaders or aspects of their culture, nothing to do with Britain. Why some countries do better than others is a complicated question but to chalk it all up to internal reasons is ignorant.

For example, in 1885, Belgium's King Leopold II began a 75-year colonial period in the DRC (the country has been called several names over the years, but for ease I'll consistently refer to it as the DRC), which brought with it the exploitation of natural resources, forced labour, disease and mass killings.[40] It is estimated that the DRC's population may have been reduced by as many as ten million people during this period.[41] Even after the country's independence, Belgium continued to shape the DRC's destiny. In 1960, Patrice Lumumba was elected the DRC's first prime minister. Four months later, he was overthrown in a military coup and killed. With assistance from Belgium and the US, a later coup in 1965 brought a brutal dictator, Mobutu Sese Seko, to power. His 32-year reign brought another era of pain and destruction for the country.[42] So many of today's problems in the DRC can be traced back to the horrors and exploitation of King Leopold II's rule and Belgian colonisation.

Of course, it is not just Belgium that has this dark colonial history. From the Palestinian struggle to the plight of Aboriginals in Australia, to the Indian caste system, the British have played a major historic role in global inequality. I can see why my family's geographical mobility seemed a little odd to my old primary-school teacher, but there is a thread that connects Fiji with Pakistan, and both countries with the UK: the British Empire. The adage went that there was a time when the sun never set on the empire and my roots are a living embodiment of that legacy of British colonisation and rule across so much of the globe. Pakistan was part of India before the British hastily drew a line down the country in 1947, forcing my mum's family to leave everything in India to take the long journey to the newly created Pakistan. The Fiji Islands were brought under British rule in 1874. When my aunt wanted to travel the world as a nurse, she was networked to other countries formerly under British rule; first she went to Libya and then on to Pakistan. Had Mrs Woffington known the history of the UK — something most of us still don't study in any depth or with much truth in the UK — she perhaps would not have been so surprised at my global connections. It is not so weird that both my parents ended up in the 'motherland'.

Growing up, my dad always taught us to be proud of our heritage, giving us long explanations about the British Empire and how much our family's history was intertwined with our place of birth, the UK. The Queen's appearance on our TV screen was an opportunity to teach us about the various Crown jewels that were stolen from our ancestors, as well as from the African continent. In fact, he would use any excuse to give us these lessons. For example, as a small child I had a naughty habit of trying to eat sugar from the sugar pot when no one was looking. Rather than just give me the standard parent spiel about how my teeth would rot, he would also go on to tell me of our legacy of picking sugar cane as indentured labour in the Fiji Islands a hundred years ago.

Today the history of the British Empire has become part of a so-called 'culture war', which can be described as the clash of people with different social viewpoints, often around identity, racism, sexism and societal norms. To talk about Britain's history negatively means you are likely to be accused of distorting the past or hating the country. While an honest conversation about Britain's past and our ongoing impact in the world would mean admitting mistakes, the empire can also be seen as a point of connection. There were times during the 2019 election that I wanted to shout, 'I am also the granddaughter of someone who fought against the Germans and Japanese in the Second World War!' Admitting that our histories, and hence our present day struggles, are heavily intertwined need not be a combative conversation. It would further serve to remind us why there are such huge gaps in life chances around the world.

## MOVING BEYOND LUCK

Here's the bottom line: where you are born in the world is the biggest reason as to where you end up in the economic hierarchy. So, if you think everyone deserves a fair chance in life it follows that you have to start thinking about the factors shaping the geography of opportunity and fight for the solutions that disrupt these inequalities.

During one of the few times I visited Pakistan on my own, my mum sent me as the family representative to offer condolences to her cousin in Lahore. Her cousin had experienced an atrocious year of loss and hardship. First her husband had died of a heart attack, then her daughter – my wonderful cousin who was so loved by everyone in the family – had died after being given the wrong injection. As a disabled child, with a forever youthful mental age, the doctors had promised my aunt that they would help her with some physical ailments using a new treatment. Instead, they killed her. It is hard to write this without thinking about her laughing face and cute way of calling me '*Baji*' which means sister. And the time we rode in the rickshaw together with my sister and my great-aunt, having to squeeze into the two-seater rickety car. We literally couldn't stop laughing. It's a memory I will treasure for ever.

Then death struck a third time. My aunt's daughter-in-law, who also lived with her, had felt unwell a few days after childbirth. Wanting to avoid the costs of further hospital treatment they waited, thinking she just needed time to recover. It turned out she had internal bleeding. By the time they took her to the hospital nothing could be done for her. Years later, when I would return and see her two beautiful daughters and son, none of them would speak about her. Yet, the two daughters who were certainly old enough to remember their mother spoke endlessly about their aunt who died. It was as if the pain of losing their mum had been buried.

As I took the long car ride to my aunt's house, winding through the back streets of the old city of Lahore, feeling all the ups and downs of the many potholes, I wondered what I could possibly say to my aunt. Especially as my Urdu wasn't sophisticated enough to be able to do justice to how much sympathy I felt for her and how upset I was about never seeing these treasured members of my family again.

As we sat, drinking tea, my aunt told me about how difficult times had been. The silence in the house, the difficulties of raising the three children left behind now without their mum. As I tried as best I could to express my sympathies, she would simply reply about her efforts to find solace in God, of having to accept it was 'Allah's will' and hence was how it was meant to be.

I wanted to shout at my aunt – no, this isn't about God, this is about your government not having the money, this is about corruption at the top and the Pakistani government prioritising military spending because of futile conflict with India, in part created via the British when they hastily drew new borders; this is about the Pakistani elite not paying their taxes; the impacts on the country from the multiple foreign wars in Afghanistan; and, of course, the interest that Pakistan has to pay on its debt repayments to global lenders in a deeply unjust financial system. These are all problems that can be fixed. At the very least, your daughter and daughter-in-law would both be alive today if these solvable problems were seen as just that – solvable. I wanted to tell her, don't just accept the world as it is, but instead the best I could conjure up in Urdu was that the world feels very unfair.

In the UK, while knocking on doors during the 2019 campaign, I would constantly hear a similar pessimistic assumption about what could and couldn't be done. It would often end with the conclusion that people might as well vote for their own self-interests as we are all doomed. The idea that an individual just needs to be at the top of the food chain so they don't get eaten. Yet, history tells us that we will only truly prosper if we prosper together: clubbing our money together through taxes to pay for joint services, owning our public assets so that everyone gets a fair price, supporting people through a strong welfare system when they go through hardship, coming together through trade unions and collective bargaining to check the power of the bosses, and protesting to pressure or remove governments when they are no longer delivering for the majority.

What if life wasn't shaped primarily by luck? What if we made sure that you live a good life wherever you are born and to whatever circumstances? Yes, there would be a lot that would need to change – the global financial infrastructure, the availability of medicines, more support on climate action and education – but it is not beyond our capabilities. One of the first places to start is to redistribute wealth.

# 4

## WEALTH: THE SOCIAL ENGINEER

When I went to university in the early 2000s, fees were introduced. They started at £1,000 per year, which is relatively low compared to now. Still, my mum lamented that if my siblings and I had been born a bit earlier, we would have got grants to go to university. Instead we would end up in debt. Coming from a low-income family I qualified for fee exemption and also received a full loan of over £4,000 a year to cover living expenses and books. I tried not to think about how long it would take to pay back and was glad that it at least had a very low interest rate. Now, thanks to David Cameron and Nick Clegg's coalition government (May 2010–May 2015), the same education costs at least £9,250 a year. This is only serving to increase the opportunity gap between students from rich and poor backgrounds.

For example, I paid off my debt after around ten years. One of my university peers, a good friend, told me she had also taken the loan, despite the fact that her parents had paid for her education. They had advised her to put it in a high-interest account, so it would accumulate some extra cash. She then paid off the full loan using money from her family and pocketed the interest. This same friend's parents also bought her a house to live in while she studied and they rented another student a room, so the renter was paying off the mortgage.

By the time my friend was twenty-seven she had a four-bedroom house in one of the most expensive neighbourhoods in Oxford. Yes, I was jealous! But that's not why I'm telling you this. It is an illustration of how the introduction of fees can compound the gap between rich and poor – a version of this story is happening in every tutor group in the country. Even after getting into the same university from radically different secondary education experiences, the playing field is even less equal by the end of the degree. Their wealth does the work for them – and the gap between those with and without can grow exponentially. And this policy of tuition fees was made worse by the Cameron–Clegg coalition, two privately educated men who had attended Oxbridge – for free.

After my mum died in January 2017, I had a really odd conversation with a solicitor. Looking at the date on which she died he pointed out that the inheritance threshold had gone up not long after, explaining 'If only your mum had passed away in April instead of January, you wouldn't have to pay any inheritance tax.' I was shocked by the perverse logic. Of course, I wish my mum had died on a later date, but not because of money! But looking at the cold, hard statistics, perhaps this dark obsession with keeping and accumulating wealth is rational given the difference it makes to you and your off-springs' life chances. However, the fact that this is what comes to mind for some people when someone dies says a lot about the type of society we have become.

Where does this model of wealth get us? It means a huge gap in life chances, security and power between those with huge stores of wealth and those that rely primarily on their wages for life expenses. The richest 1 per cent of households in Great Britain have £3.6 million per household on average, 230 times higher than the £15,400 or less found in the average households in the bottom 10 per cent. When taking into account property, pensions and all other financial assets, the most recent data from 2020 shows the wealthiest 10 per cent of households owned 43 per cent of all the wealth in Britain, while the bottom half of the population held only 9 per cent.[1] In the midst of the cost of living crisis in 2022, the annual *Sunday Times* Rich List found that the number of billionaires in the UK had swelled to a new record of 177, with the wealth of the richest 250 individuals increasing by more than 8 per cent.[2]

Wealth is far more unequally distributed than income, so its role is far more important in social mobility. Even if you land a decently paid job, because of the way wealth multiplies you are very unlikely to catch up with someone that has the same wage but also £100,000 invested in a house. As a leading public policy thinker in the 1990s, Michael Sherraden, put it, 'Income only maintains consumption, but assets change the way people think and interact in the world. With assets, people begin to think in the long term and pursue long-term goals. In other words, while incomes feed people's stomachs, assets change their heads.'[3]

In the UK, in recent years wealth inequality has been at least twice as high as income inequality, and the speed at which wealth at the top is multiplying is linked to the overin-flated housing market. Meanwhile, multiple cases of worker exploitation and poverty pay rates have been posited against various employers, including the likes of Amazon's Jeff Bezos, one of the richest men in the world. When winning means extracting and hoarding so much wealth, there is very little left for everyone else. Margaret Thatcher's promise of wealth at the top flowing down to make everyone better off – so-called trickle-down economics – has not only failed to materialise, but has actually worked in the other direction with wealth flowing upwards.

We have all heard the obscene statistics and I fear we have become a bit desensitised to them. The rich getting richer? Well, duh! But these aren't just figures, they capture the way the economy is working and how having money is nothing to do with how hard you work, but how many assets you can grab.[4]

## UNDERSTANDING WHO IS RICH AND WHY

Are the superrich innovation superstars and 'job creators' whose businesses help society by generating new jobs that benefit us all? Or are they largely making money off assets that already exist (also known as rent seeking) and hoarding wealth at the top in a way that disrupts opportunities for everyone else?

The answer can be found by looking at the *Sunday Times* Rich List which provides details of the top thousand wealthiest individuals in the UK. For this book, I gathered publicly available information for each of the people on the list, using any credible sources, including company websites, to build a database of what the most common sources of wealth were: if they had inherited money, if they had attended private school and which universities they had gone to. Of course, it is littered with people who are rich because their parents were rich and their parents' parents were rich. My calculations found that over 4 in 10 of the individuals for whom information could be found had a significant source of inherited wealth, and more than 1 in 3 went to private school. However, what was more interesting were the most common sources of wealth. While it is hard to differentiate sources of wealth because the rich tend to hold a large portfolio of financial assets, we can isolate the following key areas:

## 1. Property

Property, and the assets associated with property development, are a clear top source of wealth. This category includes property developers and those with big property portfolios. Property developers acquire land, develop it into residential areas and then sell to the housebuilders or keep the land and build themselves, indeed some even manage the rental properties at the end of this process. Or at least this is the simple version. Big developers were once focused on offices, backed by insurance companies and pension funds. Now, as housebuilders, they have access to an arsenal of global capital from the Saudis to the Chinese. They use intensive political lobbying and their increasing integration with the finance sector to dominate housing markets. If that sounds nefarious, it's because it is. Leading property developers are not a positive force tackling the housing crisis – they are the opposite.[5,6]

The *Guardian* reported that one of the top ten UK builders, the Berkeley Group, built 3,536 homes in 2017.[7] The average price of these homes was £715,000 – far from affordable. By challenging the viability of local authority targets, Berkeley has consistently reduced the amount of affordable housing on its developments across London. Meanwhile, over eight years from 2012, Berkeley made a profit of more than £3 billion. The former chairman of the group Tony Pidgley was one of the few in previous rich lists who actually did come from very humble beginnings,[8] but he used his position to support a system that locks the poor out of decent long-term housing.

## 2. Finance and hedge funds

The financial sector incorporates all kind of functions, including investment bankers, accountants, financial analysts and hedge fund managers. Given London's dominance in international finance and its ability to make people very rich, it is no surprise those working in the sector feature so heavily in the Rich List. As with property, this sector is one that has been failing society. Instead of servicing and growing the economy for the majority, it is the sector that hides taxes for the rich, encourages a movement of money and investment from productive job-creating assets to property and brought us the global financial crisis of 2008.[9,10]

How do people in hedge funds make their money? Well, the short answer is they charge a fee on assets, and depending on their performance, often between 2 and 20 per cent. But what are they doing to 'earn' this fee? For those not entirely clear on what hedge funds do (i.e. most of us), they are complex financial instruments that place bets on the rise and/or fall of stock prices, currencies and commodities. Their aim is to preserve and grow investors' capital under all market conditions.

So, if you want to get rich this way, you will need to be comfortable with making money from things getting worse. For example, George Soros and the successful $10 billion bet his Quantum Fund (the first ever 'hedgie') placed on the downfall of the pound on Black Wednesday in 1992 was a move that cost the Treasury – and hence the UK taxpayer – around £3.3 billion and won Soros the infamous title of 'the man who broke the Bank of England'.

How rich are those working in hedge funds? Well, in 2020, the twenty-five highest-paid hedge fund managers made a total of $32 billion – an all-time record. Of those, fifteen earned over $1 billion each, according to *Institutional Investor*'s Rich List.[11] When you earn this much, it very quickly adds to your store of wealth: after all, there are only so many Prada suits you can wear in one day. And remember, many of these hedge fund managers already come from a wealthy background.

The chief executive of the Finance Innovation Lab, Anna Laycock, sums up the problem with both hedge funds and the way the financial sector works more generally, 'This isn't to say that the basic concept of hedging – i.e. limiting your exposure to risk – is unethical in itself, but as is common in the history of finance, something originally developed to serve a useful economic or social purpose has lost that sense of purpose and instead become focused on speculative, short-term profit. Financial services should be just that: services which support a thriving, sustainable economy, not mechanisms to extract value and serve only a few.'[12]

### 3. Construction

This is not people that started off as bricklayers and worked themselves to the top, these are the people that own the machines and the materials to build. Lord Bamford, who owns construction equipment manufacturer JCB and who was a big donor to Boris Johnson and the Leave campaign,[13] is a prominent name on the list. Lord Bamford and his family's total wealth is estimated at £4.32 billion. Of course, construction can include a lot of things – residential construction, commercial space and public infrastructure projects – and can overlap with the work of property developers as described above. Compared to other sectors in this list it does directly generate jobs for non-graduates and because of relatively high union density, the pay is comparatively good.

However, there are still major issues with workers' rights. The British construction industry was the focus of the largest investigation into fraud and corruption ever carried out by the Office of Fair Trading, after years of complaints that workers were being blacklisted or essentially blocked from working across the industry if deemed 'troublemakers' who were organising workers to raise legitimate workplace issues. Blacklisting was found to be endemic. The government discovered a substantial database containing the names of over three thousand construction workers, stretching back over thirty years, which was accessed by large corporations in order to deny 'militant workers' jobs on building sites. It was alleged that Balfour Beatty, Laing O'Rourke and Sir Robert McAlpine bought the personal details of workers.[14] After years of fighting, some of those most acutely affected were rewarded compensation in 2016[15] and 2019.[16]

## 4. Food, hotels and fashion

Looking at the other industries listed, there are several that stand out as sectors notorious for low pay and zero-hour contracts. Food, hotels and fashion are all sectors run on a model of squeezed wages. A survey of workers in the food industry by the Bakers, Food and Allied Workers Union in 2021 found that almost 1 in 5 (19 per cent) had run out of food at home because of a lack of money. Forty per cent of the respondents said they'd eaten less than they should because of a lack of cash while more than a third (35 per cent) were eating less so that others in the household got enough to eat. The trade union's general secretary, Sarah Woolley, commented on the irony of the situation: 'The very people going out to work in food factories and shops to keep shelves stocked and fridges filled are coming home to find their own cupboards are bare.'[17]

The fashion industry has an even wider issue, with the problematic supply chains well documented. When I worked at Save the Children, I used to get emailed the details of the companies vying to make the Christmas jumpers to help raise money for the charity. It was shocking how few could fully account for their supply chains.[18] It is estimated that less than 2 per cent of the people who make the clothes on our bodies earn a living wage,[19] with 75 per cent of these workers being women between the ages of 18 and 24.[20]

### 5. Music

Far less contentious are those present in the rich list who have made their money from their artistry. A lot of the names that make it are old-timers like Paul McCartney, Elton John and Sting.

Even for someone like Paul McCartney, his combined wealth of an estimated £865 million is nothing compared to those at the top, like the £10 billion that Michael Platt has from hedge funds or the £11 billion the industry and finance tycoons the Hinduja brothers have putting them at the very top of the list.[21] One problem for wider society in the future is that musicians and actors are increasingly coming from high-income backgrounds, with a dwindling budget to support cultural activities in state education.[22]

You might start to notice some common factors in the industries producing the wealthiest people. One way or another, they squeeze the average person – whether that's employees, consumers or both – and are built off the suffering of others. I haven't even mentioned the significant number of Russian oligarchs that are still on the list even after sanctions. Too often, if you were to 'make it' as one of these wealthy elites, you would be involved in activities that are at best unhelpful or more likely extremely damaging for society and that are making inequality worse.

The Rich List points to a deep problem in the balance of the economy. Even where they are creating jobs, they tend to have adopted a Mike Ashley Sports Direct model of 'innovation', i.e. finding new ways to exploit the workforce creating wealth for the business. The Sports Direct-type model is associated with various actions undermining workers' rights, including paying as little as possible (and sometimes less than the minimum wage), involuntary zero-hour contracts when workers have regular hours, major health and safety issues in warehouses, worker humiliation, and being fired for taking sick leave. Today's economic system is increasingly designed to produce immobility, and the rich get richer by creating and reinforcing this system.

Despite the rhetoric, industries have not become profitable through innovation, in fact it is often the opposite. The biggest players maintain their stranglehold through lobbyists for these sectors who make sure regulations are shaped to ensure the same players remain highly profitable, while forcing out innovation and diversity.[23] Of course, there are the few in the Rich List that have done great things without tarnishing their names, but there are simply too many stories of individual wealth intertwined with exploitation, politicking and wealth hoarding for it to be a coincidence.

## BORN RICH OR SELF-MADE?

'Prince George must have been really grinding a lot harder than the rest of us to be worth £2.77 billion before the age of 10. I wish I possessed the determination and work ethic to earn another million every time it's nap time.'

Pistachio @HarleyShah, tweet, January 2022

The most glaring British example of inherited wealth and privilege through birthright is that of the royal family. When Queen Elizabeth II died in September 2022, there was a huge transfer of wealth and assets to her children, and in particular the royal heir, now King Charles III. Shortly after the Queen's passing, the *New York Times* published an article on how the new King had amassed a huge fortune as a prince, investing in financial managers to grow the worth of the assets he was given in his early life.[24] The numbers were eye-opening. His private estate, known as the Duchy of Cornwall, alone covers a total of 130,000 acres – an area nearly the size of Chicago! These assets had allowed the then Prince of Wales to invest and profit further. It is strange that we don't ask about the origins of this wealth, who should really have it and indeed why the King isn't subject to the same inheritance taxes as the rest of us.[25]

While this form of inherited wealth and power is extreme, the transfer of social status and connections, as well as wealth, is common among the rich and leads to dramatic differences in life opportunities. When Oliver Daemen, eighteen, joined Bezos to go to space in 2021, he was celebrated as the youngest person ever to fly to space.[26] Daemen's father is Joes Daemen, founder and CEO of the Dutch investment company Somerset Capital Partners. This generous father paid handsomely for his son's ticket to the stars. While they didn't reveal the exact sum, we do know that the anonymous person who had originally won the bidding war for the seat but had to drop out due to a 'scheduling conflict', had paid $28 million for the eleven-minute trip. That is equivalent to $2.545 million per minute. Or $42,424 per second. It would take 400 years for the average worker in the US to earn $28 million. The company said that the flight will 'fulfill a lifelong dream for Oliver, who has been fascinated by space, the Moon, and rockets since he was four.' Well, of course, what 4-year-old doesn't dream of going to space? But most of us don't have a family with the money and connections to make that dream come true.[27]

The proverbial silver spoon in life can open the door for you in all sorts of places. In recent years a new term, 'nepo baby', short for 'nepotism baby', has been introduced to the cultural lexicon. In this iteration, a nepo baby is the child of an actor, musician, producer, industry insider, etc. who has likely bene-fited from their parents' fame or connections while launching their own career. *Vulture* did a family tree of the many actors and musicians from different generations that have had family connections in the industry.[28] The article caused a big stir, with even a few nepo babies writing tweets defending their privi-lege, pointing to their hard work,[29] and stating that nepo babies are not confined to the entertainment industry, and that indeed perhaps these are not the ones we should be worried about. British singer-songwriter and actor Lily Allen, the daughter of actor Keith Allen and film producer Alison Owen, tweeted: 'The nepo babies y'all should be worrying about are the ones working for legal firms, the ones working for banks, and the ones working in politics, if we're talking about real world consequences and robbing people of opportunity. BUT that's none of my business.'[30] I wouldn't disagree that the nepo baby phenomenon is not just an entertainment industry problem, but having seen my working-class husband struggle in the industry I wouldn't downplay the issue here – we are missing out on a lot of talent across society and it is robbing us all.

One study found that it is better to be born rich than naturally talented. Using one new, genome-based measure, economists found that while genetic endowments are dis-tributed almost equally among children in low-income and high-income families, success is not. The least-gifted children of high-income parents graduate from college at higher rates than the most-gifted children of low-income parents.[31] Another study in the UK found that someone who was born well off, went to private school, but then didn't graduate at all, is *as likely* to end up in the elite than people from a working-class background who went to Oxbridge.[32] Wealth, and the contacts it brings, is the engine that gets people to where they want to be.

Maybe this is a bit unfair. There must be at least some self-made billionaires. In its rich list for the US, *Forbes* has been assigning each billionaire a 'self-made score' from 1 to 10. While the scores are categorised further, a score of 1 to 5 broadly means an individual inherited their wealth, while 6 is a slightly different category defined as a 'hired hand who didn't create the business', and 7 to 10 indicates they built their own company or established their fortune on their own.[33]

In 2021, this scoring system deemed 70.5 per cent of the list of 400 as 'self-made'. However, 160 people scored an 8, indicating that they came from a middle-class or upper-middle-class background, which in my view means that they didn't make it on their own. They had relatively more wealth and privilege than the majority of the US population and while the score doesn't go into details, it is likely most of these now billionaires got some form of family financial support and a private education. The four richest people in the US – Amazon founder Jeff Bezos, Tesla CEO Elon Musk, Facebook CEO Mark Zuckerberg and Microsoft co-founder Bill Gates – were all assigned 8s. As well as questioning whether these rich men really are self-made, there is much that can be said about some of their corporate practices, including the treatment of staff, and the public investment that has helped these companies thrive (we will come back to this).

A score of 10 is reserved for those who came from

disadvantaged backgrounds. One is George Soros who, as we have already discussed, made a lot of money helping to collapse the UK currency. Another with a score of 10 is Noubar Afeyan, who is the founder and CEO of life sciences innovation firm Flagship Pioneering and chairman of the board and co-founder of biotech firm Moderna. Moderna became a household name after its Covid-19 vaccine, which was authorised by the US Food and Drug Administration in December 2020. Born in Beirut, Lebanon in 1962, Afeyan and his family fled the Lebanese Civil War and moved to Montreal in 1975. He has received multiple awards for his contributions to humanity,[34] but his businesses have run into ethical problems. For example, Moderna worked hand in hand with government scientists on the Covid-19 vaccine, but instead of honouring this contribution and the $10 billion in taxpayer funding, Moderna claimed it was the sole inventor in order to make all the financial gains on a key vaccine patent application.[35]

Overall 'self-made' is itself a misnomer, not only because there is often some kind of privilege or luck that we can point to, but also because all of these individuals have relied on others to get to where they are, whether that's a team within their business, or taxpayers' investment, or indeed their underpaid staff. There is a pyramid of workers, public investment and favourable regulation that prop up these billionaires.

## SITTING BACK AND WATCHING YOUR HOUSING WEALTH BALLOON

It is not just about the superrich: it is also about the widening gap between those that have some wealth, primarily through owning their homes, and those that do not. Today, many earn more from the increase in value of their house than their yearly wages. The average house price in the UK is 65 times higher than in 1970 but average wages are only 36 times higher.[36] I covered those that are property developers earlier but owning a house in general puts you in a much better position in terms of wealth. Housing has become the pipeline for intergenerational wealth and a driver of inequality overall.

London house prices rose 86 per cent between 2009 and 2019.[37] Overall, the estimated total value of the housing stock in England in January 2017 was £6.8 trillion – an increase of £1.5 trillion over the previous three years – equivalent to 3.7 times the GDP of the UK, and nearly 60 per cent of the UK's entire net wealth.[38] Of that housing stock, £1.7 trillion is in London.[39]

Why is housing generating so much wealth? Is it because there has been a home improvements programme that has added £1.5 trillion of wealth to the housing stock? The answer is nothing to do with what homeowners have done. Rather, the answer is asset inflation. Asset inflation – where asset prices rise more than their real value – has happened because of more than a decade of low interest rates and macroeconomic policies such as quantitative easing, where the Bank of England prints money or increases money supply to encourage lending. Again, wealth begets wealth.

It is a remarkably positive story for those of us who are lucky enough to own a home; it's also inseparable from the housing affordability crisis for those who don't. According to the National Centre for Social Research, 86 per cent of the British population wants to own their own home,[40] but given that houses are now 9 times the average wage in England and 11 times the average wage in London,[41] owning a house is out of reach for an increasing number of people. Even with house prices falling in 2022 and 2023, the cost of mortgages has meant that they are no more affordable to many earners.

There is another story of housing that is relevant to the narrative of social mobility – that of generational differences. Increasing house prices mean that millennials in the UK face much higher housing costs (relative to incomes) than older generations did when they were making their way in the world. In large part this is driven by the rise and fall of home ownership. UK home ownership rates surged by 29 percentage points between the greatest generation (born 1911–26) and the baby boomers, but this generation-on-generation progress has been all but wiped out for millennials. Their home ownership rate in their late twenties, at 33 per cent, is 27 percentage points lower than the rate for the baby boomers at the same age (60 per cent). For generation Z the problem is going to be even worse.[42] Housing – the provider of wealth for the last two generations – will be the downfall of social mobility.

This is why expanding home ownership and keeping rents low is so important to addressing social mobility. The only thing our government has done in recent years is first-time buyer deals that inflate prices higher.[43] A few years ago, on the BBC's *Newsnight*, I proposed that we could at least stop the global elite that don't even live in the country from buying properties and leaving them empty – some countries like Australia and Switzerland already impose some restrictions. Such a move would help ease the housing crisis by dampening demand, as would putting extra taxes or other restrictions on second homes. Another more fundamental change would be for the public sector to build more homes through a non-profit construction company. This would undercut the private developers who currently can get away with supplying insufficient numbers and sometimes exceedingly small dwellings that aren't even very affordable. Some councils and authorities have been bold on this, with the Welsh government creating a publicly owned construction company,[44] which has the potential to loosen the grip of private developers.

## 'HOW THE OTHER HALF LIVE': POVERTY AND DEBT

*'People know that when their [energy] bills arrive, they can either cut their consumption or they get a higher salary, higher wages, go out there and get that new job. That's the approach the government is taking.'*

Jake Berry, Conservative MP, speaking on Sky News,
October 2022[45]

Just as parents' wealth is a huge factor in whether their children will be rich one day, being poor is too. The situation isn't just that parents do not have the money to send their children to private school, but that they grow up in more stressful environments and potentially don't have access to the best foods for development.[46,47] Children who have lived in persistent poverty during their first seven years have cognitive development scores on average 20 per cent below those of children who have never experienced poverty.[48] Sixteen-year-olds who are eligible for free school meals are still around 27 percentage points less likely to achieve good GCSEs than less disadvantaged peers.[49] Childhood poverty is one of the most serious issues society faces. It is hard to take any government seriously when they claim to want to increase social mobility but do very little to address poverty.

These facts are particularly worrying given that poverty is increasing, in particular in-work poverty, meaning even those employed are not able to get by. The total number of workers in poverty has reached record highs in recent years. The Joseph Rowntree Foundation (JRF), a charity focused on poverty in the UK, found that of the 4 million workers in poverty, 1.9 million are full-time employees, 1.4 million are part-time workers and 0.7 million are full-time self-employed workers.[50] Seven in ten children in poverty are now in a working family, the charity's annual UK poverty report found in 2022. The cost of living crisis will push an estimated 1.3 million more people into absolute poverty by the end of 2023, including half a million children.[51] Earning a poverty wage is now a reality for millions. Working hard to be in poverty is completely incompatible with a society that promises you that if you work hard you will be rewarded, and yet this is the UK as we find it today.

It is not just that these households and individuals are income poor, it is that they are often increasingly finding themselves in unsustainable levels of debt. Just as wealth has ballooned, so too has household debt. The JRF found that 1 million low-income households had to take on new or extra debt to cover an essential bill even in the early parts of the cost of living crisis in 2022. Just six months earlier they had found that the number of low-income households in arrears has tripled since the pandemic hit, and 4 in 10 working-age low-income households fell behind on bills during the pandemic.[52]

To get by these days, you need to go into debt. This is in part about low wages, which I get into in Chapter 8, but it is also about the economic model we have that emphasises buying things. How can there be so much wealth among so much poverty? We have a system that makes some rich by making others poor.

## GREEDFLATION AND THE COST OF LIVING CRISIS

The cost of living crisis started with the supply chain problems caused by the Covid-19 pandemic and Brexit, and these were compounded by Russia's invasion of Ukraine in 2022, resulting in a squeeze on the supply of wheat, energy and fertiliser, causing inflation to rocket further. However, even before the disastrous set of actions under Liz Truss and Kwasi Kwarteng, price rises started to occur at levels greater than the supply issues would have suggested and across goods even where no such supply side issues existed. Rents started going up by 10 and even 15 per cent, although mortgages did not rise at this point. Energy bills saw a record increase, while energy companies were making record profits.[53] BP's profits for the first half of 2022 were more than double the profits for the same period of 2021.[54] The big grain producers also had record profits. The large increases in Big Oil and agribusiness firms' profit margins indicate that they raised prices on energy and food well beyond any level that could be justified by their own cost increases.

While working in the US, I noticed a particular theory gaining currency and being used by President Biden. The theory is, that in a time of extraordinary disruption, dominant corporations are taking the opportunity to jack up prices more than they otherwise could, which is squeezing consumers and supercharging inflation. It is an opportunistic exploitation of the situation designed with only one end in mind: to maximise their profit. The thesis was named 'greedflation'. That so many companies are choosing to put an additional mark-up above the actual cost, rather than absorb the cost or share the costs with customers in an honest way, is not just immoral but hugely disruptive for the economy.[55] This profit-focused approach was found to be responsible for over 50 per cent of consumer price inflation, and that without the greed, prices would be much more in line with wage growth.[56]

What has been happening in the financial sector takes greed-flation to an even more grotesque level. Speculation is the trading of commodities for profit; the more wildly commodity prices swing, the more money speculators can make on those price changes. In the US, experts predict that deregulated speculative activity is responsible for somewhere between 10 to 25 per cent of food prices.[57] Speculators have rushed into the grain market,[58] worsening any existing supply shocks. Similar activities have been taking place in the energy sector.[59]

It took months of advocacy in the UK to get a simple levy on energy companies' excessive profits, and this was only a short-term measure. Raising taxes on the richest is a legitimate way to reduce inflation and financial regulation could stem speculation, yet this hasn't been happening. Why? Because money buys influence.

WHEN MONEY AND POWER MIX

A day after losing the election in December 2019, I was stupid enough to go on *Newsnight* to talk about it. I asked why it was that for my whole life, the only prime ministers that had ever come to power were those backed by Rupert Murdoch. The presenter accused me of saying the public were stupid. That's not what I was saying, I was pointing out that when so much of our press is concentrated in the hands of a few billionaires it undermines our democracy. An actual free and unbiased media would challenge the establishment, uncover corruption and inform the public. The manipulative power of the media is immense, so if you can hold those channels of public communication, and limit critical media, you help protect your power.

The rich and powerful know this and as a result have invested heavily in controlling the main media channels. The increasing concentration of wealth has sinister ripple effects that don't just rig the system to protect the rich, but fundamentally skew the direction of progress for all of us. With increasing wealth the rich can do this by influencing government, as well as media – both traditional and social. Elon Musk's takeover of Twitter is the most obvious example.

We learned in Chapter 2 about how politicians are rigging the system in favour of the rich, a phenomenon sometimes referred to as 'state capture'. During the Covid-19 pandemic, Conservative politicians gave valuable contracts without proper vetting to their friends,[60] reminding us that rich countries, including the UK, are not immune to corrupt political actors and those trying to weaken institutions. The Johnson government tried to undermine the judiciary in several ways when coming to power in 2019, including openly questioning the impartiality of judges.[61] It would be wrong though to think of Boris Johnson as the main and only culprit. There are examples of dodgy and corrupt behaviour by our politicians and elites published every week. It can be the type of direct influence that Johnson applied, as well as helping your friends get peerages and jobs, like when Jacob Rees-Mogg's former business partner, Dominic Johnson, was appointed as a minister in the Cabinet Office and the Department for International Trade,[62] and King Charles III being allowed to vet a proposed Scottish rent freeze law which affects housing on the Balmoral Estate.[63]

All of these examples demonstrate how close the rich have got to power, shaping the rules and making sure the system gives them even more power and privilege. This is all pernicious and damaging, but there is another form of this capture, and that is by those in big business. Rich people at the top in both politics and business are combining their efforts to rig the system and ultimately maintain the system as it is. For example, in Bob Colenutt's book *The Property Lobby* (2020), he discusses the actors who are protecting the status quo, including professional bodies, landowners, housebuilders, financial backers and politicians who work together to focus on their own interests, rather than those of everyday people.[64] These actors have colluded to rip up building standards, keep efforts to build affordable housing at bay and to slow housebuilding through a process known as land-banking or hoarding land.

Our political system has long been hijacked by the super-rich, but in recent years it has felt like their influence is ever more present.[65] Even if it was true that they deserved all their wealth, they shouldn't have that much power to shape the lives of everyone else. At some point inequality and wealth concentration starts hurting us rather than acting as a way to encourage competition, and all the signs are telling us we have long crossed that line. The UK proudly calls itself a democracy, but this is not how a democracy should function.

## PHILANTHROPY IS NOT THE ANSWER

So many of those that get rich today do so in industries such as finance, property development or retail, which are designed to create inequality and exploit people and resources. Even if someone from a poor background makes it to the top of these sectors, their success is too often predicated on entrenching their childhood communities in hardship. Furthermore, those at the top are increasingly seizing control of the institutions that shape the rules of the game, making sure that the system keeps people where they are and creating a vicious cycle of privilege and power among a select few and their families at the top.

Those defending wealth at the top often point to philanthropic activities by the richest. When the *Sunday Times* print their Rich List, they also print a Giving List, highlighting rich individuals who give a share of their wealth to charitable causes. Of course, supporting good causes is one way for the rich to give back, but this does not make up for bad behaviour and lack of wealth distribution in the first place and can seem tokenistic. Take Rishi Sunak; he literally has the power to increase taxes on the rich, place more regulations on the financial sectors, push property developers to build more truly affordable housing and increase spending on education, but instead of all that he has given more than £100,000 to his old elite school, Winchester College, to provide scholarships for kids who can't afford to go there.[66] Given the cost of the school is £43,335 per year, he is barely creating a few more exceptions to the rule.

There's a whole list of problems with this approach of letting the rich get superrich off the back of questionable behaviour and then applauding them for giving a little back. A great book on this is *Winners Take All* (2018) by Anand Giridharadas. He comments that the rich can be doggedly wedded to profits, even when they shouldn't be involved, like Bill Gates's defence of big pharma.[67, 68] These philanthropists act like they can 'disrupt' themselves out of social problems and ignore the experts and democratic mandates of governments because they have the money and arrogance to do what they want. In fact, when you look closer at what a lot of the big global philanthropists are doing, it seems a lot like they are trying to make themselves look like agents of positive change, while solidifying their wealth and power and using these 'good deeds' as a cover for their misdemeanours.[69]

Individuals like footballer Marcus Rashford and rapper Stormzy, who both give to charitable causes, including Stormzy's funding of Black scholars to the University of Cambridge,[70] actually campaign to change legislation or vocally support politicians trying to give power and wealth back to the majority.[71] This is the difference between systemic change and charity – the former means tackling the root of the problem and taking on the establishment, the latter lets a few people feel good about themselves but means we are stuck with this mess.

The answers must include the wealthiest paying more taxes, as well as efforts to stop this much accumulation of wealth at the top in the first place through higher wages for the rest of the workforce and increased employee ownership. The justification is threefold: that this wealth is never the outcome of just one person, but of public investment and employees; that this level of wealth accumulation is blocking efforts to increase mobility because of the way it creates powerful vested interests that fight to keep things in their favour; and finally, that too many of the biggest fortunes come from exploiting others. It is not just the rich that stop bold action on redistribution: too often the wider public buys into the idea that the rich deserve all their billions. We need to demolish our deference to the elite classes if we are to see greater equality.

# 5

## 'She can't even speak properly': Class, Prejudice and the Struggle

**Jon @Donjon611**
'Sorry but listening to you gave me a headache. You don't speak properly with your givin, listenin and letting. Also better, bitter, butter, etc have a tt- this needs a "t" sound at start of the 2nd syllable.'

**Paul Harrison @PrestonsWomble**
'Not realising the irony that it is people like her, with little real work-life experience, going into Parliament without having a clue about anything, that has led to the current situation where we have the worst cadre of MPs ever.'

**Quote tweeting Megan Wills @ MeganWi90287242**
'@adamboultonSKY Someone tell Faisa there's a 't' in the alphabet!'

**Adam Boulton @adamboultonSKY quote
tweeting Megan Wills**
'Not in the right on Labour lexicon there isn't.
Dropping it shows you are embarrassed about
being posh.'[1]

Is she posh or not posh? Yes, all of these tweets are about me.
One saying I can't speak properly, one saying I'm too middle
class with no experience of how difficult life can be and the
other, from the former editor-at-large of Sky News, Adam
Boulton, saying I'm faking how I speak in order to sound more
working class. Confused? I was too. It was weird to be told I
wasn't speaking properly while being told I was putting on a
working-class accent during the same programme. It shows
both the class snobbery that exists and that there are so few
working-class people on TV that people don't believe it when
one appears.

These tweets are tame compared to some of the letters I got.
People were so angry about my accent that they took the time
to write letters, buy stamps and go to the postbox. This backlash is the level of wrath not saying your 't's evokes! I started
to find this response mildly entertaining, telling myself that I
must be doing something right to elicit anger from people who
are clearly snobs. At the beginning of a lecture on issues of race
and class at Birkbeck, University of London in 2018, I read out
one of the letters I had happened to receive that very day, in
particular a section reading: 'My mum used to call people like
you who lived on our streets slags.' It was such an extreme reaction that I couldn't help but laugh! I thought it would also bring
some humour to my talk, to break the ice at the beginning of
my otherwise technical lecture, but instead the lecture theatre

fell silent, with many shaking their heads and looking shocked. I realised that it wasn't funny to be receiving this type of abuse.

An old colleague of mine reminded me recently about the people who would also call the main line in the office, shouting at my staff that they needed to speak to me to correct my English. How can so much anger be generated because I sound working class? After all, the vast majority of the population, 97 per cent of us, do not naturally speak in a received pronunciation accent, so you would think we would be used to hearing regional accents.[2] Of course, some of this aggression was undoubtedly down to me also being a Muslim brown woman talking about what some deem as 'radical lefty ideas' — it seems I embody many identities that can set specific segments of the population off.

One time I engaged with one of my accent haters online, asking why he was so against someone with my class experience speaking the way I do. He responded that it would be okay if I were on *Match of the Day*, implying that the only place working-class accents should be heard is on sports programmes and not talking about politics! Working-class people, or people with working-class backgrounds should know their place, which apparently is not speaking on political shows. Not to mention the ignorance this shows of the crossover between sports and politics. Imagine if Manchester United's Marcus Rashford hadn't inserted himself in politics. There would have been a lot more children going hungry during the pandemic.

Adam Boulton ended up looking foolish when it was revealed that I hadn't actually been putting on the way I spoke as some ploy to get people to see me as one of them. He apologised on his show a couple days later. I should have asked that he also reply to @MeganWi90287242 to say that there's a 'z' in Faiza.

In some way, I can understand why Adam Boulton assumed

I was putting it in on. Statistically, it was unlikely that I was being authentic. After all, people working in television are twice as likely than the average person to have attended a private school.[3] However, every time I reply to Twitter haters saying I'm the daughter of a car mechanic who spent part of my childhood on benefits, the tweeter will either go silent or reply finding some other fault with my identity – usually my race or religion, or that I'm a Londoner – that meant I wasn't a legitimate voice on these issues. You can't win.

But of course, this isn't really about me and my Twitter hate. The British class system – through its links to income and wealth inequality, prejudice and power – is a crucial determinant of where people end up and what our conception of 'making it' is. The class system in the UK has long been a way of sorting people into a social hierarchy. Your name, the way you speak, the school you went to – these types of human hierarchies can only exist if they are promoted and legitimised through narratives like 'anyone can make it as long as they work hard enough'. If, as we've discussed, social mobility is a method of sorting the winners and the losers, deserving and undeserving, the hard-working and the lazy, the class system is tacitly endorsed by the social mobility narrative. It is a narrative that tells us that the poor are poor because they are lazy. It is a way of dehumanising some and justifying extreme inequalities.

You might wonder why the relationship between class and social mobility needs a separate chapter, as it may be assumed that it is simply the corollary of wealth. However, the specifics of the class experience remind us why some people make it and some don't. It is not simply down to the amount of homes you own, but the confidence that comes with being born into money, who your parents invite round for dinner, growing up with cleaners in your giant house versus cleaning your own mess. These life experiences all shape you into the person who has to play the game of 'making it'.

## WHO ARE THE WORKING CLASS?

What makes a person working class? Being Northern? Working in a factory? Being a plumber? Being white? Voting for Brexit? If you watch TV or read a newspaper you will probably think all of the above. Those studying the issue often get stuck on this question, spending hours on what jobs count as working class, deciding whether to ask someone what jobs their parents did when they were growing up, or debating the old Marxist definition about the people that own the means of production compared to those that get paid only for their labour.

In 2017, tired of clichés and working-class myths, my friend and former director of the race equality think tank the Runnymede Trust, Omar Khan,[4] and I, decided to combine our knowledge to do some work on the area. We wanted to inform the debate through the voices of the diverse working class themselves, looking instead at their everyday lives rather than trying to tie down a strict definition. Funding meant that the first phase of our research was based in London, which according to a number of Conservative politicians and their friends is dominated by 'the metropolitan elite'.[5] Apparently the nearly 1.5 million people who make up hospitality, retail and care workers[6] aren't legitimately working class. The work was then followed up by other researchers with interviews and focus groups in other parts of England and Wales in 2021.[7] We sought to meet the class mythology built by a misinformed, or indeed purposely misleading, elite with the truth of the over-lapping nature of class and race.

Listening to these interviews I was struck by the repetition, regardless of where in the country someone was. Working-class people include Black people, white people, old and young, people in social housing, people in private rented accommodation, migrants and many others. What unifies them is their life experiences. They live precarious lives, face prejudice and have very little power and voice in their day-to-day interactions with work or the state. Those in frequent contact with public services also spoke of being 'dehumanised' by impersonal and judgemental housing and benefits officers. They also showed real pride in the places where they lived. The only difference between regions was that housing and gentrification did not manifest in the same way for working-class people outside of London. We summarised their experiences under four 'P's: precariousness, power, prejudice and place. Being working-class isn't just an economic condition but a broader struggle of respect, of having a say and of that voice counting.

As other studies have demonstrated,[8] our research found that the stereotypical idea of 'working-class jobs' was largely obsolete – as was a lot of the romanticism that used to be associated with them. While working-class material conditions, with the help of unions, improved over much of the twentieth century, this trend has reversed in the past forty years. Zero-hours contracts have grown exponentially, children growing up in poverty are now more likely to have a parent working than not[9] and housing is taking up an ever larger share of an ever smaller pay packet.[10] Rather than the promised social mobility that 'hard work' and 'aspiration' are meant to bring, we have a system that maintains privilege at the top and leaves working-class people in low-paid, insecure work, often in social care and hospitality. Our model of capitalism and its supporting infrastructure chews working-class people up and spits them out.

And yet, despite the evident hardships and inequalities faced by the working class, I was particularly interested to note the number of people who claim to be working class and who aren't. According to the British Social Attitudes Survey, 47 per cent of Britons who would be officially classified as in middle-class professional and managerial jobs identify as working class.[11] Furthermore, a quarter of this group identify as working class even when their parents did professional work.[12] Why? In many countries, including the US, most people prefer to say they are middle class even though they are working class,[13] so why are we different? The primary reason for this is that people like to see their success as due to their talent and hard work rather than having been helped by education and family wealth and connections. Sam Friedman, professor of sociology at the London School of Economics, who became interested in the topic at a young age when noticing the growing gulf in outcomes between him and his working-class friend,[14] found professionals would reach into their family history to portray their humble origins and 'tell an upward story'.[15] The social mobility myth is so powerful and such a badge of personal triumph, that people want to say they've been mobile even when they haven't. They want to be the hero in the movie, making up a false narrative to show they worked hard to fight for a better life, managed to beat the odds and therefore deserve everything they have.

Two hundred and fifty years since the creation of the term 'working class',[16] through the Industrial Revolution, we are now confronted with a new class reality. And no, it is not that class doesn't matter any more, or even that what it means to be working class has changed in the post-industrial age. Rather than 'working class' being redundant, as the British prime minister Margaret Thatcher notoriously suggested forty years ago,[17] it has mutated from being a term used to foster solidarity and to describe those working in industrial jobs, to being a concept within which the 'white working class' are pitted against immigrants and the minority ethnic population. Post-2016, a new caricature of the working class – as male, white, racist, Brexit voting and residing only in the north of the country – seeped into the public psyche, creating a phase of class politics that is both toxic and wholly divorced from reality.

Brexit further politicised and distorted the term 'working class'. We sometimes hear about the 'betrayal of the working class'[18] in relation to delivering Brexit and not investing in white working-class communities in the north of England. Yet when you look at the figures, a higher proportion of the home-owning middle class voted for Brexit and indeed many of these Brexit voters were in the south east.[19, 20] While there is evidence to show that working-class people have been increasingly voting Conservative,[21] the story is not as extreme a s the political narrative suggests.

The truth is that the British working class has always been incredibly diverse. My great-grandmother was – as the legend goes – tricked on to a boat from India as a 16-year-old and taken to Fiji by the British where she was told she had to work in fields to cut sugar cane. The work was physical and required being on your feet for long days in the heat, and of course women also had to keep the living quarters clean and the workers fed. But this wasn't about a contribution to the Fijian economy, but to the Colonial Sugar Refining Company (known as CSR) who owned the fields, and the produce. The wealth created by my great-grandmother's labour ultimately flowed back to rich white Australians and Britons rather than staying in Fiji. The profits of the CSR were so reliant on cheap and exploited labourers, that when the practice of indentured labour stopped, so did the profits, which in turn led to the demise of the CSR. From the indentured labourers working in sugar cane fields in Fiji, to those working in the mills in Wigan, a global British working class was contributing to the wealth of the British elite.

So why isn't this diversity or history reflected in our perception of the working class? One reason is the classic political tactic of divide and rule. It creates space within the working class for hierarchy, so that those without recent immigrant backgrounds can feel more worthy than others, even though the realities of their economic experience have more that unifies them than divides them, especially when compared to the rich. Nigel Farage and indeed many Conservative MPs would never have made it to prominence if people had rejected a division between the Black and the white working class. Far from the technical conversations about what it means to be working class today, it has turned into a political construct to undermine class interests and, yes, to support the idea that those who are at the top deserve to be there.

I could see how this division works in the way my Conservative opponent, Iain Duncan Smith (IDS), was associated with ideas of 'Britishness' at the 2019 general election, and I was its antithesis. The words 'Vote IDS' with the Union Jack next to them would appear multiple times on my Facebook page. One time, I was cheeky enough to reply with 'Vote Faiza Shaheen' with a Union Jack next to my name. I hadn't anticipated the barrage of abuse accusing me of making fun of the flag and asking me why I was running to be a British MP when I didn't like the Union Jack. Of course, this was also about questioning my legitimacy as a Brit. I had to point out, that more than fifty years after independence, the Union Jack still sits at the top left-hand corner of the Fijian flag. Liking or not liking the flag is irrelevant; I am British.

## WHO ARE THE UPPER CLASS?

The class prejudice issue also goes the other way, with an apparent deference to an old monied elite in the UK. The people at the top are not held to the same standards as the rest of us – witness the behaviours of Boris Johnson. Our narrow view of what power looks and sounds like means that Johnson was our twentieth Etonian prime minister. That one tiny private school has produced *over a third* of all our prime ministers tells us a lot about an entrenched power structure in the UK and how often we accept the upper classes – people who very clearly have no experience of what life is like for everyday people – as our political leaders. David Cameron brought us rapid cuts to our public services and a disastrous Brexit vote that polarised the UK politically and has had multiple economic costs; Boris Johnson lied repeatedly, shirked responsibility during a global pandemic and failed to even get close to delivering his major policy goal which was to 'level up'; and short-lived chancellor, Kwasi Kwarteng, also an Eton boy, tanked the pound with his first fiscal outing.

These people believe that government is their rightful place, even when they have no idea what they are doing – what else explains Boris Johnson rushing back to try to become prime minister again only a few months after being ousted from the top job? A group of US academics designed an experiment to measure overconfidence among the elite, and our reactions to this group.[22] The team of academics conducted a series of investigations, including one with more than 150,000 small business owners in Mexico who were applying for loans. The researchers obtained information about the applicants' income, education level and perceived standing in society to measure social class. The experiment included a flashcard game, where participants were shown an image that went away after they pressed a key and it was replaced by a second image. They then had to determine whether the second image matched the first. After completing twenty trials, applicants had to judge how they had performed in comparison with others. When the researchers compared the scores with their predictions, they found that people with more education, more income and a higher perceived social class had an exaggerated belief that they would perform better than others.

In another investigation, undergraduate students were taped in a mock hiring interview. Randomly selected judges watched one of the videos and rated their impression of the applicant's competence. Once again, the researchers found students from a higher social class tended to be more overconfident, but they also discovered that this overconfidence was misinterpreted by the judges who construed their performances as greater competence.[23]

This overconfidence and belief in the skills of the rich are two explanations for the disproportionate number of people at the top from private schools. I remember the moment that I realised that my tutorial partner at Oxford University was saying the same thing as me but using more complicated English and saying it with a lot more confidence. This confidence converts into employment, in part explaining why so much of our media, politics and courts are heavily dominated by those that attended private schools, and especially those that attended both private school and Oxbridge. For example, a third of regular newspaper columnists attended both private school and Oxbridge, which is especially out of proportion when you think just 7 per cent of the population are privately educated and roughly half of those also end up at Oxford or Cambridge.[24]

Another way in which the middle and upper classes convert their privilege into getting ahead in life is their networks.[25] You will have heard it said a million times, that it is all about who you know. It begins early on: parents ask their friend who works in a prestigious company to give their child an internship, the person feels obligated to their friend and also knows they would return the favour. This child can then write about this internship on their university or job application. They get to be at the right parties and meet the right people who give them further connections. This continues throughout life and on to the next generation. It's LinkedIn on steroids, but without much need for listing your skills. While unpaid internships are now illegal, it would be naive to think the practice of internships for friends' kids has vanished. Of course, those from working-class backgrounds don't tend to have the same favours to call in.

## CLASS MATTERS

In 2017, I agreed to help create a TV show with a documentary company on social mobility. The idea was that we would put kids from different backgrounds in real-life work situations – running magazines, in estate agencies and making chocolate. Their interactions and confidence in the workplace would illuminate the class differences and demonstrate the vast gaps between the upper, middle and working classes. I had a few difficult conversations with the director of the show, as well as the director of the production company, both of whom were, unsurprisingly, privately educated white men, as was the person who had commissioned the show at Channel 4. The irony that a show on social mobility was put together by a few of the beneficiaries of the system was not lost on me.

They seemed intent on filming class clichés, playing into ideas of aspiration that I wholly disagree with and trying to get me to say that today's inequalities could be solved simply by better work experience! They told me the show was apolitical – which in my experience is code for saying 'we don't want to say anything that upsets the rich'.

In the end my role became very minimal because I didn't want to legitimise an approach to social mobility that I disagreed with, but there is one part of the project that stays with me. During the filming of the trial, we took a group of ten kids aged from about eight to twelve years old, all from different parts of the country, and brought them together in London. They were very obviously from different backgrounds and wore it on their sleeves in the way they walked around the studio. They were asked to run a restaurant, to decide among themselves what roles they would play – from the manager to waiters to dish cleaners. Very quickly, some of the more affluent kids declared they should be the manager. As they were fighting over who would be the boss, one of the working-class kids went straight to start washing dishes. Asked why, he simply replied 'Because this is the type of job I'd do.' It was heart-breaking. This child, not more than ten years old, had already internalised the class system. He had put himself at the bottom of the social hierarchy.

Like race, dominant stories about the working class also affect our own perceptions of others. In 2016, UNICEF (United Nations Children's Fund) put out a video that captured the way in which we all internalise the class system.[26] They got a child actress, Anano, aged six, to dress as a rich girl and a poor girl to see how people would respond on the streets of Georgia (the country, not the US state). You can probably guess what happened. Passers-by stopped when they saw her dressed in a smart coat and boots, looking confused, they asked her how old she was, if she was lost and where she lived. In contrast, when make-up artists put black marks on her face and gave her dirty clothes, people walked on by. Anano burst into tears when one man in a restaurant told her to go away. People behaved so badly, that the social experiment had to be called off. UNICEF used the video to point out that 'Every day, millions of children living in poverty are ignored, pushed aside and deprived of everything they need to thrive.' But I think the video also demonstrated class prejudice and the power of dehumanisation.

The problem is that perception is an amorphous enemy to fight. In 2015 a study emerged from the London School of Economics[27] that looked at how class affected pay. They used Britain's employment survey, which captures the data of almost one hundred thousand people and looks at the backgrounds and pay of those in the very top occupations.[28] What they found was revealing. It turns out that those in elite occupations whose parents were employed in semi-routine and routine working-class jobs, who they describe as 'long-range upwardly mobile', earn on average £6,200 a year less than their colleagues from higher professional and managerial backgrounds. And no, this wasn't because of education, or gender, or hours worked, or firm size – all those things were controlled. Essentially, regardless of other factors, if you are from a working-class background you will get paid less than your peers doing the same job. This gap goes up to £9,440 in media.[29]

The authors chalk this difference up to several factors, in particular class codes. Things like knowing when to wear trainers, and when not; being able to talk about the fancy things people are doing in the evening; in short, being fluent in middle-class culture. As such, the people that can 'make it' are those able to switch class codes, those who can act more middle class when they need to. I hate to admit it, but I think I do this all the time in the workplace. I married someone from a working-class London background, something I feel I did unconsciously to ensure I had a reprieve from all this pretending. There are only two places where I haven't had to pretend: firstly, when in the company of trade unionists, who for the most part themselves are working class or have working-class backgrounds; and secondly, when working in America, where people simply thought my accent was 'cute' and had no idea about the class significance of me not saying my 't's.

Social mobility in this sense requires a change in accent and losing any marker of being working class. This inherently implies that there is something wrong with coming from a working-class town or background. This is not a surprise. We are constantly told that the jobs that working-class people do – like caring for our children and aged relatives, or driving lorries – are 'low-skilled'. Social mobility makes you embarrassed to be working class, it implicitly says that to 'make it' you should forget where you came from.

You might notice a contradiction here: while the actual working class try to act less working class, the middle and upper classes claim to have working-class roots even when they don't! How can being working class be a badge of honour and shame at the same time? The story of upward mobility and the romanticisation of working-class existence being employed by the middle classes is because actually they have never had to suffer the consequences and hardship that come with the working-class struggle. They get the best of both worlds: saying they've done well through hard work, while having all the privileges of a middle-class upbringing. In contrast, those with real and obvious working-class signifiers find themselves having to tone them down or lose them all together to fit into middle-class spaces.

## THE COST OF CLASS

The air smelled of death. I looked up to see the building smouldering. Around me I could hear people crying, deep painful moans, clutching their heads, some unable to stand from the weight of the pain. A man with desperate eyes stopped to show me his poster of a family that hadn't been found. 'Have you seen them?' We both knew the likelihood was zero.

It may sound like a warzone or an incident in a low-income country but we were in the Royal Borough of Kensington and Chelsea, one of the wealthiest places in the world.

On 14 June 2017, I woke up to the news that a fire had broken out at a block of flats in West London. As an East Londoner, I don't know the area. My natural inclination was to think that there wouldn't be many casualties. After all, these days there are so many fire safety standards and our fire brigade is well trained. I couldn't have been more wrong. The next day, in my capacity as a think tank and political commentator, I had to speak about the horrifying fire and why it had happened while standing outside the still-smoldering building. It was one of the most devastating scenes I've ever experienced.

It was Britain's deadliest fire in living memory – seventy-two people lost their lives. Within hours, we learned that warnings about fire safety from residents had been ignored. Later we heard about the safety failures at national and local level and about companies hawking unsafe building materials unchecked. We heard about how a council had subsidised the opera festival so that it was free, while cutting costs of cladding, reminding us that it was the cultural pursuits of the residents of Knightsbridge and Holland Park that mattered more than the lives of those in North Kensington. We learned too that the local council covered the building in cheap, highly flammable cladding to cloak what wealthy constituents in Kensington and Chelsea described as an eyesore.[30] And when we saw the faces of those killed, we saw that the majority were Black and brown – Muslim, Arab, African. The first victim named was a Syrian refugee, Mohammed al-Haj Ali.

While of course there was much heartbreak in those days and a community from all walks of life that came together to help survivors, you couldn't help but notice the many comments that would pop up on Twitter and in comment spaces under articles that explicitly or implicitly suggested these lives were worth less because they were the lives of migrants and children of migrants. One of the most disgusting examples came more than a year later in November 2018, when a video emerged of a group of people laughing as they burned a cardboard model of Grenfell Tower. The incident took place in someone's back garden, in which an English flag was mounted on a pole. The group could be heard sarcastically saying 'Help me, help me!'[31]

The Grenfell Tower fire was for many the outcome of a collision of class and race prejudice with public spending cuts and an unfit housing system. Being working class can be deadly.

After the Grenfell Tower fire, many argued that the atrocity should signal a turning point in housing policy and in how seriously we take inequality. We have yet to see this turning point. It took more than a year for the cladding used at Grenfell Tower to be banned. Indeed, it took eleven months for Theresa May to commit £400 million to remove existing cladding from tower blocks. Even this modest and long overdue announcement was revealed as a sham: the £400 million was to be taken from affordable housing budgets.[32] This political disregard for social tenants is rooted in state disinvestment from public housing and in the riches of the property developers that line the rich lists discussed in the previous chapter. Our estates are being run down and demolished while public assets are sold off.

More than five years after those apocalyptic scenes that should for ever scar Britain, the Grenfell Tower Inquiry has failed to conclude. Even when the report of the first phase of the inquiry, focused on the events of that night, was released,[33] the forty-six recommendations were voted down by Tory MPs.[34] Some of these recommendations included for danger-ous ACM cladding to be banned and removed from buildings, for a national evacuation strategy, and for improved safety for residents in tower blocks.[35] No arrests have been made. To the disgust of many, the fire service has received the most blame so far; meanwhile, firefighters on the scene that horrific night are now increasingly being diagnosed with cancer.[36]

We shouldn't be surprised it is taking so long for the Grenfell Tower victims and survivors to get justice, given that it took thirty-two years for the survivors of the Hillsborough disaster – the horrific crushing of football fans at Sheffield's Hillsborough Stadium that occurred during the 1989 FA Cup semi-final – to be compensated for the cover-up. Before the Grenfell Tower Inquiry, many of the same recommendations had been made previously in the investigation of the Lakanal House fire in 2009.[37] If the findings from this had been implemented, the Grenfell Tower fire may never have happened. The second phase of the Grenfell Tower Inquiry started in 2019 and is ongoing. It is looking at evidence on the 2015–16 refurbishment that made the block a firetrap, how residents' earlier complaints were handled, the testing, certification and marketing of the cladding panels and external insulation. So far the companies and architects behind the cladding decision have evaded any blame, despite evidence showing they knew it would fail in a fire.[38] But then this government projected a green light on to

Parliament on the anniversary of the Grenfell Tower fire, so I guess they did their bit.

The Justice4Grenfell organisation put the ongoing injustice succinctly: 'Public inquiries are meant to hold the government, and others, accountable. But right now, the Government doesn't actually have to make any changes in response to what inquiries find out. Lives are lost, people are investigated, statements are made . . . but absolutely nothing changes.'[39]

Being working class is not just about money, far from it. It is about gradations of respect, of dignity, of the right to a good life and access to justice. These factors of judgement and repression work together to erect a formidable system against social mobility, including everything from housing and how public services treat you, to how you are spoken about. When people talk about an issue being systemic, this is what they mean. The prejudice is inbuilt into the system at every level.

## DO WE JUST NEED TO GET MORE WORKING-CLASS PEOPLE INTO TOP JOBS?

So what happens when you have a combination of the dehumanisation and disrespect of the working class teamed with those who perpetuate these views holding the most powerful positions? When I was nineteen I did an internship at the Home Office. It was part of a Civil Service summer scheme for underrepresented groups. I had to apply and be interviewed like others, and I was over the moon when I learned I had an eight-week relatively well-paid job for the summer. I was placed in the youth offenders unit, a policy team within the Home Office. I learned a lot in those months – mainly that I was too opinionated to be a civil servant! I also got to observe youth courts. I saw the rich men and women judging the poor kids, who sometimes had no parents with them, for what seemed to be petty crimes. As I looked at these judges pointing their fingers I couldn't help but think *What would you know about their lives? Who are you to judge?*

This is where class privilege can become dangerous. Systems are built on the experiences and therefore prejudices of the rich. In the days after the Grenfell Tower fire a spotlight was shone on inequality in a way I hadn't seen before. Finally, questions were being asked. The new Conservative leader of Kensington and Chelsea Council, who had been voted in after the former leader left in shame, found herself confronted with a question about whether she had ever gone into a tower block in the area while doing media rounds. Her answer was 'No, I have not been inside a tower block.'[40]

But more diversity at the top of public institutions is not enough. Yes, it would be better to have a leader of the council who has at least gone into a flat in a high-rise building in the area, who has some understanding of the specifics of residing in social housing, but this is not enough on its own. I've seen that even with a diversity of representation, nothing really changes, indeed the situation for migrants and the working class has only worsened with the increase in diversity at the top of the Conservative Party. Unless these people are also willing to do things differently, to fight developers, to change the prison system, to root out the myriad ways in which class prejudice is concretised into the fabric of our country, they are at best a figurehead and at worst the legitimising face of a system that keeps people in their place.

Parts of the private sector have also started to think about representation as an answer to their social mobility problem. Big corporations have faced increasing pressure to look at the demographic make-up of their teams, to ask difficult questions about why there are not more women and people of colour in top positions. A smaller number of firms have also looked at the proportion of their staff drawn from private schools and working-class backgrounds.

Corporations taking this route and receiving accolades for it are PricewaterhouseCoopers (PwC) and KPMG – two of the biggest accountancy firms in the world. Together with Deloitte and Ernst & Young (EY), they are known as the Big Four accountancy firms in the UK. In 2021, after working on collecting gender and race/ethnicity data about their staff, which revealed notable pay gaps, especially when comparing ethnic groups, they decided to also look at class differences. PwC found that more than four-fifths of their employees came from a higher socio-economic background; only 14 per cent of its staff came from a lower socio-economic background, based on parental occupation, and they were paid less than their colleagues, with a 12.1 per cent median pay gap.[41] KPMG found that 23 per cent of its partners came from a working-class background and pledged to bring this up to 29 per cent by 2030.[42]

So, here's the thing. While many will applaud these companies for both doing these studies and making these pledges, it is not just their workplace practices but their actual *raison d'être* that is the problem when it comes to inequality. The Big Four accountancy firms are the goliaths of corporate tax planning, designing and selling tax avoidance schemes to multinational corporations. Furthermore, the Big Four played a vital role in the financial crash of 2008, failing to ring the warning bell about banks they audited, signing off on their accounts just months before their collapse triggered years of austerity across Europe.[43]

Then there is the issue of the obscene pay packets for those at the very top. While in 2021, PwC's revenue rose 2 per cent to £4.4 billion in the year to 30 June, the distributable profit per partner rose more than a quarter to £868,000. Chair Kevin Ellis was paid £4.4 million in the year, up from £3.4 million the year before, resulting in a pay ratio with that of the median PwC employee of 82:1.[44] So while these studies appear very worthy, if a company was taking social mobility seriously they would distribute increasing profits to those on lower wages within the company. The best thing firms like PwC could ever do for social mobility is stop their lobbying to protect the wealthy and big corporations. They should also pay their cleaners and security guards much much more.

Unless we are more honest about the problem and who's to blame, we will continue to see superficial approaches being applauded. Articles that congratulate companies while conveniently leaving out the part where the company has made the world the way it is are continuing to perpetuate the problem.

## WHERE NEXT?

'What does class mean to you?' I was asked this recently by someone writing a book about race and class. I didn't really know how to answer this question but related it to my own life experience, talked about it being part of my identity and some rubbish like 'It's the prism by which I see the world.' Entirely unsatisfied with my answer, I later asked my husband, Akin, the same question. He said, 'It means, I'm fucked.'

Class was always political, but the issue has become even more politically toxic recently. From the BBC's David Dimbleby declaring on the night of the EU referendum result that working-class votes were the decisive factor to TV dramas depicting the lazy and criminal, the mythology built about working-class people is wide-ranging, divorced from the economy and power, and damaging. This is important in the story of social mobility, because the hierarchy that social mobility endorses and supports protects the class status quo and vice versa.

The UK class system has been centuries in the making, just like caste in India, and it is not going to change overnight. But what is the alternative to hierarchy? How about being able to be proud of your working-class community, being able to enjoy a decent quality of life regardless of your income, and instead of individualism having community-led solidarity? This is possible. Higher wages, public ownership of water, energy and trains to ensure a better distribution of wealth, a shift in our cultural output to celebrate rather than berate working-class people, a celebration of working-class talent and hard work instead of focusing so many of our national celebrations on the monarch. It would be worth the effort, not just for the working class, but for the whole country.

# 6

## RACISM

When my siblings and I were growing up in the eighties and nineties, my dad thought it was inevitable that we would face racism at school and in life in general, so he wanted us to be prepared for it. How? By learning how to punch fast and punch hard. Sports were a constant on the TV and boxing was one of the many sports my dad loved to watch. My father was a huge fan of the charismatic Muhammad Ali and I think he was trying to channel the spirit of Ali into our little fists. From the tender age of four, he would line my siblings and me up, and tell us to take turns to punch him as hard as we could on his belly or arm.

'When they call you "Paki", punch them like this,' he would demand, hitting his own bare knuckles against a brick wall so hard that it felt like our whole house would collapse.

My mum, being of a very different disposition to my dad, was horrified. 'Just tell racists that in Urdu, Paki means clean,' she would say. To which my dad would laugh and respond, 'That won't do anything.'

My dad was right. It wasn't long before someone called me a Paki at school. I remember it clearly. Aged five, in the playground, and this boy called Barry called me a Paki. He was standing in the doorway, irate and angry about something and knew this was an offensive term. It was one of those out-of-body experiences – yes, I had been preparing my whole short life for such an encounter but I was conflicted. On the one shoulder, I had my dad telling me to punch Barry straight in the face, and on the other, I had my sweet mum chanting in Urdu 'Paki means clean'. Being skinny and not the type that liked getting told off by my teachers, I decided to go with Mum.

'Paki means clean, *actually*!'

Poor Barry, he looked so confused in that moment. I had totally disarmed him without having to punch my bony hand in his face. My friend had told the dinner lady that Barry was being mean, to which the dinner lady – Mrs White – and yes that was her name, told me to remember that 'Sticks and stones may break my bones, but names will never hurt me.' Can you imagine? The eighties approach to racism was so laughable! I remember a few years later another well-meaning teacher, Mrs Sheridan, told the class that they shouldn't be racist, after all, she was 'jealous' that I was always tanned. Even at age nine I knew that as well-meaning as Mrs Sheridan was, it wasn't the right thing to say.

It was clear in early life that I would have to stick up for myself, but also that I would have to be inventive. I didn't realise it at the time, but that moment with Barry in the play-ground was a life-defining moment. I did fight back, but in a way that suited me. In some ways though, this type of racism, overt and in your face, is much easier to deal with than the type of racism that means you get lower school grades, longer jail sentences and stops you from getting jobs. When racism is built into the system of opportunity there are hurdles erected at every junction of life.

In recent years there has been a growing reckoning in our country and elsewhere that means we have started to see visible change in a way that we haven't in the past. The mass protests, the high sales figures of excellent books like Reni Eddo-Lodge's

*Why I'm No Longer Talking to White People About Race* (2017) and increasing representation on our screens of different stories that better reflect our diverse communities are all hopeful signs that something is shifting. There are so many inspiring people of colour out there leading the charge, showing how much beauty and strength there is within communities that have been traditionally sidelined. We must do more to ensure this talent can flourish by addressing some of the structural barriers to equality and, importantly, connect this struggle to that of class.

## RACISM THROUGH THE LIFE COURSE

As I mentioned in the Prologue, in 2016 I was asked to help put together a documentary looking at the likelihood of the United Kingdom ever having a Black prime minister. I mapped the typical path to becoming the PM – i.e. born wealthy, does well at school (most likely private), goes to Oxford or Cambridge university, gets a top job, joins a political party, gets elected – and tracked the odds of a Black person passing each one of these hurdles. The conclusion of *Will Britain Ever Have a Black Prime Minister?* was that if you were lucky enough to have been born white and into priv-ilege, been privately educated, went to Oxford or Cambridge university, or indeed any university, and got into a top pro-fession, then the chances of you becoming the prime minister were 1 in 200,000. Meanwhile, for a Black state-educated child, the chances of becoming PM are 1 in 17 million. I found that a state-educated white child is 12 times more likely – and a privately educated white child 90 times more likely – to become prime minister than a Black child.

But it's not just about who gets the top job. The statistics are skewed throughout our entire social system, affecting the opportunities of children from as young as preschool age and compounding throughout life. I was the geek running through some of the numbers in the show, with the British Hollywood actor David Harewood asking me questions about the data – and these numbers raised a lot of questions. Why is it that Black children are almost twice as likely to be poor as white children?[1] Why does Oxbridge still have so few Black students? Why are ethnic minority applicants to prestigious Russell Group universities less likely to receive offers than their equivalently qualified white peers, even after controlling for applicants' chosen degree subject areas and even after the numerical competitiveness of courses has been taken into account?[2] What explains differences in employment outcomes when Black and white applicants have the same credentials? It had been some years since I'd looked at race equality statistics in real depth and I was shocked by some of what I found.

For instance, I knew that Black kids were more likely to be excluded from school, but as I looked through the Department for Education data, I discovered how early this starts – with 3- and 4-year-olds being excluded from nursery! Some will try to notch this up to Black children being 'more naughty' but this is a racist trope.[3] During the show we spoke to parents who said that they felt their child was being racially stereotyped. Prejudice can live in all of us and because we are socialised in myths and stereotypes about 'others' from so early on in life, these shape our views, whether we like it or not.

The level of school exclusions appears to be directly related to educational underachievement and both are linked to involvement in the criminal justice system. The evidence that high levels of school exclusions and underachievement played a major contributory part in young Black people's involvement in crime is instructive.

Underachievement and exclusion are key causes of continued socio-economic disadvantage among Black communities and have come to be known as pipelines into the prison system. This is where you can clearly see discrimination on top of discrimination play out in the outcomes of people's lives.

Exclusion and academic underachievement also play into employment prospects. Black people of Caribbean origin experience, on average, significantly higher unemployment and lower earnings than white people. After the Race Relations Act of 1965, sociologists conducted an experiment in which they sent a pair of CVs with identical qualifications and experience but different names – one having a 'white-sounding' traditional English name and the other an 'ethnic' name – to the same employers. The 'white-sounding' names received far more favourable responses.[4] Unfortunately, the same bias was found in research published in 2019.[5] It found that minority ethnic applicants in the UK had to send 60 per cent more applications to get a job interview than their white counterparts. For people of Nigerian origin and people of Middle Eastern and North African origin, it was 80 per cent and 90 per cent, respectively.

As this table highlights, race plays into a feedback loop, with Black kids more likely to be born into poor households, more likely to be excluded, more likely to be on a zero-hour contract and therefore more likely to be poor. Then they have children and the loop begins again. (I've used 2019 exclusion and A-level results here because of the disruption caused by Covid-19, which meant teacher assessments were used.) It is notable that some statistics point to non-elite young white people falling behind other ethnic groups in admissions to the top universities, and university in general.[6] The reasons for this are complex but geography is a big factor. Successful efforts in London, where half of the Black British population live, to address attainment gaps has resulted in a boost for this group and others in London.[7, 8] While these statistics look at the experience of Black and white individuals, I should add that poverty rates for Pakistani and Bangladeshi children are even higher, at 47 per cent and 41 per cent respectively.[9]

### Probabilities in outcomes by race – a cycle that repeats itself

| | Black | White British (non-private school) | White British (private school) |
|---|---|---|---|
| Grow up poor[10] | 3/10 | 2/10 | 0 |
| Permanently excluded from school[11] | 3/10,000 | 1/10,000 | Data unavailable |
| Average point score per entry for A level[12, 13] | 28 | 33 | 41 |
| % of applications to Russell Group met with offers of a place[14, 15] | 40% | 52% | 71% |
| Time it takes to find job after graduation[16] | 5 months | 3.1 months | Data unavailable |
| Likelihood of working on a zero-hour contract at 25 years old[17] | 6.5% | 4.7% | Data unavailable |
| Unemployment rate[18] | 7.1% | 3.2% | Data unavailable |

The day after the show aired, I came into the office to be confronted by my Black colleague working at the reception desk. 'Faiza, I watched your show.'

'What did you think of it?'

'I don't know what to do with that information. I've got two girls in school.'

What was I meant to say? I could only listen and agree that the situation was terrible.

The part of the show that had really got to my colleague was when we had put up a graph showing the difference between white and Black groups from the age of 7 to 16. It wasn't as simple as Black kids doing worse than white kids. Kids of both races generally started at a similar level, but then the performance of Black students declined on average until age 14, while white children performed as expected given where they started. The big mystery was why, between the ages of 14 and 16, there was a notable uptick in the performance of Black children, with Black African children outperforming white children on average by the time they reach the age of 16, even though they were lagging behind just two years earlier. What had happened? Well, turns out this is the first time that papers are anonymised and marked outside of the school. The first time that someone marking the paper doesn't know the child is Black.[19]

I decided to show these statistics to a conference of primary school head teachers in south London, and at the Black Workers' Conference for the National Education Union. The room fell silent at the head teachers' conference, and while they did not act defensively, they were shocked. At the Black teachers' conference, however, there was no shock but there was anecdotal evidence of how they had seen this prejudice play out for their pupils.

I too had seen this difference in treatment when growing up. When I was at college in Walthamstow doing my A levels, career advisers gave me completely different advice compared to my Black Caribbean friend, despite her getting good grades. While I was encouraged to follow my career aspirations, she was told that she should lower her ambitions and rather than train as a lawyer become a legal secretary instead. A reminder also of the difference in racial stereotypes between a brown and Black girl.

## RACIAL STEREOTYPES

'Looks tough and dangerous. Violent tendencies.
Middle Eastern accent.'

'Dark skin. Looks like a terrorist, dangerous,
you dislike him as soon as you see him. Middle
Eastern accent.'

'Middle Eastern. Strong, physically imposing.
Pure evil.'

While Hollywood is the biggest propaganda machine for social mobility, with rags to riches stories being a staple of the industry, it is also, ironically, a machine for deeply embedded racial stereotypes – the sorts of stereotypes that then feed into our system. The above quotes are a few character descriptions that my husband, Akin Gazi, has had to deal with. He is an actor of Turkish Cypriot origin, born in London, and he has played a few 'evil' roles over the years. The stereotypes above are ludicrously ignorant. The Middle East is a huge land mass and there is no such thing as a 'Middle Eastern accent', it is code for generic foreign accent. 'Looks like a terrorist' is similarly thinly veiled racism.

My husband has a litany of stories of racism to choose from. On one production, the lead actor joked about being unable to pronounce some of the actors' names (Iraqi, Turkish and

Afghani actors in this case) and joked 'Maybe I should call you Akin Bhaji.' I was enraged. Here was a white actor cast in an Arab role, unable or, more accurately, unwilling to learn how to correctly pronounce the names of the actors actually from the region. Another time my husband was humiliated by a producer and director in the back of a car travelling between filming locations, when the director snorted, 'You actually look just like a terrorist.' The producer agreed and laughed. Both were posh and white. Now someone else might have said something, or not taken the role at all, but working-class actors cannot afford to turn down work, even if that work reproduces negative stereotypes about Muslims or people from the Middle East. But this is not just about the treatment of my husband, it is about the way these negative stereotypes shape society and frame who is good and who is bad, who is worthy and who is not.

The best example of this was when my husband Akin portrayed Bayezid II in a popular historical drama. Bayezid was an Ottoman sultan who ruled the empire from 1481 to 1512. He offered Jewish people dispelled from Spain during the Inquisition safe passage and protection in the Ottoman Empire. He wanted these refugees to be given a warm welcome and threatened death to anyone who harmed these new arrivals.[20] This, however, was not in the script. Instead, he was chopping off heads and trying to force Christians and Jews to become Muslims on pain of death.

It's no secret that Hollywood and the industry in the UK have fed into negative depictions of people of colour, women and the working classes. Marlon Brando famously rejected his Best Actor Oscar in 1972 for his legendary performance in *The Godfather*. Brando wrote in the *New York Times*: 'The motion picture community has been as responsible as any for degrading the Indian and making a mockery of his character, describing his as savage, hostile and evil."[21] Even if there is more of a push for diversity now, the decades and decades of racism on our screens is implanted in society's psyche.

It's a similar story in our news outlets, which are also guilty of demonising some while humanising others. In 2011, riots kicked off in several English cities after a young Black man – Mark Duggan – was shot and killed by the police. Even before any evidence of what had happened emerged, a photo started circulating of Duggan. It was a picture that appeared to show him to be unsmiling, hard-faced, even thuggish.[22] It gave a sense that he was in the wrong and probably deserved to be killed by the police. But weeks later, the full photo emerged. In the initial photo the image had been cropped to only show his face, but when you could see his body he was holding a heart-shaped plaque saying 'Daughter, always in our hearts.' Photos – and how they are manipulated – matter; they inevitably shape our reading of the news stories they accompany.

Racism and double standards have also been clearly on display in regards to Ukrainian refugees. Journalist after journalist on TV stations as mainstream as the BBC and Sky blurted out how 'these aren't typical refugees', that they are 'civilised' and look like us with 'blond hair and blue eyes.'[23] The inferred comparison is plain. The fact that we have a government that plans to allow Ukrainian refugees in, while deporting those coming from Afghanistan, Iraq and other countries where we had a clear hand in making the country terrible to live in, to Rwanda, tells us all we need to know about the hierarchy of humanity as dictated by our government and media. Portraying Iraqis and Afghanis as subhuman, as dangerous, evil terrorists is not a mistake. The dehumanisation of these people is part of the plan, it's part of the justification for draconian immigration laws, it's woven into the fabric of our minds. This is not to argue for a race to the bottom, but rather for equal humane treatment regardless of race or ethnicity. Ukrainians deserve our support, as does everyone else.

Sometimes this stereotyping comes from places you wouldn't expect. When I worked at a global development organisation, I had a disturbing meeting in relation to some work on inequality I was leading on. I was told that it was better to use a photo of a Black child on the cover of a report on inequality not because this image would represent who was most affected by inequality, but because images of Black babies 'raised more money'. I had already handed in my notice and this moment only made me more pleased that I had. This sort of imagery of Black babies with flies on their faces are harmful to the continent, providing a one-sided impression of Africa and erasing the historical context, any agency and the success the continent is having. Through the constant use of these pictures, people associate abject poverty with the continent. Later, working at the same organisation, I noticed how every time there was talk of education, an image of a girl wearing a hijab was used. I asked why this was and my colleagues looked confused, but it is not the case that it is only Muslim girls that aren't being educated, indeed the main factor in understanding why children aren't being educated is poverty not religion.[24]

The summation of this racial stereotyping and demonising in every part of public life is a deeply racist system of empathy, of justice and of accountability. When I discovered that a local Tory councillor had horrific Islamophobic tweets on his Twitter account, I challenged him by raising awareness of what he had tweeted, yet I received very little support, including from the Labour Party, in trying to hold the councillor accountable. Even with my media contacts it took a while to get it into the press.[25] It was as though it didn't really constitute 'news'. People don't care when they believe the stereotypes to be true.

Stories that play into approved and accepted bigotry, however, are headline news. In 2014, an anonymous whistleblower leaked to the British press a photocopy of what appeared to be a secret communique, one that supposedly revealed an Islamist conspiracy to take over schools in the English city of Birmingham. It dominated the news for the next few weeks and months. The document would later come to be widely regarded as fake, and the court case against the teachers and governors accused of being involved collapsed, but that didn't stop a nationwide panic over Islamic extremism infiltrating schools and beyond. In the years that followed the 'leaking' of the letter, the Conservative government hardened the country's counterterrorism policy, revamped school curriculums and banned educators. Birmingham has since been labelled a 'no go' area for non-Muslims in far right media and rhetoric,[26] and the careers of many of those working in the schools have been ruined.[27] There had been some attempt to correct the narrative in the intervening years, but it hadn't received any traction.[28] It was only in 2022, when a podcast series was produced by the *New York Times*, *The Trojan Horse Affair*, that people came to see how Islamophobia was a critical part of the story.[29]

On the face of it, the podcast was a simple investigative piece trying to find out who actually wrote the letter that sparked the whole affair.[30] But along the way, the co-hosts Hamza Syed and Brian Reed had to confront just how quickly people were willing to believe the contents of the letter — as if they wanted to believe it was true because it confirmed their inherent suspicions. It also sheds a cruel light on the quality of the journalism at the time. The podcast was a huge success, topping political charts. Many of my US colleagues wanted to talk to me about it and yet – perhaps because it showed how systemic Islamophobia is in the UK – it got very negative reviews and severe backlash in the UK press, including in the usually sympathetic *Guardian*.[31]

This stereotyping doesn't just affect how society sees different groups, but also how these groups view themselves. We begin to see ourselves in a negative light. It acts as a double whammy against the possibility of people's upward mobility, crippling both opportunity and motivation. Similarly to what we found in the class work I did for Channel 4, experiments have found that discrimination and undignified treatment may result in children internalising inequality, believing they are inherently worth less than others. In a controlled experiment in India, boys from high and low castes displayed the same ability to solve mazes under monetary incentives, but low-caste boys performed worse if the name and caste of the participants were announced at the beginning of the session.[32] Another study found that female university students who read scientific essays asserting that there are no gender differences in mathematical ability perform better in mathematical problems.[33]

The role of algorithms and artificial intelligence (AI) has provided another dimension to racism.[34] Multiple scandals, including the photo-enhancing algorithm that changed a grainy headshot of former President Barack Obama into a white man's face, have popped into the headlines in recent years. However, perhaps more worrying is the way facial recognition is designed to target criminal suspects or those without official immigration papers on the basis of skin colour.[35, 36] These technologies are also making the difference as to whether or not you get a mortgage.[37] Yes, we are programming our technology to be prejudiced, but that is only because we are ourselves programmed to be racist, misogynistic and classist. It is people who first create the program or application, and machine learning or AI that takes it from there.

Sometimes it can feel like the system is rigged against you – and that is not an irrational feeling. When hate and demonisation is all around you, should you 'rise above it'? Or is it the ruling systems that need to change? To change the programming of AI, we need to change our own programming.

## RACE/RACIST SCIENCE: WHEN IT GETS ULTRA-UGLY

In 2018, I was asked to join a panel including the son of Michael Young, the man who coined the term meritocracy. His son, Toby Young, has been called out in the past for lewd comments about women,[38] is an advocate of eugenics[39] and is an old friend of Boris Johnson,[40] so I knew it would be interesting. We were all meant to reflect on how Michael Young's book (*The Rise of the Meritocracy* (1958)) and the ideas of meritocracy, had gone from satire to a policy desire. Young, of course, was asked to go first, but rather than reflecting on the fact that his dad's book, which was meant to be a warning, had been misused, he started referring to 'academic papers' that had found that the reason why certain children were behind was because of genetics. I couldn't believe what I was hearing. I looked across at the audience; some of them looked confused, a couple were looking at me reflecting my own disbelief and disgust. After taking a couple of seconds to recover my composure, I shouted 'What are you saying?' He stopped speaking, looked at me and said, 'Oh, I suppose you're now going to say I'm a racist.' Well, duh, what he was saying certainly sounded racist and classist! You might have thought this type of thinking would have been confined to the twentieth century, thrown in the dustbin for good, but no, the thinking still pervades.

Eugenics is defined as 'the study of how to arrange reproduction within a human population to increase the occurrence of heritable characteristics regarded as desirable.'[41] It is thinking that has justified genocides from the Holocaust to indigenous people in Canada, and beyond. In the US, eugenics policies were enacted from 1907 and over most of the next century in thirty-two states. An estimated 80,000 people – mostly Black, Latina and indigenous women – were sterilised by the state in the name of 'purification'. Only eight states have apologised.[42]

But the rationale that underpins eugenics has also taken other nefarious forms. Eugenics needs a legitimising bedfellow and 'race science' is happy to oblige. Race science, or as I like to call it *racist science*, claims that there is a link between race and intelligence. As explained by the author of a book on the subject, Gavin Evans, 'race scientists claim there are evolutionary bases for disparities in social outcomes – such as life expectancy, educational attainment, wealth and incarceration rates – between racial groups. In particular, many of them argue that Black people fare worse than white people because they tend to be less naturally intelligent.'[43] It is both completely wrong and extremely dangerous, but despite widespread derision from the majority of scientists it still carries favour with those who need to find excuses for their prejudice. In particular, it has found its way into the rhetoric and thinking of the alt-right. The murderer in the school shootings in Buffalo, New York, in May 2022, cited specific academic work in his deranged manifesto. The killer drove to an area that had the highest Black population in his vicinity and shot dead ten mostly elderly Black people. He was a believer and supporter of race science and a self-professed white supremacist.

When I was working on my PhD, I came across a book that had repopularised racist science among the policy elite in the 1990s – *The Bell Curve*, by Charles Murray and Richard J. Herrnstein (1994). It uses different racial averages in IQ scores between Black and white test takers to forward an agenda of white supremacy. Of course, these IQ tests are flawed, and there is little consideration of the social and economic context of different test takers. The scariest thing is where the book takes us in terms of policy. It argues that we should stop trying to improve poor kids' material living standards because doing so encourages poor, low-IQ women to have more children. It also concludes that the United States should curtail immigration from Latin America and Africa. Reading it, I could feel my insides turn! But then I was even more disgusted when I read that it had been a bestseller, used by those on the political right to justify cuts to welfare spending in the US.

The biological differences arguments have deadly outcomes. Multiple studies have found that Black women are more likely to die in childbirth in the UK, with a study in 2021, using statistics from 2016–18, finding that Black women are four times more likely to die in childbirth, and Asian women twice as likely, than white women.[44] Part of this is to do with Black women being more likely to be poor, but another explanation is that medical professionals are not listening to Black women and taking their pain seriously. One survey of white junior medical staff found half endorsed false beliefs about biological differences between Black and white people. Those who did also perceived Black people feel less pain than white people, and were more likely to suggest inappropriate medical treatment for Black patients.[45] Prejudice results in medical bias, which ultimately hurts people.

If you believe that poor people are poor because they are inherently less intelligent or biologically less human, then it is easy to leap to the conclusion that liberal remedies, such as welfare support, affirmative action or foreign aid, are doomed to fail. If it is all nature and not at all about nurture, then it is simply the fault of the individual and any intervention would be wasteful. These racists would totally hate this chapter and this book!

Oh, by the way, Toby Young got into Oxford because his dad called them after he failed to get his grades; so much for meritocracy.[46] Even after all his disgusting comments over the years he got asked to be on the board of the Office for Students in 2018. After an uproar, he resigned.[47] But it goes to show how close these guys and their warped views get to power, and how many of those in power don't see anything wrong with his views. Scary stuff.

## THE INJUSTICE SYSTEM

The justice system is meant to be the recourse by which citizens are able to uphold their rights and ensure the rule of law is applied, but not only is access limited to those who can afford lawyers, the rulings are often not in favour of the poor and marginalised. It should be a tool to correct for inequalities, a system where people can see anti-racist principles upheld and where your income does not matter; instead it is a system that perpetuates inequalities. We don't have a justice system, we have an *injustice* system.

Just look at the differences in stop and search rates. In England and Wales between April 2020 and March 2021, there were 697,405 stop and searches (excluding vehicle searches). There were 7.5 stop and searches for every 1,000 white people, compared with 52.6 for every 1,000 Black people. So Black people were seven times more likely to get searched as white people.[48] Deputy CEO of Transform Drug Policy Foundation, Jane Slater, told the *Independent:* 'As the evidence demonstrates stop and search has proved ineffective at reducing drug use, curtailing drug markets, or reducing drug related harm. Rather it has led to disproportionate criminalisation of marginalised communities – particularly inner-city black youth, fuelling stigma and inequalities.[49]

When we progress to the next stage of the injustice system, prosecution, Black people are 12 times more likely to be prosecuted for cannabis possession than white people.[50] This on its own is troubling, but then you see that Theresa May's husband Philip's Capital Group is an investor in a UK medical cannabis exporter[51] – it's literally one rule for the rich, powerful and white, and another for the poor, underrepresented and Black. One makes money, the other gets put in jail.

After prosecution, the injustice continues. Looking at length of custody, the average in 2019 was 27.1 months for offenders from Black, Asian and minority ethnic backgrounds, compared with 19.5 months for white offenders. This is in part explained by white offenders being much more likely to plead guilty, as a guilty plea carries a discount of up to a third of sentence length at the sentencing stage.[52] However, the 'Lammy Review' (2017) found that this difference in guilty pleas was in part down to Black people being less likely to trust the justice system and due to less experienced legal representation.[53]

Legal aid – an instrument that is meant to give people the ability to access this hugely imperfect system, specifically those who cannot afford private lawyers – has suffered unprecedented cuts since the Conservatives came to power in 2010. The 2012 Legal Aid, Sentencing and Punishment of Offenders Act saw £350 million knocked off of the £2 billion legal aid budget, resulting in vast numbers of people losing access to much needed legal support.[54] Expenditure on criminal legal aid reached a peak of £1.2 billion in 2004/05 but by 2019/2020 had fallen to £841 million, a decline in cash terms of around 30 per cent and a decline in real terms of around 43 per cent since 2004/05. In 2020/21 the pandemic had a serious impact on many providers and continues to do so.[55] Of course, these cuts have affected all those on lower incomes, but 72 per cent of legal aid clients are from BAME backgrounds.[56] For women this issue is also pressing. Emma Scott, director of Rights of Women said: 'We know already that in family law women are the majority of applicants for legal aid. In 2006, 62 per cent of all applications for legal aid were for women. If you remove legal aid for women to sort out the finances after marriages break down, we know it's really difficult to represent yourself. We say ultimately it will increase women's poverty because they will not be able to reach satisfactory arrangements.'[57] Amnesty's 2016 report concluded that 'cuts to legal aid have decimated access to justice for thousands of people.'[58]

When my mum finally got a divorce from my dad, I saw these disparities play out in real life. She had to rely on a legal aid lawyer, whereas my dad – with all his experience of the criminal and legal system – had a top lawyer. We were told it would be a simple case, with my mum deserving of half of everything, and yet my dad managed to delay and bully, hide assets and even attempted to take my mum's pension. When my dad tried to make my sister and mum homeless by sending bailiffs to the house (I had already moved out), we had to represent ourselves in court. We were lucky that the judge took pity on us and threw the case out, so my mum and sister were able to remain in the house. It took years for my mum to get even some money and it was nothing close to the 50 per cent she should have got. Not only had my mum gone through almost thirty years of documented emotional and physical abuse, she now had to contend with a system actually stacked in favour of my dad! The whole thing was so stressful and unfair, it made me hate the UK legal system. Even then, before the bulk of the cuts, I could see that a two-tier system had been created.

You can see how injustices beget more injustices in a system riddled with bias and underfunding, but this isn't where the issues with the legal system ends. Privatisation of prisons has created a new system of perverse incentives to make matters even worse. The so-called prison industrial complex (PIC), defined as the overlapping interests of government and industry that use surveillance, policing and imprisonment, is often spoken about in a US context, but the UK is not immune. In fact, Britain was the first European nation to open for-profit prisons, with 15 per cent of the prison population now in private prisons – the highest proportion in Europe and higher than the US.[59]

A UK campaign group focused on the benefits of public ownership, We Own It, lays out the disturbing facts about our private prisons. The private companies running our prisons aim for around 8–10 per cent profit margins.[60] This requires them to drive down cost by paying staff less or having a smaller workforce. This cost cutting is partly what explains the higher incidence of assaults in private prisons versus public ones.[61] Meanwhile, companies like G4S encourage prisoners to work 40 hour weeks yet can pay them as little as £2 a day. And no, the privatisation of prisons isn't about cost saving for the government; there is no evidence of reduced costs, indeed given the various issues they may even cost more.[62]

The US has found that when states turn to private prisons, the number of criminals incarcerated rises and the length of sentences increases.[63] One study found that private prisons lead to an average increase of 178 new prisoners per million of the total population per year. At an average cost of $60 per day per prisoner, that costs states between $1.9 to $10.6 million per year, if all those additional prisoners are in private prisons.[64] While we haven't seen similar figures in the UK, it doesn't take a PhD to work out why for-profit companies running prisons might create incentives to lobby government to go harder on crime.

Then there are the ways in which the relationship between private prison companies, such as G4S, have a very cosy relationship with government. In 2012, it was reported that G4S had a former home secretary and defence secretary on its board.[65] This type of revolving door between politicians in government and private sector companies that get huge public sector contracts represents a conflict of interest and wholly undermines trust in institutions that are meant to be delivering the best and most cost-efficient services. The introduction of profit incentives into the country's incarceration system crosses a troubling line that puts financial gain above the public interest of safety and rehabilitation.

In 2013, Serco were overbilling the government on electronic tagging contracts, charging for offenders who were already dead; they were fined £70 million. Then, in 2019, they were fined £22.9 million for false accounting.[66] However, they are still rewarded contract after contract in prison and immigration detention and beyond.[67] It is interesting to say the least that the people imprisoning people for a profit are actually criminals. Yet another example of white-collar crime being treated completely differently.

From who gets stopped and searched to the way prisons are run, the system hammers inequality further into our institutions and the lives that are caught up in it. Not only do we not have a system that rewards merit fairly and equally, we have a system that punishes unevenly. The consequences for those that get caught up in this system are dire – 'working hard' to escape a system designed to trap you is a big ask. The end point is a 2020 prison profile where 13 per cent of those incarcerated are Black, even though they make up just 3 per cent of the population, and, even more disturbingly, where 32 per cent of all children in prison are Black.[68]

## THE ECONOMY FEEDS OFF HIERARCHY

*'Imagining away the existence of races in a racist world is as conserving and harmful as imagining away classes in a capitalistic world – it allows the ruling races and classes to keep on ruling.'*

Ibram X. Kendi, *How to Be an Antiracist* (2019)[69]

In one of my first ever policy jobs I worked with people who were obsessed with looking clever. And in this environment at this time, looking clever meant being focused on the economy and economic growth. It was as if there was no such thing as society. Suffice to say I would find myself at odds with many of the people there, especially the senior staff. The worst came out when we discussed immigration. I was working on a report about Eastern European immigration, looking at what industries they were employed in. I had found that in Hull, they were predominantly in food manufacturing and were especially concentrated in meatpacking factories. These are typically low-paid jobs in difficult conditions and I was told that these jobs were notoriously hard to fill before the influx of Eastern Europeans. With the financial crisis of 2008 and related recession, there was a question of how manufacturing in the city would be affected and hence what would happen to the Eastern European population.

'Well, they will be like the Pakistanis that came here to work in factories, then as those jobs went they became obsolete,' the head of research of the organisation, himself an immigrant from Canada, said. I looked around to see if anyone also felt this was rude and offensive, but no one seemed to have noticed. Instead, another member of staff piped up to agree. 'Yes, [name] is right, these workers will be like those that came from Jamaica and Pakistan, they will be unnecessary for the British economy and hence unneeded here.'

I wrote down what I had heard in my notebook. I felt the blood rush to my face and steam come out of my ears like we used to see in cartoons. Did they think of people only as accessories for the economy? And were they really so ignorant about the histories of immigration from Pakistan and Jamaica as to dismiss those populations and only value them for what they could do in the economy? As a junior member of the team I decided to wait until the end of the meeting to say something, partly because I needed to control my anger! So, just as everyone thought the meeting was ending, I gathered my courage and told them how upset I had been to hear the way that people, including my own family, had been spoken about in this meeting: 'Immigrants are not just cogs in your economic machine.' I think they were embarrassed, they couldn't look me in the eye for a couple of weeks.

Like so many times in my life, if I had not been in this elite space, no one would have said anything. This is because the dehumanisation of certain groups is completely normalised. People do not even notice. But this dehumanisation has worked for our economy. Throughout history, and most notably in the case of slavery,[70] capitalism could only take root and prosper off the backs of free or at least very low-paid labour. Racialised exploitation and capital accumulation are mutually reinforcing.

Racial capitalism is a concept coined by Cedric J. Robinson in his book *Black Marxism: The Making of the Black Radical Tradition*, published in 1983. It provides 'a conceptual framework to understand the mutually constitutive nature of racialisation and capitalist exploitation'.[71] The idea is that capitalism only values that which – and those who – add capital to an economy, and that policies strip people of colour of their ability to do this, thus devaluing them to society as a whole. In the UK, like so many other places, economic inequality is both racialised and gendered, with Black and brown people and women consistently at the bottom of the economic hierarchy, often in less-desirable jobs, with lower earnings and higher poverty rates. Once, during a conversation with a Brazilian-born Uber driver who had come to my local advice surgery to talk about the difficulties of earning a decent living from the platform, he asked if I thought that it was a coincidence that most of the drivers were immigrants. I said no. The general rule seems to be that where society values certain groups less so does the economy.

Even when people of colour do own their own business, there are persistent disparities in outcomes. After starting a business, Black business owners have a median turnover of just £25,000, compared to £35,000 for white business owners.[72] Lack of access to finance is a key reason why people of colour say they stop investing in their business ideas.[73]

Generations of these disparities mean that in the UK, for every £1 of white British wealth, Pakistani households have around 50p, Black Caribbean around 20p, and Black African and Bangladeshi approximately 10p.[74] It is important here to make a class distinction to explain differences between minority ethnic groups in the UK. Indians, especially those that came via East Africa, were much more likely to migrate to the UK to be doctors and accountants, rather than nurses and factory workers. The difference for this group is 90–95p to every £1 of White British wealth.[75]

We often think we can overcome racism with a bit of antiracism training, but that will not solve issues of racial disparities and unequal life chances. We need to think more about how the economy works, who it works for, who it rewards and why. (We will get deeper into this in Chapter 8.) The question is: can we run the economy without rising inequality and the exploitation of certain groups? The answer is yes, but we have to do much more to redistribute wealth, improve the quality of and access to public services, and increase wages and workers' rights. What we are certainly not striving for is to have a few more Black and brown faces at the top of society, upholding and even fighting for a system that taxes the rich less, rips off workers and holds on to a rigid economic hierarchy. The aim here is not to have as many poor white people as poor Black people, rather it is to eradicate poverty altogether.

## CARING ABOUT RACISM AS A BAD THING

In 2020, in the wake of the murder of George Floyd and the mass protests on racial equality it sparked across the world, there was a growing call to remove statues of historic figures that had been involved in the slave trade or otherwise responsible for racist oppression. In Bristol, local protesters took action into their own hands, pulling down a statue of the slave trader

Edward Colston and throwing it into Bristol docks. The act divided opinion nationally with the Conservative government voicing strong opposition. The then culture secretary, Oliver Dowden, told museums that they risked losing public funding if they took down statues as a result of pressure from campaigners[76] and the right-wing press chastised the National Trust and others for being 'woke'.

In the same year, the Equalities Minister, Kemi Badenoch, declared that the government is 'unequivocally against' the teaching of critical race theory. 'We do not want to see teachers teaching their white pupils about white privilege and inherited racial guilt.' At the height of the Black Lives Matter protests after the murder of George Floyd, the then foreign secretary, Dominic Raab, belittled taking the knee as having originated in *Game of Thrones* and said that it was fit only for proposals of marriage or meeting the Queen. A year later, a slew of Conservative politicians joined him to complain about the England football team taking the knee during the European Championship, with the then home secretary, Priti Patel, refusing to criticise the England fans booing them.[77]

Why so much antagonism towards those taking a stand against racism? These examples are part of a broader narrative about those fighting for the rights of discriminated and marginalised groups, which is to pit them against one of the largest social groups: the working class. The argument goes something like this: asking for women's equality, gay rights, trans rights, racial equality or any other form of group-based rights, somehow equates to fighting *against* more attention and better material conditions for the working class. You are the enemy of the majority and only there to posture for groups of people who are taking up too much political space. You are, in countries such as the UK and the US, the 'woke mob'. This thinking is the reason why the government is able to put out reports saying institutional racism doesn't exist,[78] with significant public support. Rather than the acknowledgement of systemic racism we have systematic denial. We are in a deeply damaging phony war of the working class versus the 'woke-ing' class but there is: (a) nothing wrong with being 'woke' if that simply means being aware of structural disadvantages certain groups face; and (b) group-based inequalities and economic inequalities do not contradict each other; rather they overlap, with many of us fighting against both.

In a situation like that of the UK, where racism is still a problem and where we have never confronted our colonial history, we are stuck. We are also likely to repeat huge and inhumane mistakes like the Windrush scandal, when the descendants of those people that came from the Caribbean to help rebuild this country after the Second World War were wrongly deported.[79] A society that doesn't see race – not because we live in a utopia, but because it is too painful to look at it – won't make any progress. Not seeing race is not looking at the reality of the construction of our society. Exorcising the demons of the British Empire might be difficult but it is necessary to build understanding. The ongoing culture wars cast wokeness as the villain, but being woke is understanding our history and having empathy for each other. That is something we should want.

Luckily more people are waking up to the realities of racial discrimination, especially in the wake of the brutal murder of George Floyd in the USA. The constituency I ran in, Chingford and Woodford Green, is roughly 70 per cent white[80] and yet when local protests were organised a sizable number of people turned up on Chingford Green. Later, when I organised a more in-depth conversation with young people, I was surprised that so many turned up and delighted that they engaged and exchanged information with each other. These young people gave me so much hope. Educating yourself is key, but so is changing the economic system.

## INDIVIDUAL ESCAPISM WON'T SOLVE STRUCTURAL RACISM

During a trip to Hollywood to visit a cousin, I randomly found myself at dinner with film director Antoine Fuqua (*Training Day*, *The Equalizer*). Being clueless about films and nervous about being in the vicinity of someone who knows Denzel Washington, I thought I would turn the conversation to my strength – inequality (yes, I'm obsessed and annoying!). I asked about his journey to becoming a famous director in Hollywood. I thought he would talk about parental support or being inspired by watching a certain movie, but he told me instead about a big piece of luck that came his way. While he grew up in the ghettos of Pittsburgh, his destiny changed because his name was picked in a school lottery that meant he was literally bussed out of his poor neighbourhood to a rich one. I had read academic papers about these programmes during my PhD and I was stunned to be confronted by one of the beneficiaries in real life. He told me about how this richer neighbourhood gave him access to people doing jobs of all kinds, and that these friendships and connections had a dramatic impact on what he thought was possible for his life.

I couldn't get over how easily we could have been deprived of this talented director, one of very few African American directors in Hollywood when he started making movies in the 1990s, and it made me think about how much we are missing out on as a society more generally. The solution, though, cannot be bussing a few more working-class Black children into a white neighbourhood, because what about the ones that don't get picked? Escape for a few with hardship for the many is surely not the end point we are aiming for.

Even for those who do escape, it turns out that it is harder for them to climb the stairs of success, and easier to find themselves pushed back down. A study in the USA was able to compare like-for-like for white and Black people. They found definitively that most white boys raised in wealthy families will stay rich or upper middle class as adults, but Black boys raised in similarly rich households will not. For poor children, the pattern is reversed. Most poor Black boys will remain poor as adults, while white boys raised in poor families fare far better on average. The *New York Times* provided a powerful visualisation of the data in which you can see clearly how much more frequent it is for Black men to fall from the wealthiest 20 per cent to the poorest 20 per cent in terms of income.[81] This is no doubt linked to the differences in family wealth to fall back on if things go wrong, but it also shows that discriminated-against ethnic groups are more likely to face extra scrutiny in the workplace.[82] Work hard, do everything right but one misstep and you're sliding back down the snake. You are never safe from a racist system.

Imagining life as a game of snakes and ladders, it is not only the dice that is loaded against working-class people of colour, they are having to play a game with twice the amount of snakes as ladders. The game is rigged, so why do we force people to play it?

While working out the probabilities of a Black person becoming prime minister,[83] I also had to look at the life paths of previous prime ministers. Three-quarters of all our prime ministers went to either Oxford or Cambridge – including Liz Truss, Boris Johnson, Theresa May, David Cameron and Tony

Blair. Every university-educated prime minister who has won a general election since 1937 went to Oxford or Cambridge, with John Major being the only prime minister without a university education, and Gordon Brown having not won a general election. I don't think we want to be endorsing this path. These elite routes are not just exclusionary of all those not born rich, but also why we get the wrong types of politicians. We should try to move away from these elite pathways altogether.

People may look at Obama and say 'Well, he did it.' But again, he was the exception. Also, Obama was followed by arguably the most explicitly racist president in modern history – Donald Trump. A focus on the exceptions means we are not looking at how we change the system or do the hard work on reducing racial prejudice in society. Recently, the Conservatives have been extremely self-congratulatory with their ethnically diverse Cabinets, but as discussed in Chapter 1, these ministers often went to private schools and have spent a lot of their political careers pulling up the ladder for migrants and working-class people. It feels like people of colour are accepted at the top of politics only when they represent or uphold the same economic and political system that oppresses everyone else.

The last four chapters on global inequalities, wealth, class and race have pointed to what is driving differences in opportunities. Often the answer suggested is education. However, as we have started to discuss in relation to race here, too often our education system is part of the problem.

# 7

## EDUCATION:
## THE GREAT UN-EQUALISER

One dark December night during the 2019 election campaign, I knocked on the door of a large house on the edge of East London. I was greeted by a woman who turned angry at the mention of the Labour Party, telling me her main priority was being able to send her children to private school. She felt that Labour's proposed policy to take away the tax break that private schools receive would put that in jeopardy because of a potential increase in fees. I replied with what I had said to other parents, and indeed to pupils in private schools, that while there was a possibility that the cost could go up, it was the educational well-being of all children that the Labour Party had to consider. A tax break to private schools was simply unfair to underfunded state-run schools who were not able to claim charitable status.

She didn't buy it. 'What does that mean for my daughter?' I saw her daughter lingering in the hallway and asked if she wanted to say anything. The mum answered for her, 'All she cares about is her school.'

'That's understandable. But there is also the wider question of what kind of society you want your daughter to grow up in. Which political party will deliver on the climate crisis, on equality, on bringing people together?'

She stared at me blankly, then explained that all that had nothing to do with her, and her only focus was ensuring her kids could get ahead.

This mindset is a cornerstone of the society in which we live. It is a society that has cultivated the values of individualism and winning at all costs, so it is unsurprising and even natural that parents will want their kids not to lose in this game. The consequence is that rather than being the great leveller, education is a route by which people maintain their family's advantage and inequality reproduces itself. On another doorstep, I was told by a parent that he was 'highly aspirational' and that is why he sent his kids to private school. As if working-class parents who can't afford private school fees don't want the best for their kids! Parents' desires for their child to get ahead often creates or reinforces educational hierarchies. These parents shouldn't be demonised, as at the end of the day they are behaving rationally given the way the system works, but we should recognise that the system is rotten.

Everyone agrees with equality of opportunity in principle but we simply can't give people more equal access to opportunities without more equal incomes. If we had to make a guide to social mobility in the UK, it would include being born into a wealthy family, preferably white, and then being educated at a private school where class sizes are significantly, sometimes 50 per cent, smaller.[1] How can even the best of state school teachers make up for these key determining factors? Poverty, overcrowded housing, parental stress, poor access to the internet and computers, insufficient food – all of these factors have an impact on a child's success[2,3] yet even with the right funding schools can only provide better meals within school hours, and potentially a laptop and dongle. The pandemic has also widened the underlying economic differences between households.[4] We are simply asking too much of teachers and state schools.

Despite these facts, we persistently cling to the notion that education can solve it all and be the great social leveller. But how can an education system, with its own hierarchies based on private, selective, non-selective schools and elite universities possibly provide equal opportunities? Simple answer – it can't. As the sociologist Basil Bernstein famously wrote, 'education cannot compensate for society'.[5] However, as we will discuss, while education is not the silver bullet for social mobility that policymakers present it as, it could be key in developing a new model of success.

## THE GOLDEN PATHWAY?

Once upon a time I volunteered for schemes that aimed to increase applications from those from low-income backgrounds to the University of Oxford. It involved going from state school to state school, encouraging young people to apply. I would give big speeches about how even though it was difficult to fit in to the institution if you are working class, we had to attend to ensure the views of everyday people were represented in the jobs that came after coveted degrees from Oxford – politics, business and the media. I was pretty smug about the voluntary work – I featured in *CosmoGirl* at the age of nineteen as a 'teen changing the world'. But through the years, I've come to see championing this narrow idea of success as not just inadequate but deeply problematic. These institutions are steeped in colonialism, elitist rituals and intellectual snobbery – how can they ever be bastions for the working class or progressive change? Of course, having more people from working-class backgrounds there could help to remake the culture and at least open doors for those able to enter. However, I saw more of my working-class peers assimilate into elite cultures and ideology rather than be made more class conscious by being at the institution. Thinking you are superior to others is alluring – even for those who should know better.

What I learned at the time was designed to make me think only about me, to think that rich nations were 'developed' and superior, that poor countries were poor because of their own mistakes, that welfare systems were not economically optimal and that issues of inequality were secondary to economic growth. I didn't really have the vocabulary to articulate my anger, but I knew I hated it.

Thankfully, the teaching of economics has been questioned since the financial crisis of 2008,[6] which no mainstream economist of the time saw coming. A few economists outside of the mainstream had pointed out that we were on shaky ground,[7] but they were roundly dismissed and ridiculed. When students started walking out of economics lectures in the UK and USA,[8] the discipline had to do some self-reflection.

Yet, people that went through Oxford are seen as somehow superior. I studied philosophy, politics and economics, the famous PPE degree that so many of our prime ministers also studied. I can tell you that in my experience many of the people who studied PPE are among the worst, most arrogant and entitled people around. I would go as far as saying that reading PPE at Oxford should be seen as a red flag, not a sign of superiority. Fundamentally, the principles I learned stemmed from a belief system that had created imperialism, empire and poverty in a world of plenty. I spent ten years after university trying to take everything that I learned out of my head. I re-examined it and then replaced it with something closer to the reality of the world, power and class.

\*

In this chapter we are going to look at inequalities in education outcomes, but sometimes when we have this conversation we revert to assuming that the 'best route' into adulthood is to go to a top university. This is how social mobility is conventionally measured, but in presenting solutions we need to go beyond thinking how many others can follow this route and think about how we can redesign the whole system. Currently, our education system promotes the types of hierarchies of success and academic talent that we need to bin if we are to give everyone the dignity and livelihoods they need for a happy life.

## EDUCATIONAL OUTCOMES: WHERE YOU CAME FROM IS WHERE YOU END UP

Ask any politician what should be done about social mobility and I'm pretty sure the first answer they will give is something about education. One noticeable example was New Labour's mantra of 'education, education, education'.[9] The cuts to public services since 2010, under the guise of austerity, has further diminished the purchase that education can have against growing wealth inequalities. In 2019, the respected think tank the Institute for Fiscal Studies (IFS) found that since 2010 schools and colleges in England have suffered the worst fall in spending since the 1970s. The report found that adult education, further education and skills spending on young people have been hardest hit by austerity since 2010, with spending on classroom-based adult education and apprenticeships down by more than a third since 2009–10.[10] The government, under Boris Johnson, had in 2019 committed £14 billion over three years to increase spending on schools in England.[11] The IFS calculated that the extra money will 'just about reverse' the 8 per cent cuts in spending per pupil since 2009.[12]

The response to the report from Boris Johnson's government at the time? A press release from a spokesperson at the Department for Education said its new funding was 'the biggest cash boost for a decade. The prime minister is clear that education is one of his main priorities, and we want a system that boosts productivity, improves social mobility and equips children and adults with the skills and knowledge they need to succeed.'[13] So, after cutting for a decade, the government wanted to be applauded for bringing funding barely back in line with what it was over a decade ago.

The impacts of these cuts, and wider educational reforms, have been profound for inequality. The gap between rich and poor students attending university is wider than it's been for more than a decade.[14] Wherever and however you look, our education system is not correcting inequalities, rather it is exacerbating them. Research by the Sutton Trust highlights how few are mobile through our education system, finding that even when those from deprived backgrounds do get into a top Russell Group university, they can still find themselves back in the bottom half of the income spectrum.[15] The trends can be divided into four key types of journeys:

- Group 1. Going nowhere: most of the richest and the poorest are on a conveyor belt. The most affluent groups are on what looks like a straight path from high-income families, through top universities to high incomes (defined as the top 20 per cent of earners) in their thirties. This conveyor belt trend is true for the most deprived group too, who start at the bottom and stay there.
- Group 2. Stuck at the top: even those who don't go to university from the most affluent group are still likely to end up in the higher income categories.

- Group 3. A bumpy ride: the few from the poorest group who go to the top universities still don't necessarily end up in the most affluent group. Instead, they seem to be on a roller-coaster ride, reaching their peak at university. Statistically, their university education does not pay off the way it does for their more affluent peers in terms of jobs and incomes by age 30.
- Group 4. In the middle: this group also tends to see a reversion to the same level, whether they have been to a Russell Group university or didn't attend university.

This is not a picture of an education system driving social mobility. Instead it paints the same picture as the other statistics in this book – that we live in a society where most people stay in their place.

## INEQUALITY SQUARED

While they get the lion's share of the blame, as well as the focus for solutions, universities are neither key to educational problems nor where the main solutions are. The problem starts way before university and every step in the education process heaps more inequality on top of inequality.[16] A simple resource breakdown of education from nursery and early years to further education helps to demonstrate this point.

### Nursery and early years

Study after study tells us that early childhood is a vital life stage that can shape a child's later path through life.[17] Research from neuroscience shows that during the early years of a child's life – from birth until around six years of age – their brain has extraordinary capacity for learning. By the time a child is six, the same time most early childhood education programmes end, their brain has already reached about 90 per cent of its adult volume.[18]

Since 2010, there have been cuts in spending on the early childhood services targeted towards disadvantaged families. Most notably, Sure Start children's centres, which were local hubs providing health advice, parenting support and opportunities for play and learning, experienced devastating cuts. These equated to 70 per cent between 2010–11 and 2018–19. Since 2010 there has been an expansion of free and subsidised childcare for working parents, but this excludes the most disadvantaged.[19] Meanwhile, as the rich have got richer, so have the resources to stimulate and nurture children in wealthier households.[20]

*Primary school*

Even at the age of five there are significant differences in achievement at school. Only 57 per cent of children who are eligible for free school meals are assessed as having a good level of development in meeting early learning goals, compared with 74 per cent of children from better-off households.[21]

During the Covid-19 pandemic, 15 per cent of teachers from deprived schools reported that more than a third of pupils would not have electronic access to schoolwork compared to 2 per cent at more affluent state schools.[22] All the signs indicate that the pandemic may have increased the educational gap, as disadvantaged pupils are less likely to remotely access resources that promote learning and enable contact with teachers.

Across England, Wales and Northern Ireland, 1 in 8 schools do not have a library. Schools with a large number of pupils eligible for free school meals, where libraries would be most beneficial, are twice as likely to be without one.[23]

It is worth noting too, that teachers in England lost 17 per cent of their real-terms pay between 2010 and 2021.[24] An OECD survey comparing the working lives of teachers across 45 different countries, found that teachers in England are some of the most monitored and scrutinised of any rich country. However, they rank as one of the lowest when it comes to being consulted on curriculum and assessment.[25] And it is not just the teachers that are over-monitored: children in the UK face testing from the age of 4 upwards. The UK is unusual in its emphasis of statutory standard assessment for children at ages 7 and 11. Published school league tables also add to this emphasis on testing and test scores. This relentless focus on academic monitoring has made it less likely that we consider other aspects of education, such as children's well-being and creativity.[26]

Overall, the UK is the world's fifth economy yet ranks twenty-third in educational inequality in primary schools.[27]

*Secondary school*

Private secondary schools in England receive substantially more income per pupil than their state school peers. In 2017–18, on average the private schools had a mean per pupil income 3.6 times higher than their local state-funded schools, even where those schools were in the same local authority. The mean income per pupil for private schools found in the same study by the think tank Common Wealth was £21,664, compared to £6,024 in state-funded schools.[28] So children living in the same area, even on the same street, could be having completely different experiences of education.

The economic gap in school incomes varied across the country and between different private schools. For the most elite boarding schools, the per pupil income was substantially higher. The study found that 23 schools had per pupil incomes 7 times higher than their local state schools. At the top of this list, Marlborough College had a per pupil income 12 times higher than state schools in the same local authority and Eton College had an income 10 times higher.

According to the Programme for International Student Assessment, which considers the overall knowledge and skills of 15-year-olds including literacy, reading, mathematics, and science, the UK was 13th in the world in 2018.[29] It ranks 16th in inequality in secondary schools, behind less affluent countries, including Romania and Poland.[30]

### University

On a freezing cold morning in December 2017, I found myself giving a speech outside Goldsmiths, University of London. Lecturers were on strike over a pensions dispute, which was the latest assault on their pay and benefits. Among the large crowd stood disgruntled academics alongside university support staff and students who were united in their anger at the direction of travel in higher education. Looking around at the striking lecturers, underpaid staff and debt-ridden students the obvious question was: who is higher education working for? The situation has not changed since 2017: in fact at the time of writing more strikes are being planned as the wages and working conditions of university staff are being further eroded.

The extreme hierarchy of UK higher education – with Oxbridge at the top, followed by other Russell Group universities, then old universities pre-1992 and finally post-1992 institutions – perpetuates inequalities in terms of who applies and who is accepted. It is worth remembering the difference this makes to earnings for graduates. Back in 2014, six months after graduating, Oxbridge graduates earned £25,600 on average; this is approximately £7,500 more than those that went to a post-1992 university[31] and this gap continues to open over careers.

Furthermore, those who attend higher education earn a lot more on average than those who do not. At age 29 the average man who attended higher education earns around 25 per cent more than the average man (with 5 A\*–C GCSEs) who did not. For women the gap is more than 50 per cent, largely because women with graduate degrees tend to work more hours than non-graduate women.[32]

## Further education

Higher education is of course not the only route for adults wishing to remain in education. Further education – the colleges and institutions that provide education below degree level for people above school age – is an alternative, but it gets less attention and even less funding. In the era of austerity we have seen cuts ideologically applied across the country and further education increasingly undermined, with 16- to 18-year-olds in education facing the sharpest cuts in the sector. Communities that have been left behind, and in reality held back through bad policy, have seen local adult education centres shut, which has left them further isolated and unable to learn locally. All this at a time when automation is leading to a reduction in well-paid middle-level positions, which means that we need more, not less, adult education.

Each stage of education carries a huge unequalising force. The end point is an accumulation of inequality, not equality. Figure 1 overleaf highlights the huge disparities in educational attainment at the age of 26 by group.

*Figure 1: Highest level of educational attainment among 26-year-olds by socio-economic status, and if went to an independent school, in England 2016*[33]

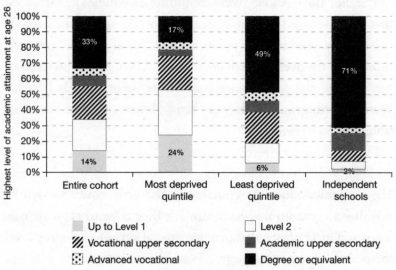

No recent event brought home the issues of a rigged education system more than the use of an algorithm to 'normalise' the distribution of A-level grades. Due to the Covid-19 lockdown, pupils were unable to sit exams in 2020, so instead teachers were asked to submit the grades they thought their pupils would get. The exams regulator Ofqual then used an algorithm with the aim to keep grades in line with previous years. Thousands of young people were left devastated when they opened their results to find their grades had dropped from As to Cs, and from Cs to Us – but this disappointment was not evenly spread. Not one person got downgraded at Eton and in terms of upgrades those at private schools saw an increase of 4.7 per cent in the proportion of students getting As and A*s, while state-run further education colleges – like the one I went to – saw an increase of just 0.2 per cent.

Angry pupils flooded the roads around Downing Street and the Department for Education demanding a government U-turn to return grades to teachers' assessments, chanting 'Justice for the working class'. The government finally relented. What many failed to notice was that even when the algorithm was not involved in both 2018 and 2019, there was more than a 20 percentage point difference between the proportion getting As and A*s at A level at private schools versus state schools.[34] The algorithm was mimicking the inequalities already in the education system.

Even with the grades, relying on educational success to get your kids ahead is becoming a harder game. People in the highest positions who get paid the most rarely have the highest education. Educational achievement means much less than it used to and is rarely a passport to the top. There are no education ladders to climb to become the Duke of Westminster!

The idea that we can turn this system around without systematic change, without addressing the obscene advantages of attending private schools – especially the very top private schools, followed by elite universities, is farcical. It is simply impossible.

## WHO GETS TO BE ARTISTIC?

It is important not to limit our understanding of the biases within the education system to just academic outputs. Music and art are other areas where investment in state schools has sharply declined. Michael Gove's introduction of the English Baccalaureate (EBacc) led to subjects being downgraded and secondary schools had no incentive to offer them as GCSE subjects. The result is that 1 in 5 schools have given up teaching music entirely, with only 35,000 pupils completing

GCSE music in England in the summer of 2018, representing a decline of 23 per cent since 2010, while entries for A-level music have fallen by 40 per cent since 2011.[35] This stripping of music from our state schools is showing in our national musical institutions, with 70 per cent of the members of the National Children's Orchestra coming from private schools and only 30 per cent from state schools.[36] Less than 1 in 10 students studying music at university are from the Black community or other ethnic minority communities, which is quite something when you think about the dominance of Black culture in our pop music charts.

In 2021, even after eleven years of cuts, the Office for Students (OfS) and the then education secretary Gavin Williamson proposed to cut funding for 'high cost' subjects, including music, dance, drama and performing arts, and art and design by 50 per cent. The consultation stated that these were not considered 'strategic priorities' by the government.[37]

What does this say about the pipeline of talent for the future? Expect Eton boys rapping and putting on Northern accents as they play working-class caricatures. This is not just about opportunities for young people to be whoever they want to be, it is about the stories that will be told and the mirror that will be held up to our society in the future. Cultural outputs are fundamental in social education and entertainment and without a diverse set of people producing these outputs our country will seem extremely flat and one note.

## GRAMMAR SCHOOLS ARE NOT THE ANSWER

Whether it's Theresa May or Liz Truss, politicians keep coming back to the idea of grammar schools to solve our social mobility problem. More grammar schools – which historically select children by ability at the age of eleven – would actually make things worse. The evidence is clear that grammar schools do not lower educational inequalities – not when they were introduced over sixty years ago, and not today. One of the times this came up as a policy option, in 2016, I had to go on TV and argue why it was such a bad idea. While I talked about the evidence, my opponent was almost overcome with nostalgia, the sort of 'when I was young' grandparent lecture, talking about what it was like in the 1950s when they were at school. A classic case of anecdotal bias, which is not how we should be making policy.

Firstly, very few of the poor attend grammar schools, even in areas where there are multiple grammar schools like in Birmingham and Kent. Their intake is primarily from the upper middle class. Only 2.6 per cent of pupils have free school meals in existing grammar schools, compared to 15 per cent across the UK. Even in the 1960s, when 26 per cent of children were from the 'unskilled working class' at grammar schools, a high dropout rate meant that they represented just 0.3 per cent of those achieving two A levels or more.[38]

Secondly, the evidence shows that grammar schools do not increase overall educational performance. In Kent – which retains a fully selective secondary education system – the achievement of pupils as a whole is no higher than the national average while educational outcomes are less equitable than elsewhere. Furthermore, outcomes for pupils from backgrounds of social disadvantage in Kent – the group least likely to attend local grammar schools – are markedly worse than the national average for similar pupils. Internationally, evidence from the OECD shows that the best-performing education systems are those with 'comprehensive' school systems and those that tier children by school have less equitable outcomes without an overall performance advantage. In other words, grammar schools do not lead to higher academic standards overall and create greater inequalities in achievement.

One of the most egregious problems with the grammar school selection process is the way it makes children feel about their capabilities. There is a real worry that just as in the 1950s, 60s and 70s, grammar schools will separate children at age eleven, essentially telling many that they are not good enough. Parents need to ask themselves not only how they would feel if their child got in to one of these schools, but also if they did not. Creating winners and losers in the education system so early on in life is likely to strengthen class divides and inequality outcomes. All children deserve the best chance to fulfil their potential.

The bottom line is that grammar schools would only complicate the system further and act as a distraction from increasing the quality of comprehensive education. We must stop harking back to a mythical era in which grammar schools helped lower educational inequality. An educational system that allows only a lucky few to escape low incomes while leaving everyone else behind is not the kind of education system we should be aiming for. It is genuinely depressing that we keep having the same argument. We need forward-thinking policy instead of looking to the past to fix today's problems.

## THE SECRET TO INCREASING LIFE CHANCES IS GIVING PEOPLE MORE CHANCES AND MORE SKILLS

The educational route needs to be widened, with many more good options for young people. In other countries the vocational route offers this, but not here. In the UK, around 700,000 people are training to be apprentices, with under-19s making up less than a quarter of this total, meaning under 5 per cent of young people.[39] In Germany, the number is closer to 60 per cent – in fields as diverse as advanced manufacturing, IT, banking and hospitality. In Europe, what's often called 'dual training' is a highly respected career path.

The quality of the apprenticeships available also varies considerably between Germany and the UK. In Germany, apprenticeships usually last three years with a mixture of hands-on work experience and in-classroom training at specialised schools. By the end, apprentices are deemed licensed tradespeople with a status that means great job prospects and a decent income.[40] Electricians, for example, earn an average of €36,000 per year, which rises to €45,000 with more experience and training. In the UK, meanwhile, this salary is around £35,000 at the top end of the scale.[41,42]

The beauty of the apprenticeship or further education route is that it also gives people opportunities to retrain as they get older. Our current system relies on people having to get everything right during their teenage years – for many of us that is just not possible. What if a parent gets sick? Or you have to move house because a parent loses their job? Even one bad emotional break-up at the wrong time in the exam cycle and life is suddenly a lot harder. Not to mention that it is a lot to ask a 16-year-old to pick the subjects that will lead to the career they want for the rest of their lives. We need a system that is kinder.

There are a number of countries not only making efforts to train non-graduates, but also to combine this with greening the economy. Looking at South Korea, Sweden and Germany, we find that there are several key attributes of this approach: the mix of in-work and specialised skills training (including via digital education platforms); the provision of financial support including childcare for those wishing to train or retrain; special efforts to recruit women and individuals from marginalised groups; an emphasis on the specific demands of the labour market; and

public investment in green job creation.[43] The UK would do well
to look at these experiences to implement similar policies here.

## HOW SCHOOLS COULD BE THE ANSWER

*'You can be anything you're good at, as long as they're
hiring . . . and even then, it helps to know somebody.'*

Chris Rock, *Total Blackout: The Tamborine Extended Cut*, 2021[44]

We have spoken about the power of who you know in a few
places in this book, but it is important to emphasise just how
big a factor this is. New studies using Facebook data in the US
found that the mixing of income groups is crucial to giving
children from low-income backgrounds the contacts they need
for educational and economic uplift. Strikingly, one particular study found that when low-income children grew up in
neighbourhoods where 70 per cent of their friends were from
higher-income families, the lower-income children's future
incomes went up by an average of 20 per cent.[45] It turns out
that this sort of socio-economic mix is a stronger predictor of
later upward mobility than a neighbourhood's poverty rates,
family structures or school quality.

So, there is some good news here. Schools could help boost
the chances of lower-income kids by bringing together children
of different backgrounds and income levels. Of course, this
would require better integration between kids from different
backgrounds to avoid social segregation in the classroom or
playground. The issue is that current selection processes, and
the ability of those with more money to game these processes,
mean that there isn't a lot of mixing across class groups. One
suggestion is that we use a lottery system for children to

determine the school they go to.[46] This method would help distribute school places and, ultimately, because middle-class parents don't know where their child will end up, it would increase the pressure to improve the standard of all schools over time.

## EARLY YEARS INVESTMENT

How can we dismantle the elitism of education and create a system that promotes the values of justice and equality? As well as the ideas above, we must focus on what can be done in the early years. We must learn the lessons of the period between 1997 and 2010, when extra welfare support for those with children, more generous maternity leave, and Sure Start centers together contributed to better outcomes across child poverty, health and education.[47] These are the types of policies we need to bring back, but alongside them we must learn from other countries that provide better starts for children. Most notably, we must consider introducing a free or very cheap at the point of use universal early-years education system, rather than a 'childcare provision' whose terminology makes it seem like a babysitting service (I return to this in Chapter 10).

## THE DIFFICULT QUESTIONS

As I found out first-hand on the doorstep in 2019, private schools are a touchy subject. But we simply cannot address the inequalities in education without addressing their role in strengthening privilege. Abolishing their charitable status is an obvious starting point to level the playing field, but we need to think more about how to incentivise upper-middle-class parents to send their children to state schools.

Education is a process of teaching and learning, of producing and transmitting knowledge, values and skills from one generation to the next, or from one person to another. At its best, it pushes the boundaries of what we know. I was very lucky to have a mother that never spoke about education as a route to get more money, but rather to gain knowledge and have more to give back to the rest of society. However, university fees have moved us to thinking more about the monetary returns on investment and made students consumers. The repercussions of this thinking have been wide-ranging for the education sector and its role in locking in inequalities. The Labour Party manifestos of 2017 and 2019, in which there was a clear commitment to free higher and further education, would have helped the process of rolling back this ugly and costly commodification of education.

In addition to the situation with universities there has also been a marketisation of school-age education, where schools compete with one another for pupils and government funding, in the same way in which businesses compete for customers, sales and profits. The overnight proliferation of academies for example – which meant primary and secondary schools, including the land they sit on, were handed over from local authorities to privately controlled conglomerates – has recast our education system's values. There is now ample evidence showing many of these academies have cut school budgets by increasing class sizes, hiring fewer staff, undermining wages by replacing permanent, unionised, qualified staff with more casual, temporary, unqualified workers, and some even have connections to tax havens.[48, 49] Education isn't just exacerbating existing educational inequalities, it is increasingly adopting the same types of business models that result in the huge differences in development for children walking through school doors on day one of their formal education.

As a new candidate for MP, a few parents got in touch through a local party member, worried about their children's school and asking if I could help. Around ten parents of different ethnicities, genders and jobs, came into our little Labour Party office. It was a hot summer's day, near the end of term. Our office had posters of various Labour campaigns, socialist quotes and leaders from over the years. I could tell most of the parents had never been somewhere like this before. They felt like there weren't many options left. The academy trust running their school had bled it dry; with standards falling and less pupils enrolling, the situation was going from bad to worse. I worked with them to put out a video about the issue and to put up a petition to save the school. I was surprised by just how quickly these outputs were shared, with over sixty thousand people signing the petition, which eventually prompted the academy in charge of the school to step down and let another academy take over.[50] Perhaps because of the strength of parental engagement, the new academy and head teacher took a different approach with the parents, being more open and transparent. These incredible parents had fought back and they had to be listened to. I increasingly think that this is the only way anything will change, through everyday people having enough, coming together and fighting back, just like teachers and university staff have done by striking for better wages and working conditions. This is as true on education issues as with the NHS. The elites aren't going to change a system that benefits them, unless we make them.

# 8

## WHEN WORK KEEPS YOU
## IN YOUR PLACE

'Get your fucking ass up and work, it seems like nobody wants to work these days.' This is the straightforward advice to women who want to be successful from American socialite, media personality and businesswoman Kim Kardashian, who added in the same interview: 'if you put in the work, you will see results, it is that simple.'[1] There was an immediate backlash to these comments.[2] This is a woman who has undoubtedly worked hard and is excellent at what she does, but her dad was a multimillionaire with great connections. One of my favourite comments was from the then *Daily Show* host Trevor Noah, who said 'Kim Kardashian works hard, but you know who else works hard? Most women.'[3] Kardashian later apologised for the comments.

Just eight days after Kim Kardashian's pearls of wisdom, some hospitality staff at ferry operator P&O, owned by Dubai-based DP World, illustrated the point that hard work doesn't always pay off. One seemingly normal morning, 786 members of staff were on the ferries ready for a day's work, only to be confronted with a mass sacking on the spot. To add insult to injury, the announcement was made over Zoom. Later a spokesperson for the company said it was a 'very difficult but necessary decision' to secure the future viability of the business.[4] Laid-off employees initially refused to get off the boats, but 'handcuff-trained, balaclava-wearing' security guards were ready to march them off the boats and usher on cheaper agency staff to replace them. Despite efforts to overturn the decision, these staff were out for good and the company faced no criminal proceedings.[5] These discarded workers were victims of a system seeking to squeeze wages and increase profits, regardless of the human consequences. It didn't matter how hard they worked: they were expendable.

While this may seem like an extreme example, work life has become increasingly insecure for millions of people. Politician after politician will tell us that work is the best route out of poverty, yet, just like education, work is trapping people in their economic positions. In truth it is the kind of job you do, not how hard you work, that decides whether you are fairly compensated or not. The reality of the working world – shaped by the economy, corporate power and legislation – makes it near impossible for people to start at the bottom and work their way up. The right advice for Kim Kardashian to give would be to ask business owners, especially big corporates, to shape businesses differently, to put workers' health and well-being first, to tell everyone to join a trade union and to fight for political leaders that believe in workers' rights.

Changing the structure of our labour market is at the heart of truly extending opportunity for all. Starting again on how work is structured, including pay, working hours and the ability to do things that produce real value for society, offers us a way out of the narrow ideas of success we currently have.

## THE FUNDAMENTALS: WORKING HARDER TO GET PAID LESS

*'The best route out of poverty, to avoid food bank usage, is to make sure more people get a job.'*

David Cameron, Radio 1 interview, April 2015[6]

Work and jobs are fundamental to understanding social mobility and the idea of 'winners' and wealth accumulation, as well as race and class inequalities. There are some trends worth considering when laying out the mechanics of social mobility in today's increasingly harsh, unjust and unbalanced job market. From wage stagnation, the shrinkage of middle-income jobs and ballooning CEO pay, the functioning of the labour market shows us that the old adage of 'working your way up' and job security have fallen by the wayside. It is not just this generation of workers that is hurt – keep in mind that there are children growing up in these wage- and work-poor households, children who face the double whammy of seeing their schools absorb a real-term decline in funding and their parents struggle on low pay and insecure contracts.

### Wage stagnation

In 2021, more than a decade on from the financial crisis, average UK workers were still earning £75 a month less – in real terms – than in 2008.[7] Compared to other rich countries, including our European neighbours Germany and France, our workers have been left with their wage packets shrinking in real terms, even before the cost of living crisis. Indeed, the fall in wages in the decade between 2010 and 2020 was the biggest fall in average wages in peacetime since the Napoleonic Wars more than 200 years ago.[8] Then, on top of this poor decade of wage performance, UK workers were predicted to see the 'worst real wage squeeze' among G7 nations.[9] Analysis found that real wages in the UK were forecast to shrink by 6.2% (-£1,750) over 2022 and 2023 – the tightest contraction in pay of any of the G7 economies. Meanwhile, prices are soaring.[10] This is not because UK workers are not working hard enough. Explanations instead link to increasing inflation in part spurred by supply chain disruptions after the Covid-19 pandemic and Russia's invasion of Ukraine, prolonged public spending cuts with associated public sector pay freezes and falling investment in the sorts of technologies that increase worker productivity[11] – factors all out of the control of any individual worker.

*Labour share versus profit share*

Since the 1970s, the UK has seen a dramatic decline in the proportion of the total amount of national income going to workers, while there has been a simultaneous increase in profits. This is even when including the increases in wages at the top of the distribution, which means that the resulting fall in the wage share has been borne by those in the bottom half of the wage distribution. Estimates show that the wage share in national income has fallen from 74.1 per cent of national income in 1975 to 66.8 per cent in 2017, with a corresponding increase in the profit share.[12] While external factors, such as globalisation and technological change, which have made the labour market more competitive for those without graduate degrees, have played a part, the sustained fall in the wage share is mainly the result of a series of domestic policies, notably the weakening bargaining power of labour through falling trade union membership, leading to the squeezing of workers' wages and conditions. The other factor is the increasing role played by the finance sector in the economy resulting from the deregulation of the sector by Margaret Thatcher in the 1980s.[13]

The role of financialisation needs some examination. We have seen how important jobs in this sector are in explaining who is wealthy (see Chapter 4), but the role of the sector as a whole is important in understanding why opportunities for people to have well-paid, secure jobs are decreasing.

Financialisation is understood as the increasing size and influence of financial markets, actors and institutions in domestic and international economies. In practice, this means that there is an increased focus on short-term speculative activity, an increase in the number of financial instruments being sold and a move from delivering for wider society to delivering for shareholders – a phenomenon referred to as shareholder primacy. Increasing profits have also been associated with higher mark-ups due to the rise of corporates and falling competition.[14]

The French economist Thomas Piketty popularised the fact that the rate of return on capital (e.g. property, existing shares) is greater than the rate of economic growth (and hence wage growth).[15] The rising value of capital has distorted behaviour such that it makes more sense to invest in capital accumulation than in productive assets and job creation; in other words, investing money in money, rather than factories and technology.

Just as wages have skewed towards those at the top, so too have profits. This is all part of what has been termed a 'winner-takes-all economy' where the top performers capture a disproportionate share of the rewards. While in Economics 101 you're taught that free markets should lead to multiple competitors driving down prices, what has happened in reality is that only a small handful of large, powerful companies control a majority of market share. Think about Uber and how they have managed to push out local competitors and reduce work for black cabs. But the principle applies to individuals too. Top performers might be only slightly more skilled than the people one level below them, yet they receive an exponential pay-off.

### Stuck on low pay

As touched on in Chapter 4, in-work poverty has become increasingly common in the UK. About 56 per cent of people living in poverty in 2018 were in a household where at least one person had a job; this is compared to 39 per cent 20 years ago.[16] The problem is so severe, that of the 5.7 million people claiming universal credit in July 2022, 41 per cent actually had a job,[17] meaning that taxpayers are making up for employers' paying so little. Five out of six people on low pay are still low-paid a decade later,[18] meaning these jobs are not putting them on a ladder that allows them to work their way up. The majority of these jobs are in retail, care and hospitality. Various politicians, including Boris Johnson and Rishi Sunak, have promised to deliver a high-wage economy on multiple occasions, but instead we have an increasingly polarised labour market. Actual pay progression would require more employers in traditionally low-paying and low-skilled sectors to think creatively about the ways they can open up progression opportunities for their staff and for the government to focus in on this serious problem.

### High pay

While those on low pay struggle, the pay of those at the top of organisations has ballooned. Bosses of the UK's 100 biggest publicly listed companies have seen their pay jump by an average of 23 per cent to almost £4 million because of record bonus payments. The average pay of chief executives of FTSE 100 companies increased from £3.2 million in 2021 to £3.9 million in 2022,[19] and this has become a typical story in the last three decades.[20] This high level of pay should be considered relative to others in the company. Across the 69 FTSE 100 companies that disclosed pay ratios in the first quarter of 2022, the median CEO/median employee ratio was 63:1. This was nearly double the ratio for the same group of companies in 2021, at 34:1. The research shows that pay ratios were widest in the retail industry with an average pay ratio of 117:1, where retail workers on the shopfloor and those making the clothes are paid very little compared to those at the top.[21]

CEOs are getting more because of their power to set pay, not because they are single-handedly increasing productivity or profits. This escalation of CEO compensation has fuelled the growth of top 1.0 per cent and top 0.1 per cent incomes. Sometimes we are told that the rich will leave the UK if we tax them more or pay them less, but there is very little data or evidence to support this.[22]

It is important to remind everyone that this high pay is not the reason for all innovation and entrepreneurialism in the economy. Evidence has demonstrated that cash incentives do not necessarily stimulate innovative thought.[23] There is only a weak correlation between pay and executive performance, with CEOs awarded excessive pay rises even when their companies are performing badly.[24]

In the midst of the cost of living crisis in 2022, the pay gap between top and bottom seemed to be worsening, with pay growing fastest for the highest earners, while those on the lowest incomes are most adversely affected by soaring inflation.[25]

*Nowhere to go: the reduction in middle-level positions*

Since the 1980s, the share of employment for mid-range wage occupations (roughly £15–40,000 according to 2022 wages)[26] has decreased by more than 20 per cent, while the share at the lower and higher end of the wage distribution has increased.[27] The labour market is increasingly favouring the highly educated, while manufacturing employment has shrunk and those at the lower-paid end are more concentrated in less secure jobs in food and hospitality. This is reinforcing and escalating many forms of inequality. This has been called an 'hourglass labour market' or, more technically, 'labour market polarisation'.

Economists have explained this employment and wage polarisation by arguing that new technology is replacing a lot of routine jobs. The blame has mainly focused on automation, but during this period there have also been clear attempts to strip out jobs for cost-saving purposes.[28] This disappearance of middle-wage jobs and occupations has led to the disappearance of rungs in the middle of the career ladder, meaning people get trapped at the bottom as their careers now do not offer as many chances of progression.

*Precarious working conditions and zero-hour contracts*

As the power of trade unions has declined, the outsourcing of previously in-house public services to the private sector has increased, profit margins have grown and technology has been used to cut jobs. The number of people on zero-hour contracts rose from 200,000 to just under 1 million between 2010 and 2018, with a fall in the proportion of workers on fixed-term contracts.[29] Part-time workers are also far more likely to be on zero-hour contracts than full-time workers: in 2019, over 6 per cent of part-time workers were on zero-hour contracts compared with only 1 per cent of full-time workers. Part-timers are also three times more likely to have second jobs than full-timers.[30] This indicates that many of those in part-time work are not earning enough to make ends meet.

Some have argued that these contracts allow workers, and not just employers, more flexibility. But given the overlap of those on low pay and on a zero-hour contract, it is hard to see how this type of insecurity would be enjoyed. More likely, zero-hour contracts are a symptom of employers' increasing reluctance to pay the full value of labour and their refusal to take wider responsibility for the longer-term welfare of workers and communities.

Uber has often been associated with this type of disregard for workers – indeed its practices gave birth to the term 'Uberisation', defined as the transformation of an existing industry or economy with the help of computing platforms, especially mobile applications, and temporary employment schemes, leaving drivers unable to choose their jobs but classified as self-employed with no access to paid holidays or sick pay.[31] Venture capitalists are looking for the next big business ripe for Uber-style disruption because of how lucrative it has proven to be.[32] Amazon is another example, and here it is not just about wages and holidays, but about being pushed to be more and more productive through surveillance technology that watches and records your every move.[33] One of the more grotesque end points of this approach was a woman giving birth in a toilet cubicle for fear of missing a shift.[34]

However, workers and trade unions have begun to fight back and some of these issues arise from a brand-new way of working which has not been adequately examined yet, for example, in 2021 the UK introduced new legislation so that Uber drivers get paid holidays.[35]

*Equal pay (or not)*

Every year Equal Pay Day – the point in the year when, met-aphorically, women stop earning because of the gender pay gap – highlights just how much pay inequalities exist. In 2021, the day was 18 November, meaning that women earned almost 12 per cent less than men.[36] This is in major part because many women work in low-pay sectors – caring, cleaning, cater-ing, retail. Traditionally, 'women's work', such as caring and cleaning, has not been valued in the market. In this way, the pay of sectors such as care reflects wider prejudice and sexism in society. Worse, there is research showing that as employers instinctively pay women less, when women move into a sector, the whole sector sees a pay downgrade.[37] Equal pay is an even bigger problem for disabled people, with the pay gap between non-disabled and disabled people estimated at 17.2 per cent, or roughly £3,700 per year.[38]

*Limited well-paid jobs for non-graduates*

The sum of the reduction of middle-level jobs, low pay and increasing precariousness in working conditions is that non-graduates have found their options for a well-paid job severely limited. Instead, a growing number of non-graduates are working in low-paid, dead-end jobs. Non-graduates make up more than half of the workforce and are more than twice as likely to be unemployed as graduates. Seventeen per cent of non-graduates aged 22 to 29 were defined as economically inactive (not in work and not looking or available for work) even before the pandemic, compared to only 6 per cent of grad-uates.[39] However, the problem is not only the quantity, but also the quality of jobs available to them, with the majority of jobs that non-graduates take up being low-paid and in sectors such as retail and hospitality that rely on insecure and short-term contracts.[40] Non-graduates also find themselves competing with graduates at times of recession, weak new job creation and limited graduate vacancies.[41]

All of the above trends paint a depressing picture of the labour market today, but again it is important to underline that these trends could be halted and reversed by a different set of policies. Indeed, the introduction of the minimum wage in the late 1990s, and the increases in this wage floor thereafter, have had a real and positive effect.[42,43] However, a minimum wage is not enough on its own and has been undermined by other negative trends. A third of workers are living pay cheque to pay cheque.[44] For the vast majority of us there is little chance of building wealth and long-term security from wages alone.

## BE MORE PRODUCTIVE!

*'British workers produce less per hour than . . . and that's a combination of kind of skill and application . . . it is partly a mindset and attitude thing.'*

Liz Truss, leaked recording, reported in 2022[45]

You may have heard a lot about 'low productivity' in the news and that UK workers are relatively unproductive when compared to other rich countries. For example, we are almost 20 per cent less productive when compared to workers in the USA.[46] What does that mean? Economic productivity typically measures output per hour, per job and per worker. In the past, when a large percentage of economic activity was linked to manufacturing, it was relatively easy to understand what productivity was measuring, because we could count the number of widgets on the production line, but times have changed.

Labour productivity metrics are an outdated, counterproductive way of measuring human impact in a world where humans are focused on producing ideas, and they especially cannot be easily applied to sectors such as care. After all, part of the problem with how the care system currently works is the squeezing of more and more patient visits into one day, resulting in huge dissatisfaction in terms of both providing and receiving the care. Even those focused on high-tech industries point out its flaws. They argue, for instance, that using output over time to measure a knowledge worker's performance ignores the quality of that output and the results it leads to.[47] Instead of productivity, we should be measuring whether workers are achieving the right results for customers and whether they are happy and healthy while doing it.[48]

Even if you want to focus on traditional ideas of productivity, the solution is not to blame workers' attitudes but to invest, both in their skills and in the technology they use. The UK economy suffers from chronic underinvestment in the public and business sectors when compared to other countries and historically. The shift in economic ideology that came with Margaret Thatcher's leadership meant public investment collapsed from a long-term average of 4.5 per cent of GDP between 1949 and 1979 to around 1.5 per cent after 1979.[49] Relying on private investment alone to plug this gap is not going to work; we need a sizable government investment in upskilling and supporting workers in the UK. Furthermore, studies show that when workers are happier they are more productive,[50] again highlighting the need to put worker well-being first rather than assuming the issue is about worker 'attitude'.

ARE YOU PAID WHAT YOU ARE WORTH?

*'Nowadays people know the price of everything and the value of nothing.'*

Oscar Wilde, *The Picture of Dorian Gray* (1891)[51]

In one of my first policy jobs in 2008, I worked for an excellent think tank called the New Economics Foundation. In the wake of the financial crisis, when the bankers crashed the economy and were bailed out, leaving the rest of society to pick up the pieces, many of us felt that what had happened confirmed what we had felt for a long time: bankers were not just overpaid, they were gambling with our collective economic prosperity. My colleagues decided to try to illustrate this by asking a simple question: are you paid what you are worth? The study took three highly paid workers – a City banker, an advertising executive and a tax accountant – and to provide contrast, also included three low-paid workers – a hospital cleaner, a recycling plant worker and a childcare worker.[52]

The researchers used a method that allowed them to put a monetary value on the societal ripple effects of these roles. For instance, what were the societal impacts of an advertising exec given that their work can lead to overconsumption, debt and mental health issues? Of course, not all advertising is the same, but there is plenty of evidence to show it has all kinds of negative effects.[53] One of my friends had a short stint working for an advertising agency. Not long after she'd started working there, I met her for coffee. She joined me late and greeted me by shouting 'Advertising is evil!' When I asked what had happened, she told me she had spent all day talking about what made people feel insecure about their hair. To sell things, we often have to make people think they don't have enough or are not enough.

On the City banker, who had been part of bringing the global economy to its knees, estimates were taken based on the bailout and impacts of the recession compared to the tax take from this sector. The numbers were startling. The study found that, at that time, top City bankers were collecting salaries of between £500,000 and £10 million, but because of their negative impact on society, they destroyed £7 of social value for every pound in value they generated. For a salary of between £50,000 and £12 million, top advertising executives destroy £11 of value for every pound in value they generate. For the tax accountants who help people to avoid tax, paid a salary of between £75,000 and £200,000, the amount of social value they destroy was even higher, for every pound in value they generate they cost society £47 of value. There is no doubt that determining the right amount of tax payable is a specialist skill and often requires professional support, but with billions of pounds going missing in tax havens and avoidance every year, it is a job that can also result in less money going to the Treasury to support spending on public services.

Meanwhile, some of the lowest paid – childcare workers, hospital cleaners, waste recycling workers – are producing the greatest value for society. For every £1 they are paid, childcare workers generate between £7 and £9.50 worth of benefits to society, mainly because of how they start to unlock the potential of a small child and allow others to work. Hospital cleaners help to maintain standards of hygiene to protect against infection, but they also contribute towards wider health outcomes. The importance of these cleaners is often underestimated and undervalued in the way they are paid and treated. The study estimated for every £1 they are paid, over £10 in social value is generated. For recycling workers, the figure was even higher, for every £1 of value spent on wages, £12 of value will be generated, because of the reduction in carbon emissions and value of reusing goods.

People wrote us extremely upset, shouty, uppercase emails telling us we didn't know what we were talking about. But among the emails, there were also tax accountants and bankers who wrote to us to tell us we were right – that their jobs were bad for society. Radio call-in shows picked up on the report, with cleaners and childcare workers calling in to talk about how they felt they were undervalued in society. My colleagues had hit a nerve with their report. Their work illustrated that there is no straightforward relationship between high financial rewards and good societal outcomes. This isn't just an intellectual exercise – it has big implications for the way in which our society and economy are structured.

The bottom line? Financial incentives are very powerful and we tend not to shower them on the professions that deliver the most for society. So many of my friends that studied physics at university, even the ones that did PhDs, ended up being sucked into the City for their maths skills. This is while the world is desperate for new technologies to help with the transition to green economies and while there is so much more to learn about the universe. It feels like a waste. A break from the myth of social mobility means breaking with our current ideas of pay and worth. This can only be a good thing.

## WHAT HAPPENED TO ESSENTIAL WORKERS?

As the Covid-19 pandemic was coming into sharp focus and countries were going into lockdown, it struck me how quickly the UK government moved from calling care workers, postal workers, supermarket staff, etc. 'low-skilled' to 'key workers'. In March 2020 I tweeted: '3 wks ago we were told those working in supermarkets, social care & cleaners were "low skilled" – now these are the people crucial to managing #COVID19 outbreak. Everyone plays their part in society – these workers deserve decent wages & sick pay not just now but always.' To my surprise the tweet went viral, with family in Canada texting me to say they had seen it being shared on Facebook. The success of the tweet gave me hope that people do understand that pay does not equal worth. But three years later, pay and working conditions have not improved for the majority of essential workers; in fact for some essential workers, like carers, things have got worse.

Nowhere is the issue of higher wages more supported or warranted than when it comes to essential workers. This term was quickly dropped after the pandemic, but for a moment the people who keep us going were deemed important. Societies have applauded essential workers, but this has not translated into improved conditions of employment. Language is so important; if we had carried on calling them essential workers maybe our nurses, postal workers and train drivers wouldn't have needed to strike to get decent pay rises. The discrepancy between rhetoric and action is especially noticeable given the widespread public support for increased compensation.[54]

Ideally, the Covid-19 pandemic should have been the basis for a new settlement with essential workers. After all, we live in a world with an intensifying cycle of crises: the pandemic was immediately followed by the cost of living crisis, and extreme weather events are intensifying. Whether it is a natural disaster, large-scale terrorism, geopolitical hostilities or another pandemic, it is only a matter of time before society must again face a crisis. We need a well-trained, well-paid and fully staffed workforce of essential workers who will be well placed to support society through further hardship.[55]

## MAKING WORK A TOOL FOR OPPORTUNITY AND WELL-BEING

*'You have nothing that the humblest worker has not a right to have also. The worker must have bread, but she must have roses, too. Help, you women of privilege, give her the ballot to fight with.'*

Rose Schneiderman, speech, 1912[56]

I heard an amazing poem about living a 'soft life' by the fantastic young British Nigerian poet Sayo[57] on Instagram in 2022, and as well as making me laugh it got me thinking about how young people are rightfully questioning why we work the way we do. It turns out that this term 'soft life' originated in the Nigerian influencer community as slang for living a life that is filled with ease, comfort and intentional happiness, rejecting stress, self-sacrifice and overwork. Too many use it as a hashtag with photos of luxury living, but it's also meant to be about not having to worry about your bills.[58]

Collectively we are very far from delivering this for the majority of people. Over the past four decades, work has failed to secure stable and adequate incomes for growing numbers of people. This shows up in stagnant wages, erratic incomes, non-existent financial buffers for emergencies, low job security and brutalised working conditions. The struggle is real.

Over the course of this book we have discussed that 'making it' in society is predicated on a narrow idea of intelligence, that many of those that do 'make it' are involved in activities that are unhelpful or indeed damaging for society, activities that make inequality worse. 'Making it' puts on a pedestal the sort of jobs that favour greed and economic instability, rather than the jobs that produce social value – like those done by essential workers. How can we have arranged society so that success is so narrowly rationed and often detrimental to society itself? We have set up so many people to feel like failures. People looking after our children, parents and grandparents. The people keeping our streets cleaned and serving our food. Doing all the things that society cannot work without. Just google 'Why do I feel like a loser?' or 'What to do if you feel like a loser' and you'll see thousands of chat boards and articles. This is not the way to have a healthy society.

What if we did have policies so that we could get to a point where we have to work less? In 1930, John Maynard Keynes predicted that by 2000 technology would have advanced sufficiently that countries like Great Britain would be able to allow workers to work fifteen-hour weeks. As we seem to work more and more, it's hard to imagine how one of the most celebrated and influential economists could have been so wrong. Technology has only made inequalities worse and has not resulted in fewer working hours. Some have argued that this is in part because jobs have had to be created that are, effectively, pointless,[59] but personally I think the major flaw in Keynes's prediction was this: the concentration of the ownership of new technologies. The proceeds of new technologies have not been distributed widely, but only to a handful of billionaires.

Advocates argue that a shorter working week for all would encourage a more equal sharing of paid and unpaid work.[60] Trials have been conducted by individual companies and public bodies, and some have implemented them as permanent changes.[61] One of the most high-profile was Perpetual Guardian, a New Zealand insurance company with 240 staff. Perpetual Guardian trialled a four-day week (with the same pay) for six months, and made the switch permanent after finding staff had increased well-being and reduced stress, with no cost to productivity. In 2022, 100 UK companies employing 2,600 staff, joined a pilot scheme and various trials are ongoing around the world, already reporting positive outcomes for staff productivity and happiness.[62] Burnout is widespread right now and a move to a four-day week could be revolutionary in terms of setting a new work-life balance and a shifting of the focus away from profit and the bottom line. The key will be how this is delivered for working-class people and people on the front line rather than just office workers or those already well paid in the technology sector. If the ability to have time is also class-skewed, we will see inequalities in well-being increase.

We need to enact policy solutions that both reduce incentives for CEOs to extract economic gains and limit their ability to do so. Such policies could include having workers on boards; reinstating higher marginal income tax rates at the very top; and allowing firms' shareholders to vote on top executives' compensation.

There are many options to build a fairer labour market, but one option that we do not have is to keep things as they are.

# 9

## CHANGING OUR STORY OF SUCCESS

*'The first change that takes place is in your mind.'*

Gil Scott-Heron, TV interview, 1991[1]

It was the final week of the 2019 election campaign, and I was exhausted. The dark circles under my eyes were a permanent feature and I had to reach for my best make-up to look presentable. The good news was that I was having the time of my life. Through the campaign I had made deep and meaningful connections with people I would never have met otherwise, the kind of bond you might have with someone you go into battle with. Beyond the battle I was enjoying conversations with local voters about their everyday woes and worries for their kids, speaking at rallies, thinking about the local community projects I could put in place and national policy changes I would push for if I won.

As I got into bed on one of those final nights before the election, after a fifteen-hour day of relentless campaigning, I did what I was now accustomed to doing every five minutes – checked my social media. In my emails I found a message from a random person, saying 'My hubby and I are undecided. We'd like to have a chat with you.' It was a bit weird, but I replied suggesting we speak in the morning. Even though it was almost midnight they replied asking if I could speak now. My sister and husband thought it might be a Tory troll trying to trick me (there were lots of them), but I figured I had nothing to lose by calling the number.

A woman answered, and explained her husband was listening in. 'We were both going to vote Conservative but we saw your video and we're thinking we might not now. Sorry it's so late, but we were talking about it and I said we should try and talk to you.'

My campaign video had played into a sense of community and my upbringing in the area. It showed the woman my mum had met at an antenatal class while pregnant with my older sister over forty years ago. The now elderly lady, recalled becoming friends with my mum instantly, how she would love to sit with her and go through her sari collection, how proud my mum would have been of me and how she, as one of our oldest family friends, was proud of me too. It also featured my schoolfriend, whose dad used to pick me up from my family home in the midst of fighting and violence. Her family had given me a safe space away from my dad's frightening mood swings and my family's ongoing crisis. These people were the village that had raised me, proof that this area hadn't given up on me when I'd needed support. Photos of me in the local library that my mum would take us to every weekend as children, with my old schoolteachers and the parks we would play in as children were the backdrop to the words I had written. Words I had written through tears. It was my heart laid bare. Within a few hours the video had had over a million views and been retweeted by the likes of Stormzy and even those who weren't my natural political allies – like Alastair Campbell, who was formerly Tony Blair's spin doctor.

I was pleased to hear the video was making these potential voters waiver. As I set in bed, exhausted and exhilarated in those last breaths of the campaign, this couple told me about their lives, their kids at private school and their own journey to a comfortable, middle-class life. The husband had had a difficult childhood. His dad had died young, and his mum – an immigrant from India – had raised five children in a small council flat by herself. In contrast, his wife had grown up middle class, and her family had always voted Conservative. They were both of the view that because they had managed to do well, had bought a nice house in the suburbs and sent their kids to private school, that they should vote Conservative.

'But I saw your video and it made me think about my own childhood. My wife and I started thinking that maybe we should be voting for you.'

It was powerful connecting with this man about his journey, but as he spoke I could hear him chalking up his own escape from economic hardship to his own personal ingenuity and his mother's hard work, with no mention of the initiatives that supported his journey: the council flat provided collectively by the people of the UK as an act of solidarity and care, the welfare state, the state-funded education. Not that he should necessarily be grateful, but I wanted him to at least see that his experience shows that state support and investment pays off. I gently pointed out the way the state had helped me along the way, in order for him to reflect on his own narrative.

'But those people don't work hard,' he said about those struggling today.

'But they're you or me. That was once us and our parents were working hard and doing the best they could. I grew up on benefits, and I wouldn't be able to pay the taxes I do now had my family not had the support when we needed it,' I replied.

My callers fell silent. 'I suppose you're right,' he conceded.

I had several conversations like this with people from humble beginnings who somehow also believed that those that didn't make it were lazy, or who didn't really see the role luck and public investment had played in their lives. The myth of 'anyone can make it as long as they work hard enough' is so powerful that it is even effective on those who know from life experience that the realities are different. Without understanding why this is, we can't begin to undo the collective psychology that under-pins the social mobility agenda. And, without changing this personal narrative, we are unlikely to want to invest in others.[2]

## HOW THE INDIVIDUALIST IDEOLOGY WORKS

*'This pathologization already forecloses any possibility of*
*politicization. By privatizing these problems — treating them*
*as if they were caused only by chemical imbalances in the*
*individual's neurology and/or by their family background —*
*any question of social systemic causation is ruled out.'*

Mark Fisher, *Capitalist Realism* (2009)[3]

Given the extent to which the system is rigged, the question I constantly grapple with is why we accept society as it is. In a world where eight of the richest men have as much wealth as the poorest half of the population[4] — 3.6 billion people — a large-scale and deliberate mythology and propaganda have to have been cultivated and planted into our unconscious, both here and abroad. The systemic neglect of communities in certain parts of the country has led to what some doctors call 'shit-life syndrome'.[5] This links poor mental health as the outcome of economic decline, social stagnation and powerlessness, pinning down the neurotic chaos caused by capitalism.[6] And yet these are exactly the places that voted in 2019 for a political party who champion the myths of social mobility while simultaneously cutting benefits and avoiding paying tax on their own millions. How is this the case? A number of interlinked stories are being told by leading politicians, the media and some big corporations, all of them emphasising the individual over society.

'Anyone can make it as long as they work hard enough' is one of the foundational myths of societies like ours and most other capitalist economies that fixate on individual gain. What do I mean by foundational? You can think of the narrative of individualism as a journey – with 'anyone can make it as long as they work hard enough' as the first step. Once you take this step, you're on a path to emphasising individual attributes over community, making people more susceptible to thinking that personal character and grit are more important predictors of making it than poverty or societal factors and as such people are less likely to support public investment. This is why there is so much effort from the political right and the billionaire-owned press to get the public to take that first step and believe this foundational myth. The beauty of the narrative is that it also makes people less likely to blame policymakers in government. If people believe it is their own fault that they earn low wages because they haven't worked hard enough, then they are much less likely to rebel against the government as they are inter-nalising the blame rather than seeing fault in larger societal structures. These myths and lies, once absorbed into enough human minds, are foolproof.

The values of individualism dominate the content of the mes-sages transmitted through the mass media;[7] the idea of innate talents and stories of those who have apparently gone from rags to riches are all around us. Yet, this is far from how it works – even at a micro level. Years ago, my husband was working on a film in Malta which told the story of Saddam Hussein's body double's memoir. He was keen to have me accompany him to the set, and I was curious to see what it was like. Getting picked up at 5 a.m. was extremely painful, as was having to watch the same scenes filmed again and again and again; by lunchtime I was desperate to go home – I'll explain why. One of the scenes was set in a nightclub, where the women had been asked to strip off. Malta is a religious country and the extras refused to undress so dancers were called in from neighbouring Sicily. The film was set in the early 1980s so the make-up artists had to stick hair on the women's genital areas so they looked authentic to the time! This hilarious and strange context aside, I was shocked by what I saw, and I'm not talking about the fake pubic hair!

It turns out that a filmset is a good place to observe inequality in action; it acted as a microcosm of wider society. Indeed, the grotesque and in-your-face inequality was one of the reasons I was so desperate to leave. The extent to which the level of treatment depended on where the actor was on the casting list was immediately obvious: from the number of runners that surrounded the lead actors, to the size of the trailer, to the way you were spoken to if you were an extra. I was told that this is how it goes and that this hierarchy was reflective of who was more important to the making of the film. Yet, when I looked around I could see hundreds of people contributing. Making a film or a TV show requires huge amounts of resources and teamwork – you can't make a film without a catering department, cleaners, supporting artists, electricians, producers, writers and, yes, actors. If some of those – even the runners at the bottom of the hierarchy – were removed, the production would simply halt. My husband would often say if the catering on a production was not up to par then the film would fail.

This is true at the societal level too. We keep coming back to essential workers and their role during the Covid-19 pandemic. For the most part, those workers deemed essential have not seen their wages rise nor their working conditions improve despite being so central to our collective battle against the pandemic. Imagine if no one had picked up your rubbish, stacked your food in the supermarket, delivered your online purchases? No one is an island.

It is so abundantly clear that every member of society has value not just individually but to every other member of society. We *know* the importance of people in low-paid work. So why do we refuse to recognise them with equal pay and status? Here are seven key reasons why we persist with buying into the myth of social mobility and the associated hierarchy of who is worthy of decent wages and not.

## 1: The social mobility propaganda machine

*'It is time for a reality check and to come to terms with the fact that "Hollywood" . . . is in the business of misrepresenting everyone. It has no commitment to truth. It has made a lucrative business of deluding the world.'*

Hamid Dabashi, article, November 2021[8]

From *Rocky* to *Britain's Got Talent* and *The Great British Bake Off*, we are consuming stories of 'making it' on a daily basis. These TV diets have been linked to the degree to which we believe in the idea of meritocracy and the American Dream. One academic, Eunji Kim, found that contemporary Americans are watching a record number of entertainment programmes that emphasise rags-to-riches narratives.[9] Kim's experiments found that regularly watching TV shows like *X Factor* is a powerful driver in shaping belief in the possibility of upward mobility. Their power comes from the depiction of real people, portrayed as deserving and from humble backgrounds, who then go on to have success. Viewers experience 'transportation', defined as 'a cognitive and emotional experience in which viewers immerse themselves in a story'.[10] These shows have a deeper political message, helping to legitimise income inequality and dampen public support for redistribution.

There is a long history of Hollywood propagating these messages.[11] One part of the all-time favourite 1990 movie *Pretty Woman* which sticks in my brain is where Julia Roberts, who is playing a sex worker called Vivian, turns to her best friend Kit (Laura San Giacomo) and asks if they know anyone it works out for. Kit thinks about if any of their sex worker friends have managed to fall in love and marry a rich man. Failing to think of anyone, she says 'Cinde-fucking-rella.' The film then goes on to be that fairy tale. Of course, we all need escapism, and this is not a critique of every rags-to-riches story, more a call to recognise just how many of these stories there are in the ether and a reminder that their impact on our belief that 'you can be the exception' cannot be underestimated. This is also not about being stupid or easily manipulated. We are all susceptible to these powerful messages. If it didn't work, TV producers wouldn't spend so much time making these shows!

### 2: We are told questioning it means we are envious

'You're just jealous' will be a common response to this book and its arguments. Envy is, according to the Bible, one of the seven deadly sins and of course an undesirable human emotion. But maybe it's not envy, it's anger? Anger at a system that perpetuates inequality. Or maybe if there is a touch of envy, it is warranted. Personally, I've turned more red with anger than green with envy researching this book, but it is totally rational to be envious. Envy is actively encouraged in our capitalist society, how else could we all be convinced to keep buying things we don't need? Essayist and cultural thinker John Berger in *Ways of Seeing* (1972) describes this use of envy in advertising: 'The spectator-buyer is meant to envy herself as she will become if she buys the product. She is meant to imagine herself transformed by the product into an object of envy for others.' Envy is baked into our thinking, the poor need to envy the rich and everyone around them to keep the wheels of consumerism turning.[12]

As we saw in Chapter 4 when we discussed wealth, the rich often inherit their wealth, they get accolades for being innovative, holiday in exotic places, get on their private planes or at the very least fly business class. They often don't pay their fair share of taxes, they seemingly live above the law and pass on all their wealth to their children. Meanwhile, the people that work in their factories, shops or hotels, who care for their children, serve their coffee and clean their houses, are struggling just to get by, and are supposed to forget about the luxuries they see enjoyed by their employers. It is not surprising that a little envy might enter the equation.

In the storm of the cost of living crisis in 2022, as the majority of people were struggling to pay their bills, the then chancellor Rishi Sunak – the man tasked with dispensing financial resources, depicted as Superman by the BBC[13] and one of the richest MPs in the UK – got on a plane to his multimillion-pound LA property.[14] His Spring Statement had done nothing to alleviate the situation of rising energy and food bills. But what did he care? He was literally jetting off into the sunshine, with newspaper columnists and his fellow politicians covering his back by – yes, you guessed it – telling us all we're just jealous of his wealth.[15]

So why be surprised that some would be green with envy?

It's no wonder that people wish they had the money to buy a house outright and close the gates on a society increasingly troubled by mental health problems and doomsday scenarios on the climate crisis, that makes them work endlessly with nothing to show for it. Not even a better life for their children. Who wouldn't want to cocoon themselves into a life where the biggest dilemma is which private school to send your kids to? I'm not being trite, I genuinely overheard this exact conversation between two Tory-supporting political commentators in the BBC *Newsnight* green room before they went on air to talk about the impacts of public spending cuts. And even if we don't necessarily want a private jet, it is certainly normal to envy the security of being able to pay your bills and feed your kids without worrying.

People often defend the rich, assuming that they have earned their wealth and that they have created a lot of new products and jobs in the process. But as we've looked at in this book, this is often not the case. So next time someone just tells you that you're jealous, tell them why.

*3: We want to believe it*

In a world where making it equates to being rich, the power of thinking that could be you – or even your children one day – is palpable. The allure is a natural one, especially wanting the best for your children. People need to feel hopeful about their futures – otherwise why go on? And of course, the idea that nothing can stop you has huge romantic appeal.

The belief that anything is possible is comforting in the light of the many obstacles we see around us and is an optimistic, motivating force. It also gives us a sense of autonomy and empowerment. What this book is showing us is that our power is not necessarily just as an individual, but how we come together to change the system so the opportunities politicians promise us are no longer a myth.

*4: Because once upon a time it was true*

'These young people today have it so easy!' This is a statement I've heard from the baby boomer generation so many times, but statistically speaking it was actually members of their generation, born after the Second World War, who had a better chance of experiencing income and career progression over their lifetimes, to the extent that of those born in 1946, more than 50 per cent ended up in a higher social class than their fathers. No wonder this era is referred to as the 'golden age of mobility'.[16] The post-Second World War economic boom brought with it more jobs in the middle and at the top, wage growth and dramatic increases in home ownership.[17, 18]

In the UK those now in their sixties earn a lot more than their parents did, as did their parents, yet their children born in the 1980s earn at best the same on average, while it looks like those born in the 1990s onwards will fall further behind.[19] This is not because there were equal chances for everyone in the 1960s and 70s, or because that generation was more hard-working, but because of the huge public investments made at the time in public infrastructure and twentieth-century developments such as 'cradle to grave' welfare and the huge expansion of higher education and well-paid jobs.[20] The reversal of some of these trends since the 1980s has led to a downgrading of life chances for the next generations.

The Social Mobility Commission's 2019 survey asked participants to choose a statement that best reflected their views: 'In Britain today everyone has a fair chance to go as far as their talent and hard work will take them'; 'In Britain today where you end up in society is mainly determined by your background and who your parents were'; (there were also the options of 'Don't know' or 'Neither'). The difference in generational responses is telling, with more than 50 per cent of respondents in the 65+ age group (the baby boomers) believing that it is talent and hard work which are the primary factors in where you end up, compared to just 30 per cent of those aged 18–24.[21]

This difference in response is not mere opinion, but a reflection of life experience. Take housing: those turning seventy today were in their mid-thirties when then prime minister Margaret Thatcher expanded the Right to Buy scheme in 1980, which offered tenants large discounts to purchase the council houses they were living in. The scheme was open to a large swathe of the population as in 1979 around 32 per cent of all dwellings in Britain were council houses.[22] The result was a rapid expansion in home ownership during the 1980s and of course a reduction in the number of council houses available. However, this trend has reversed as house prices have risen far quicker than wages; currently barely 30 per cent of 35- to 44-year-olds own a house.[23]

The post-war period of structural mobility – where for the most part everyone in that generation was better off than the previous one – has dissipated, because some Thatcherite policies, like the one outlined above, were short-sighted and only offered temporary solutions to societal inequalities, while many others actively encouraged inequality.[24] But some people can only understand their life from the prism of their own experience, particularly when it comes to understanding intergenerational shifts. We need to remind them that times have changed.

5: *We are pointing the finger elsewhere*

'*It's the* Guardian-*reading, tofu-eating wokerati, dare I
say, the anti-growth coalition that we have to thank for the
disruption we are seeing on our roads today!*'

Suella Braverman, House of Commons, October 2022[25]

The term 'woke' has become a catch-all for anyone who, for
example, challenges racist systems, wants action on climate
and cares about human rights, and apparently men who talk
about their feelings.

The culture war is conjured up whenever the right wing
establishment finds it convenient. But even deeper than that, it
is used as a tool to distract us from their policy failures, their
mistakes and their protection of the rich. It is a way to get the
masses to fight among ourselves. This is why the 'white working class' narrative discussed in Chapter 5 is so important in
understanding where we are. The racialisation of the working
class as white and represented by one voice and shared griev-
ance (immigration, multiculturalism) erases the existence of
working-class communities of colour and migrants, creating
a dividing line between the deserving and undeserving poor.
The focus on the white identity plays into a cultural rather than
a socio-economic perception of inequality, which portrays the
white working class as an ethnic majority minority and pitches
their concerns squarely against those of ethnic minorities as a
clash of cultural interests. By making working-class identity
cultural, observers are also able to blame the working class for
their circumstances.

We often hear about the culture war and that we are a nation
more divided than ever, but how exactly did this come to be?

A paper from one of my old colleagues conducted a snapshot discourse analysis looking at 500+ source materials from politicians, mainstream and non-mainstream media, social media and organisations, etc. It found that the culture war narrative is inherently polarising; it forces the audience to pick one side, thereby casting the other side as an enemy to be destroyed, thus creating a moral panic among some white British people over a perceived 'loss' at the insinuation that their very way of life is under threat. They have cleverly and carefully created a false 'enemy' to scapegoat an unequal system that they have designed and maintained, pointing instead to an imaginary battle between multi-ethnic working-class people that does not exist.[26]

It is a great distraction and the perfect trap in which to catch anyone who wants to make factual points about the role of racism in society. No doubt, people will say this book is just about being woke to pigeonhole it and me. And these divisive narratives work, they help construct a story about who we are. In recent years this narrative has been further magnified through Facebook and social media, where lies spread in a matter of seconds and the liars can sit back while algorithms do their work. Polarisation in politics, in attitudes to racism and the climate crisis didn't just pop up, they were built over time. For those of us who want to address all inequalities in society, finding a way to counter this narrative of polarisation is key to the implementation of not just equality legislation and greater solidarity between groups – but a number of wide-ranging policies from higher taxes on the rich to greater investment in childcare.

## 6: Dehumanisation

*'Dehumanisation is a standard component in the manufacture of an out-group against which to pit an in-group, and it is a monumental task. It is a war against truth, against what the*

*eye can see and what the heart could feel if allowed to do so
on its own.'*

Isabel Wilkerson, *Caste* (2020)[27]

In terms of both class and race, we have explored the subtle and
not-so-subtle ways that dehumanisation of groups takes place.
One of the most stark examples of the dehumanisation that is
incorporated in manufactured human hierarchies that I've wit-
nessed was on Robben Island in South Africa. This is the prison
that held Nelson Mandela and many others fighting apartheid.
When you go on a tour of the island they show you the brutal
reality of life at the prison – not just Mandela's tiny cell where
for many years he slept on a concrete floor, but also the quarry
prisoners worked in. The white limestone of the quarry was
so bright that the prisoners would go blind excavating the rock
because they were not given protective glasses. They showed
us where the prisoners would eat lunch, which apparently was
the same spot where they would defecate during their long days
at the quarry. As if this isn't bad enough, we were shown the
menus for the prisoners. There were actually separate menus
for 'coloured' and 'black' – the lighter-skinned people would
actually get more food than those with darker skin.

These days, there is a bit more questioning of such flagrant
inhumanity, although not enough to stop the blatant racism of
the difference in treatment of Ukrainian refugees versus those
from Afghanistan and Iraq.[28] This hierarchy at which people at
the bottom are treated with disdain manifests in where nuclear
bombs and medicines have been historically tested – because
if 'those people' are hurt no one will care. Every one of these
episodes is a reminder that some lives matter more than others.
'Black Lives Matter' is such a basic reminder, it is a shame it

needs to be said. As discussed in chapters 5 and 6 on class and race, when linked to social mobility, dehumanisation makes us believe others have less value and are less capable than we are, and therefore they deserve their lot in life.

### 7: Deference to the ruling elite

*'A deferential society in the classical – that is, eighteenth-century English and American – sense is usually conceived of as consisting of an elite and a nonelite, in which the nonelite regard the elite, without too much resentment, as being of a superior status and culture to their own, and consider elite leadership in political matters to be something normal and natural . . . Deference is expected to be spontaneously exhibited rather than enforced. A slave or serf is flogged into obedience, not deference, and the deferential man is frequently depicted as displaying deference as part of his otherwise free political behavior. He defers to his superiors because he takes their superiority for granted, as part of the order of things.'*

J. G. A. Pocock, article in *American Historical Review*, 1976[29]

*'If he is blue collar, he is likely to be drunk, criminal, aimless, feckless and hopeless, and perhaps claiming to suffer from low self-esteem brought on by unemployment.'*

Boris Johnson, *The Spectator*, August 1995[30]

I have never been treated with as much respect as when I was able to flash my University of Oxford student card. 'Oooh' people of all stripes would say, immediately changing their tone towards me, sometimes followed by 'You must be very clever'. It was the closest I ever felt to being royal and a huge contrast to how I would be spoken to when working my holidays in GAP and other retailers. And honestly, there would be times that I would want to wear my Oxford University ID on my chest so as not to have to deal with people looking down on me. Of course, it is wrong to be treated differently on the basis of the elite institutions you can get into, but this experience showed me how quickly we switch into looking up to people on the basis of the class system. It helps you to understand why we have had twenty Etonian prime ministers, as well as why we aren't rioting in the streets on a regular basis about tax evading millionaires in government and the other inequalities we absorb every day.

Where does the custom of obeying the rich come from? Going back to David Hume's, Adam Smith's and Edmund Burke's understandings of authority, the term 'deference' was used in the nineteenth century to describe an idea that people should delegate power to an elite in an atmosphere of mutual respect and reciprocal obligation. In the feudal system, there was a sense of obligation and patronage between rich and poor, although also a clear power hierarchy. It describes a particular type of 'moral order' which citizens accept without being obviously coerced. It represents a set of principles, customs, attitudes and beliefs about politics on the part of both rulers and ruled.[31] In her book *Political Deference in a Democratic Age: British Politics and the Constitution from the Eighteenth Century to Brexit*, Catherine Marshall concludes that 'There is something unique about the traditional hierarchically based Anglo-British society out of which a liberal democracy grew without a codified instrument of governance, unlike anywhere else.'[32] Our deference to the rich, she suggests, has its roots in our unwritten constitution, it is the need to share a political mindset with those in charge to maintain the peace. Somehow, centuries ago, we made an unwritten deal with the elite that they could rule us with our tacit consent.

## BREAKING THE SPELL

Imagine all of the UK living in a tower block. At the very top are the penthouses, the incredible views and the floor-to-ceiling windows, the balconies, the good heating and cooling systems; the residents have easy access to a doctor and only affluent neighbours in well-paid jobs. The flats at the bottom are several floors below ground, there's no sunlight and the flats are vulnerable to flooding every time it rains. Those in the middle have it a bit better, they have windows but their apartments are still 100 times smaller than those living on the top floor and their kids are in classes of 30 rather than the 15 per class at the schools the kids of the residents at the top of the building attend.

The rich, middle class and poor living in this block enter the building through different doors and use different lifts – they know about each other's existence but never see one another. The rich believe wholeheartedly that they deserve to be at the top of the building and that the others in the building deserve to be where they are. A few 'good-hearted' rich residents will occasionally donate to charities to help those at the bottom to eat – but they wouldn't dare go down there. Those in the middle also despise those at the bottom, constantly receiving leaflets through their doors telling them that the poor are causing noise, not throwing out their rubbish and are ill-mannered.

The lifts in the building only allow most people up to the ninetieth floor. Those on the top ten floors can't access the floors below, and those on the rest of the ninety floors can't access the floors above. You can occasionally win a place on the lift to the top floors, but these are rare exceptions – with the poorest having to win a game of poker in which they have to get a full house every time.

There is a residents' committee for the building which manages the distribution of services and resources. The rich residents hold all the power and of the two people representing all the other floors on this small committee, one has been bought off with a flat on the ninetieth floor, leaving only one to speak truth to power – but without a majority, they have no power to change anything. People have been living in this building over generations and the feelings of disdain for each other have been entrenched over time. There were a couple of times when the building got attacked, at which time the residents came together as one to stop the attackers from taking over their building and for a short time afterwards there was some more camaraderie and the ability for people to move around the block. However, this didn't last long. There was another instance when a concerted effort to organise those in the bottom floors to fight those at the top resulted in a strike that meant the building went uncleaned for weeks. The top floors finally offered a few concessions but in order to stop this happening again they later separated the bottom floors by race, causing infighting by spreading vicious rumours to divide them.

Now think of this building as society as a whole; we all seem to live in this tower block and we accept things the way they are because we think this is how it has to be, that we can only make this work if we are individualistic in our thinking and our approach, destined to fight each other for the scraps. But if you reduce the narrative to a single building, you see the absurdity. Why does it have to be this way, when there could easily be a greater level of equality between every floor? How about rather than identifying ourselves by our position in the building, we start to see ourselves as part of the same structure?

We live in a system so deeply entrenched in all of us that it is hard to be objective about our place in it. But whatever our skin colour, gender or place of birth, we can all put effort and pride into what we do. Whether we are caring for loved ones, grafting between jobs or working nine to five. Certain politicians and billionaires harm us all by hoarding extreme wealth and power and they know how to maintain that structure. They rig the system to rob people of a decent wage and refuse to contribute what they owe in tax. Then they blame minorities, newcomers and families struggling to make ends meet for the hardships the wealthy few created. When we pull together across our differences, we can truly make the UK a country where working for a living means earning a decent living, where we all have what we need to live a good life.[33]

## MOVING TO A CULTURE OF COMMUNITY AND CHECKING YOUR SNOBBERY

As Covid-19 hit, all over the world various local initiatives appeared overnight to help those in need.[34] The pandemic caused disruption of all kinds, but there was also a period of community solidarity and action. Studies have shown this ability to come together is one of the reasons why some communities were more resilient than others.[35] While slogans of 'we're all in it together' can ring hollow when you consider the vast distributional differences in who has been affected by the health and economic costs of the pandemic,[36] the ability of some communities to pull together did help to build connections between neighbours and community members during this difficult time.[37]

I set up one of these community groups in my part of town with a couple of my lovely neighbours. The idea was that those having to self-isolate, particularly the elderly and sick, would be able to call us and we would get volunteers to shop for them. We reached out to the community via local Facebook pages and WhatsApp groups and overnight we went from 4 to 150 volunteers. Within hours the phone started ringing. The first few calls were either people ringing us to say thank you for setting up the helpline and those that were confirming the rules, but then requests for help quickly followed.

After a few days I had volunteers texting me asking why we hadn't been in touch with them yet. They were literally begging to be useful! I realised that people felt good signing up to be volunteers. They wanted to help. In the three months from when lockdown began, we connected dozens of people with neighbours who helped each other. Another group set up a local food bank supplying meals to over eighty families. These operations were duplicated not just in other parts of London, but across the UK and beyond. People find peace in social interactions and enjoy co-operation – it makes you feel good about yourself. After everything I'd seen in national politics that had disappointed me, I found so much hope in this local activity – in people's ability to be kind. As a community, this spirit of empathy and support meant we transformed from being defenceless to protected.

Of course, community is not a new concept. In 1377, Ibn Khaldūn, a Spanish Arab polymath and political commentator credited by some with the invention of sociology, wrote *The Muqaddimah*.[38] In this book he discusses at length the Arabic concept of *asabiyya*, which means 'group feeling'.

Ibn Khaldūn's theory was that *asabiyya* is what holds communities, kingdoms and civilisations together, that they are bound by their sense of belonging to one another. However, this sense of community breaks down when hierarchies of power emerge and strengthen through time. For example, monarchs are corrupted by their separation from the everyday life of the people, with the result that they begin to see the people as a resource to be squeezed, and not as fellow and equal neighbours. In so many ways these observations, from over six hundred years ago, are still relevant. The hierarchies we have today are undermining our sense of community and those at the top are too far removed from the rest of society to understand or care.

As someone that has worked on policy for a long time, I've only really come to understand how important the story of individual success and the need for a change of values are in recent years. Inevitably, if we are to move away from the narrative of individual success we need to replace it with something about community and belonging, and we need to tackle the inequalities and divisive rhetoric which undermine our ability to take care of each other. Tackling the issue of diminished life chances is not simply a technical problem to be solved with technical solutions, although this will of course form a part of it.

Just as we have to confront our prejudices about those of different ethnicities, of those in the LGBTQI+ community and those with disabilities, we must also confront our internal belief system that puts those cleaning our streets at the bottom of society and those running our banks and huge property developers at the top. We need to weed out our snobbery. Deeper still, we will need to build a sense of social solidarity. Instead of individualising success, we need to finally recognise and internalise that fighting for your dreams means fighting for society. This can only be done by re-educating the population with a new story of collective success.

We are a team. In the workplace and in society. We rely on each other, to deliver the food to our supermarket shelves, to pick up the rubbish from the street, to build our homes, to develop new vaccines against deadly diseases, to create art to entertain us, to look after us when we are sick. As such, all jobs are valuable. There is nothing wrong with cleaning toilets, with stacking shelves or delivering parcels. There are no 'low-skilled' people. We need to hear this message again and again from the day we are born. As the UK was in the grips of a lorry driver shortage, I tweeted that we should not be surprised by the shortage given we have told young people for decades that in order to 'make it' you have to earn lots and speak posh. Among the many replies, someone posted: 'Years ago a teacher asked us to rank a list of professions in order of importance. Most put medics at the top and bin men at the bottom until she carefully explained how one prevents disease, the other treats it and we need both. A lesson I never forgot.'[39] This is a great idea and an exercise all teachers should do. Unfortunately, there were many other replies from those saying that they had been told by teachers that wanting to be an electrician was a failure. Our curriculum must formally include exercises that show the importance of different roles in society and instead of always looking to the rich and powerful as our role models, we must provide new role models who fit with promoting a society that values roles such as care workers.

Of course, telling a different story of who we are and what 'making it' is won't suffice without policies to operationalise the idea. We need trade unions to organise collective action, ways of us having material stakes in shared assets, such as renewable energy and water (as we will discuss in the next chapter). These policies and ideas are waiting for us, we just need the political and collective will to put them into action.

# 10

## A LAND OF OPPORTUNITIES

My mum had made it on to the heart transplant list. After ten years of her heart deteriorating to the point where she could no longer walk across the front room without having trouble breathing, multiple Christmases and summers spent in and out of hospital, we were so relieved. This was Mum's route to a decent quality of life and some stability. At last, after everything she had gone through with my dad and her health, this was her chance at happiness. When the call came one late September morning, our hearts were nervous, but our minds were buzzing with the possibilities of her health improving.

As my mum and I sat in the car together on the long trip to the hospital just outside Cambridge, I could feel her anxiety. I tried to joke with her and distract her. She started giving me long speeches about how proud of me she was and texting her family in Pakistan to ask them to forgive her if she'd ever upset them. I told her off for being overdramatic, that she would be fine and would be home soon.

In our efforts to keep her calm it was only when they took her into the operating theatre that I started to let my feelings of worry flood in. A heart transplant is probably the biggest operation one can have. It is hard to even comprehend the idea that your heart is lifted out of your chest and a new one is sewn in and connected to all the right blood vessels. There is a lot that can go wrong – both during and after the operation. We were told to sit in the critical care family room and wait during the very long procedure for updates.

In the room of strangers, we all immediately felt connected through our fears and through love. One mother spoke of her son's severe asthma attack that had left him on a special ventilator. Another family, where the situation seemed particularly precarious, told us about their loved one who was in a coma. A woman my age, Fiona, had found her husband collapsed in the shower. His heart had stopped, and no one had known for how long. The question now was the extent of the brain damage and whether he'd wake up from his coma. As those lives, including my mum's, hung in the balance, we provided a safe and empathetic place for each other.

On one of those first days, I still had to appear on Sky News to do their nightly review of the newspapers. I had tried to get out of it but due to the short notice they couldn't find anyone and begged me to come in anyway. I had told the other families in the waiting room and one of the women – in the middle of all her worry – changed the channel to the news and started pointing out what might come up. It was so touching, that despite everything else that was going on, this woman, who was a complete stranger and who was going through so much, was trying to help me.

We were of different ethnic origins, had different pay packets, from different parts of the UK, but in that room of investment bankers, policewomen, construction workers, Brexit Leave and Remain voters, we were – above all – people bounded by humanity. All judgement was suspended. And when Fiona's husband died, so young and so tragically, I wept. She never knew of my mum's passing because it was a few months later. But I know it would have upset her. I still wonder how she and her daughter are getting on, and it jabs my heart to think how much pain she must have gone through.

I tell you this story because changing our system of categorising people by their job or how much they earn means rejecting hierarchy and judgement and replacing it with a system of mutual respect and empathy. To change our story, to see each other for the humans we are, to wish everyone well and see everyone as deserving regardless of their job, class or race, we need to find ways to care for each other. The NHS is one of the few places we get to do that. It is built on a principle of equality, that we are all worthy no matter our bank balance. That so many of us are happy to pay our taxes to cover the NHS is a sign of hope. At some level we know that we must support others, even though we are constantly told to look after ourselves. Living in the USA I could see how in the world of private healthcare this fundamental human right and system of humanity is undermined when you rely on individual health insurance. While funding for collective assets has fallen during the years of Conservative rule, there are many not willing to take the government offensive lying down.

Most books and studies about social mobility end up talking about how to fix the education system, with details on how to change elite universities' admission systems. Countless philanthropists reach for mentoring or scholarships to solve the lack of class and race diversity. Others promote financial programmes that teach people how to invest and manage their money, as if the problem isn't that they don't have enough money to start with. These are not without some merit, but still play into the idea that the poor need to improve themselves rather than that society needs to change, that they need to break away or even be free of their working-class

communities to 'make it'. They try to make more exceptions, instead of changing the rules. We definitely do need
more people from working-class backgrounds at Oxford and
Cambridge universities, but that won't solve or reduce wealth
or income inequality.

All the statistics in this book have shown that the barriers
for people from low-income background are not just difficult,
they are near impossible. That the story of social mobility is
built on an implicit hierarchy that devalues work like care and
retail, while elevating jobs that pay well but often deliver little
of tangible value for society, like being a corporate tax accountant or investment banker. We simply cannot rewrite our story
of success without fundamentally unlearning all we have been
taught for generations about who matters in society.

It is both ridiculous and damaging to keep centring our idea
of success on 'beating the odds'. We need to ask, what should
replace social mobility? What should society aim to do? Even
out the chances for everyone to get to the top? No, because that
would still mean misery at the bottom. We can't all be pop
stars or millionaires, so we need to have a fundamental shift in
our societal mindset. The end goal of public policy should be to
create communities and a wider society that fosters well-being;
that allows people to lead a life of dignity and respect regardless
of whether they 'rise' or not. This necessitates a focus on lifting
people out of poverty but simultaneously 'looking up', learning
the lessons from the New Labour years and dismantling pock-
ets of privilege and embedded advantage that undermine any
notion of equality of opportunity.

For the most part when policymakers talk about addressing low levels of social mobility they do not include efforts to
block the rich from rigging the system, preventing the middle
class from using their sharp elbows to gain all the remaining

good school places or addressing housing affordability or low minimum wages.

I remember being at a diversity event at Channel 4 in the 2000s and growing increasingly irritated by production congratulating each other on having a few more Black faces in their shows. At some point I mustered up the courage to put my hand up and ask them if their production companies paid their staff a living wage and telling them that if they really wanted to address social mobility they should pay their cleaners more. They looked at me confused, I could almost hear them thinking: *Who is this woman spoiling the fun? How dare she ask us to give up our privileges of cheap cleaners? Get this loony lefty out of here!* Certainly not the first time, nor the last, that I was that person in the room. We need more voices asking these questions, pushing our employers to put fair pay on the table or even, dare I say it, above profits. Raising your voice may seem like a small thing, but it is important, and it can make a difference. Imagine if five or even ten more people had joined me in asking for higher wages in that room? Suddenly my views wouldn't have seemed so bizarre.

Of course, there is even less effort spent on empowering people to stand together, through trade unions and other institutions that emphasise the collective, where the aim is to achieve better for all instead of just one individual. In the dominant story of our society, the greatest ambition is not to change the world, but to increase your personal bank balance. Indeed, our current government, and many employers, put a lot of effort into closing down the narrative of collective change.

There are also policy ideas that will deliver on expanding our ideas of success and increasing dignity for all. How would we organise society if we had no idea where we would end up?

As we have uncovered, for the most part 'making it' or not is decided before you make a single conscious decision; the majority of the factors associated with 'success' are about the lottery of birth, of the way policy has ensured that luck above all other factors defines your life. So, as philosopher John Rawls once asked – how would you design things if you had no idea where you or your child would end up? What if we were to do his experiment, that we made policy decisions and preferences behind a 'veil of ignorance' whereby you know nothing about yourself, your position in society, your sex, race, nationality, natural ability or individual tastes?[1] Common sense dictates that we would not choose the current lottery system where a handful win big while others get nothing.

The good news is there is nothing inevitable about the levels of inequality we face. Inequality of all kinds – whether income, wealth or group-based— are a product of human decisions. Although I've peppered ideas of policy change throughout the book – from closing tax loopholes to changing our focus from economic growth to good job creation, these are expanded upon here.

We can change things, and this is how.

## POINTING OUT THE OBVIOUS

Knowledge is power. I hope in writing this book, by spending the time working out some of the statistics, that I will empower others to make the argument.

It's important to ask, if social mobility is possible to solve then how come prime minister after prime minister, both Conservative and Labour, haven't been able to address it? After being the expressed policy goal for decades, why are we going backwards? Wrong policies? Or are we trying to bang a square peg into a round hole? Is it, perhaps, that it is in the interests of those in power to maintain this system of hierarchy? That in this story of social mobility, some would need to move down but for obvious reasons the people on top – the rich – won't let this happen.

The way social mobility is conceived justifies unfairness. It codifies inequality into our mindset and makes it mathematically near impossible for people to feel good about themselves. It is toxic and a tool of greed. A way of justifying the rat race. We need millions of people to reject this status quo – and that will only happen if we can offer an alternative.

As a start, tell people about your own stories. Reflect on how much of it was luck, how much was hard work, how much was state assistance. Get people to talk about what they are worried about for their kids' futures. The change we need is so obvious when you think about it for ten minutes. Use your voice to have the conversation, changing one mind at a time is better than changing no minds, and could set off a chain reaction to build support for a fairer world. Think about the progress that we have made on feminism and LGBTQI+ rights over the years. We need to see children living in poverty as being as unacceptable as racism, misogyny and homophobia.

## LEVELLING THE PLAYING FIELD, FOR REAL

While government after government makes social mobility the litmus test of their agenda, meaningful change is yet to happen. One of the reasons for the failure of policy attached to social mobility is that it often focuses purely on education. As we have discussed in this book, even when you take social mobility as a legitimate policy focus, education is not the only determining life outcome – neither is it miraculously able to correct for poverty, low-quality housing or extreme wealth inequality. There's nothing positive to report because they are taking the wrong approach.

We need new ways of living and working, sharing and caring. If the UK or any other government was serious about tackling regional inequality or any other type of social disparity, they would focus on these five things that would help us to really level up. Critically, these efforts, especially on green job creation and the care sector, will move us to truly being a land of opportunities and not just a land for those good at passing academic exams.

### 1. An actual living wage and pay ratios

How much do people need to live a life of dignity? The Joseph Rowntree Foundation (JRF) state that a 'minimum standard of living in the UK today includes, but is more than just food, clothes and shelter. It is about having what you need in order to have the opportunities and choices necessary to participate in society.'[2] The foundation's findings are derived not through a simulation model or by a few economists in a dark room somewhere, but in consultation with members of the public. They engage people in detailed discussions, in groups, about the things a household needs to achieve an acceptable living standard. In terms of their findings on the level of income that is needed, the difference between this amount and what it is possible to earn on a minimum wage is notable. In April 2022, the JRF calculated that a single person needs to earn £25,500 a year to reach a minimum acceptable standard of living. A couple with two children needs to earn £43,400 between them. However, a job paying a minimum wage, which a previous chancellor, George Osborne, misleadingly renamed the National Living Wage, would only pay a single adult £18,600 working full-time (37.5 hours a week) and a couple £37,200 between them.[3]

If we are going to be able to honestly tell children that they can be whatever they want to be, we have to remove one of the biggest barriers in their lives – being poor. We have to agree for everyone to have at least the minimum amount of money to live with dignity. I can never get my head around the fact that we know how much people need to live on, but still pay or provide social security benefits below that rate. We literally set a poverty wage and yet expect people to live good lives.

What is interesting is that while discussion of low pay tends to be ongoing, there is almost always absolute silence on high pay. While working at the New Economics Foundation we explored the possibility of a maximum wage, or at least a wage ratio. Even hugely successful professional basketball leagues in the US have a maximum wage and a ratio of roughly 20:1.[4] This is a far cry from FTSE 100 companies, where the median CEO/median ratio was 73:1 and the median CEO/lower quartile ratio was 109:1.[5]

The issue of imposing maximum wages can elicit a strong reaction, with people protesting that to do so is to 'limit aspiration'. But given the obscene differences between bosses and workers in many firms, we can't expect minimum wages alone to level the playing field for children from different backgrounds. Maximum wages or ratios at least force a conversation about how wages should be distributed within a company, allowing us to have the sorts of conversations about teamwork and the value of different jobs outlined in Chapter 8.

The very least we can do is introduce more progressive taxation. Closing tax loopholes would also be a good place to start. The wealthiest do not pay their fair share of tax, but we need to push further, with new tax levels on higher incomes and, especially, wealth introduced. Redistribution, particularly of assets and land, is an effective way both to offset inequality and to reward workers.

## 2. Housing

Housing – the way it is being used as a piggy bank for the rich and the lack of truly affordable housing for most people – is an issue both driving inequalities and undermining our ability to build community. A whole generation is being locked out of secure housing, and those on lower incomes are subject to living in substandard and overpriced housing. In terms of rent, according to the Office for National Statistics the typical English tenant paid an average of 27 per cent – over a quarter of their total gross income – on housing costs. For Londoners this figure is much higher, with an average of nearly half of their total income (49 per cent) on housing.[6] The average cost of a house is 7 times the average wage in the UK[7] – which is a big problem when you consider that most banks only lend up to 4 times your earnings.

But this is not just a British issue; the housing crisis is affecting cities from San Francisco in the United States to Accra in Ghana, as affordable housing production is not keeping up with demand and housing becomes increasingly financialised and treated as a commodity rather than a human right. Addressing this one issue alone would both ensure a better start for children while deflating the wealth balloon.

For so long we have been told we can solve this issue by just building more and that we need the private sector to build unaffordable housing in order to build a few 'affordable' properties. The result? Still not enough housing and gentrification that has pushed people out of their community. This model is a lie and a social failure.

There are better solutions, but you won't hear them from Conservative Party government ministers. They are too scared of upsetting developers and homeowners, and as so many of them are landlords themselves it does not suit their interests to change things.[8] Access to a home has predominantly been interpreted in public policy as owning one. When housing is treated as a financial asset, it seems natural for public policy to prioritise the interest of homeowners and their wealth, and to see increased housing prices as a positive indicator of prosperity. So how do we move to making housing a community asset rather than a vehicle for personal wealth building?

There are some relatively simply first moves. For instance, as mentioned in Chapter 4, London should take a page out of the policy handbooks of Australia and Switzerland, who limit what foreign nationals not living in the country can buy. Limiting what the global superrich can buy up in the city will help ease some of the house price pressures, encourage developers to build fewer luxury homes and help address corrupt money flowing into the city.

For the UK, a rich country capable of spending more, social housing is fundamental and we need to be investing more in this human right. But we also need to make sure we learn from lessons of the past by making this housing democratically governed by the tenants rather than putting them in a position of powerlessness. We could learn from Uruguay's co-operatives. The FUCVAM (Federación Uruguaya de Cooperativas de Vivienda por Ayuda Mutua) model is based on collective ownership of housing by a co-operative, to which members contribute through a non-monetary benefit or so-called sweat equity, such as labour and time of twenty-one hours per household per week. It is strongly supported by government through the provision of technical assistance in negotiations with credit agencies and the private sector, which means government can act as a guarantor. There are also legal frameworks to ensure private developers are not holding on to land and that institutionalise housing options for the co-operatives.[9]

## 3. Free universal high-quality childcare

During the pandemic a 'woman's place' quickly became being with her children (if she had them). Even when both parents were working, data showed that it was still disproportionately women doing the childcare and home-schooling.[10] The patriarchy returned in a flash. Even before the pandemic though, childcare in the UK was among the most expensive in the world[11] and of poor quality when compared to other European countries.[12] The average day nursery is roughly £137.69 a week for 25 hours, even with government subsidies,[13] and this raises to £183.56 in Inner London.[14] Childcare is priced as a luxury, rather than a public utility.

The Nordic nations – Sweden, Norway, Denmark, Finland – are often touted as utopian countries when it comes to equality, and unsurprisingly a big factor in this is the high-quality childcare everyone – regardless of income – has access to. Investment in early childhood education and care contributes to reducing the gender employment gap, with Sweden and Iceland having some of the highest levels of maternal employment in the OECD[15] and lowest overall gender employment gap. It has also been shown to contribute to reducing socio-economic inequalities by improving outcomes for disadvantaged children and narrowing the gap between immigrant and non-immigrant children.[16] Policymakers ignore this vital sector at their peril; without positive steps here, we will fail in achieving any sense of gender equality in society.

In fact, the returns on investment on childcare are one of the

highest you can get for public infrastructure. When the employment and economic benefits of investing in the care economy
for Canada were calculated in 2008, researchers found that
every Can$100 that was invested by the Quebec government
in childcare returned Can$104 to the provincial government
and $43 to the federal government through increased labour
market participation and associated income taxes.[17]

The Nordic model of the care economy stresses quality, in
terms of the nature of the care delivered as well as the pay and
working conditions and esteem of care workers across the care
sectors.[18] Universal provision is not just about access: it requires
increased standards of training and qualifications to ensure
childcare is always of high quality, and better working conditions for childcare workers, including decent wages, stable
contract hours, and career and pay progression opportunities.

This is a no-brainer. You get kids off to a good start, people
working in care have well-paid jobs with career prospects
and women with young children have the ability to return to
work – it's a win-win-win situation. There are short-term provisions like providing more free hours to parents, but we can
only have the sort of standard that the Nordics have if we have
more public provision of childcare, with more opportunity for
training and higher wages. Others have also highlighted the
need to prioritise co-location of childcare services to prevent
unnecessary travel between sites.[19]

## 4. A green new deal

On the subject of win-win situations, a large injection of
investment in the green economy – from insulating homes to
renewable energy – has the greatest potential for changing the
economy for the better while expanding opportunities. While
the climate crisis is a global emergency, addressing it gives us

the opportunity to completely restructure who the national economy works for and to create well-paid, non-graduate jobs.

Governments should accelerate the creation of jobs as they explore new sectors. Recent estimates suggest that the new renewable energy sector has the potential to reach 100 million jobs globally by 2050, up from around 58 million today, with incentives to accelerate this transition serving to address both the climate emergency and employment needs.[20] This transition should embrace the following:

1. Decarbonising the energy sector via renewable clean energy projects such as wind, hydrogen and solar;
2. Promoting new forms of entrepreneurship targeting digital and green jobs;
3. Working with private and third-sector firms to invest in new firms and jobs;
4. Focusing efforts in areas where there is high unemployment and low economic activity, so there is a regional tilt towards the areas most deprived;
5. Investing in cheaper and healthier forms of public transport.[21]

In Germany, which has been a leader on green investment, employment opportunities are not typical white-collar occupations, and the job profile ranges from engineers, scientists, financial analysts, electricians, plumbers and lobbyists, among others. From 2004 to 2013, the number of people working in the renewable energy sector had risen by a factor of 2.3. Green job opportunities involve production, installation, operation and maintenance of windmills, solar modules, biomass power plants or heating systems as well as biogas and thermal applications.[22] Germany's systems of apprenticeships and skills training has made this expansion easier but this doesn't mean it isn't a model that could be adopted elsewhere. The types of jobs created are fundamental if we are to expand opportunities away from the typical jobs that mean 'making it' – and the story we tell about this expansion is also critical if we are to give these professions the respect that make them desirable. What could be more valuable in society than ensuring the survival of the human race? People need to feel pride in their jobs, and this would not just create jobs, it would also create meaning.

## 5. Public and shared ownership and redistributing wealth

Most measures of well-being would put Norway ahead of the UK in terms of quality of life and equality.[23] But what if I told you we could have also topped 'best places to live' charts like Norway? Norway was relatively poor compared to other Western countries, until they found oil. Oil, of course, can be a curse and we shouldn't be encouraging more drilling, but the way Norway handled their oil wealth is a perfect example of how we can share wealth. And, because the UK's oil discoveries lay side-by-side geographically with Norway's, comparing the countries' two approaches is like a sliding doors experiment on how to get the best out of oil wealth.

The UK and Norway both began offshore exploration in the mid-1960s with the first oil discoveries made in 1969. Since then, both countries have produced a similar quantity of hydrocarbons.[24] The difference is that Norway established mainly public ownership of the oil with a sovereign wealth fund called Government Pension Fund Global or the Oil Fund, designed to create funding to pay for welfare programmes and investment in future generations. The sovereign fund is the largest in the world. Today,

Norway has over $1.35 trillion in assets. In December 2021, it was worth about $250,000 per Norwegian citizen. Meanwhile, the UK, under Thatcher, privatised their share of North Sea oil and gas. While corporations are taxed on drilling, this only amounts to roughly $1.3 billion a year.[25]

The example of North Sea oil wealth, and the different approaches the UK and Norway took, is a good example of what a difference public ownership can make. Inequalities today arise to a considerable extent from a single source: stark inequality in the ownership and control of assets. By broadening the distribution of rights over productive assets we can ensure a more inclusive, democratic society, and also a more productive, efficient and environmentally sustainable one.

Apply this to renewable energy. Currently less than 0.1 per cent of our renewable energy is publicly owned, which means the same companies that have made huge profits from fossil fuels are now also able to make profits from renewable energy.[26] This seems especially weird to me because how can the wind and sun be privatised? Shouldn't we all benefit? It would not be hard to make these natural assets publicly owned.

Mutually owned building societies, co-operatives and land trusts are all models in which ownership takes a more collective form, and benefits are more evenly shared. In the workplace, this can look like people owning a stake in their company, regardless of the position they hold. This type of John Lewis structure has been found to have all sorts of benefits for productivity, but it's much bigger than the bottom line. Shared capital initiatives can generate economic and social stakes which motivate and encourage more broad-based participation in society and allow for greater voice and influence.

## INTRODUCING A SOLIDARITY TAX FOR INVESTMENT IN THE NEXT GENERATION

One of the most common questions on the doorstep when I would speak about the need for a green new deal and universal free childcare provision was 'Where will the money come from?' It was hard, on those cold nights, to give the truth in a way that was concise and that would override existing misconceptions of 'maxed out credit cards' that had been cynically used by Conservatives to drive through public spending cuts. I would tell them that money creation for a country like the UK – which has the back-up of 36 million taxpayers – is not the issue. Until Liz Truss came in and decimated the UK pound, everyone wanted to lend us money, but even still we are seen as a relatively safe bet. Printing money or loans are not the only answer, however. Taxing the rich is part of the solution not only because it boosts public spending, but because it addresses rising inequality and it embeds a sense of giving back – if framed right and spent well it can bring people together.

The issue of wealth taxes has become a live topic in a way that it had not been when I first started working on inequality. Back in the 2000s, letting the rich get rich was all the rage. It was only in the years after the financial crisis, the Occupy movement and especially since the pandemic, that there was more serious discussion of the issue. Still, despite the types of arguments that Democrats such as Elizabeth Warren[27] and Bernie Sanders have made in the US, and the ballooning of billionaire wealth we have seen here in the UK, no new wealth taxes have been introduced. This is despite widespread public support for higher taxes on the rich.[28]

So, what is the problem? The problem is political will – will shaped by elite interests in maintaining the status quo and protecting the rich. But this isn't set in stone. A year after the election I was offered a role running an international project including countries such as Costa Rica, Spain and Sierra Leone, where there was leadership willing to try different things. It was so weird to be in meetings with senior civil servants and ambassadors talking about a four-day week, publicly owned Wi-Fi services and so many other policies that had been balked at in the UK. As I started the role at the end of 2020, in the midst of the pandemic, one key policy countries were thinking about was a solidarity tax.

A solidarity tax is a way of governments imposing taxes with the aim of bringing people together in how the tax is framed and communicated, as well as how it is spent on projects that build unity. Solidarity taxes can take various forms. They may be levied on corporate and individual income, as wealth taxes or as different forms of levies or surcharges. Solidarity taxes are not a new practice, especially in times of crises. Kenya used them to help address the AIDS crisis, Germany to rebuild East Germany after reunification. There is one thing I find particularly helpful about these taxes – the title. Given the massive downgrade in opportunity, lifestyle and security that the next generation faces and the strong inclination people have to provide for their children, how about a solidarity fund that connects generations? It would also be a way to normalise wealth taxes through communicating unity and responsibility.

Uruguay told us about how they introduced a Covid-19 Solidarity Fund by creating a Covid-19 Sanitary Emergency Tax to raise monies for the fund. The tax applied to gross income exceeding \$2,850 a month, at a rate of 5–20 per cent.[29] In exchange, relief in the country was largely targeted towards employment protections, with programmes aimed at including informal workers and extending health coverage to unemployed people. A cash benefit was also introduced for vulnerable families and as a top-up for family allowance beneficiaries. While this wasn't a tax on wealth, it did make recovery more progressive in the country and had broad support.

Even the International Monetary Fund has noted the scope and benefit of considering solidarity taxes to help finance Covid-19 recovery through surtaxes on personal income and on excess profits within companies, as well as international agreements on tax.[30] Our research at New York University showed that when looking across all examples of solidarity taxes, these measures need not always be temporary, so long as they are transparent as to what they are paying for and what factors will determine their duration.[31]

The amount of money raised would of course vary based on the design of the solidarity tax. An estimate by the University of Greenwich predicted that a tax on just the top 1 per cent of wealthiest households in the UK could raise between £70 billion to £130 billion[32] – more than enough to offset a new universal childcare system.

A solidarity tax for the next generation would be a great start in providing a framework for the rich to give back, correcting for the social ills and inequalities that have built up in the system, making the rich feel good about giving to the next generation, raising money, while also building connections between each other – what's not to like?

## CHANGING OUR POLITICAL CULTURE

Imagine being at work and noticing the colleague sitting next to you watching porn. Now imagine this is taking place on the green benches in the Houses of Parliament. This is exactly what happened to a female Conservative MP who noticed what Neil Parish, the Conservative MP for Tiverton and Honiton, was up to.[33] What's worse is that the identity of the man was hidden for days until public pressure meant the Conservatives had to come clean. In fact, three days before his name came out, Neil Parish was asked in passing on a radio show for his views on claims that a Tory MP had been caught watching pornography. 'We've got some 650 members of parliament in what is a very intense area. You are going to get people who step over the line,' the Conservative MP said, as if this was nothing to do with him. 'I don't think there's necessarily a huge culture [of that behaviour] here but I think it does have to be dealt with and dealt with seriously and that's what the whips will do.'[34]

Although the Tory whips refused to suspend the party whip for more than forty-eight hours after a female minister and parliamentary aide identified Parish, the truth finally came out and the disgraced MP resigned. But this sort of contemptuous misogynistic behaviour is just the tip of the iceberg, with multiple incidents of inappropriate behaviour in Parliament receiving attention in 2022.[35] The *Sunday Times* revealed that there was a 'Sexist of the Year' award presented at a Downing Street Christmas party.[36]

It is a culture driven by contempt and enabled by perpetrators thinking they are above the law. This comes from a deep sense of entitlement, which ultimately derives from the hierarchy of worthiness produced through narratives such as social mobility. Breaking this culture and dominance of privately educated elites running this country will be no small task. Changing the people in Parliament to be more representative of the population in terms of life experience is the ultimate goal, but why would anyone be attracted into that world? It doesn't exactly feel like a place that would be welcoming to most of us. Currently, reaching the pinnacle of government doesn't demonstrate people working hard to get to the top. Looking at the background of those there and drawing on my own experiences of politics, for the most part it is those who already have a lot of political connections and wealth, or at best the people most willing to fit in with the status quo. There are a few good ones, but far fewer than we need and deserve.

We need to take some bold steps. Moving Parliament outside of London and into a building that projects more open and consensual politics rather than the combative stage we have right now could help. A permanent move northwards of the seat of power could transform and rebalance the relationship – both economic and political – between London and the rest of the UK. Westminster Palace could then become the Museum of English and British History. Yes, it would cost money, but it would also bring huge benefits over the longer term in the message we send about the kind of country we are. Some may argue that these efforts would just be symbolic, but symbols have power and it is important that we ask, what symbols do we want to represent us as a country? Currently, we have inherited wealth in the form of the King and our Parliament as our symbols – not exactly the sort of symbols that make you think this is a country that is serious about equal opportunities and addressing inequality.

We should also abolish the House of Lords in its current form, either replacing it with an elected House of Lords or a form of innovative democracy, as the author and rapper Darren McGarvey has suggested in his book *The Social Distance Between Us* (2022).[37] His idea of some sort of citizens assembly, made up of randomly selected people across the country, rotated like a jury service, could help to extend our democracy and keep a check on the power of the elite.

BE THE TROUBLEMAKER — ORGANISE, UNIONISE,
STAND UP FOR EACH OTHER

The story of Amazon and Jeff Bezos has come to signify corporate greed, declining workers' rights and mass consumption.
Amazon's 1.1 million workers in the United States make it
the country's second-largest private employer after Walmart.
Watching the news in the US one afternoon, in the aftermath
of a tornado that had ripped through Illinois, I was confronted
by the brutal reality of the Amazon work model. Images of
Amazon warehouses with the roof blown off appeared along
with news of six people dead. A worker, a young African
American man, appeared for interview and talked of how they
had been taught to stand against the walls, but how this had
failed to protect everyone.

I was confused. It was the season for extreme weather; why
had these guys been working, or at the very least why hadn't
they been given proper instructions on what to do in cases
of emergency? A later investigation revealed that there had
been concerns raised about safety before the tornado and that
employees were not fully aware of protocols. There were also
reports that staff were told they were not allowed to leave that
night.[38] Jeff Bezos had recently been crowned the richest man
in the Forbes 400 and launched himself into space last year, and
here were six employees who had died because his company
hadn't taken the time, care or finances to ensure their safety.[39]
I felt furious at the injustice.

But in 2022 a different, more hopeful, story about Amazon
emerged. Amazon workers, led by a former employee who
had been sacked for organising a small walkout over safety
conditions, Christian Smalls, had won a vote to unionise the
warehouse in Staten Island, a site known as JFK8. In his victory

speech which popped up on my Twitter feed – he thanked Jeff Bezos for going to space because 'while he was up there, we were organising a union.'[40] It was perfect. But it only got better when you read into what had happened. It had all started at the beginning of the pandemic when then Amazon worker Christian Smalls planned a small walkout over safety conditions at a fulfillment centre in New York City. Of course, Amazon, like other big corporates, are highly opposed to workers organising, so the company quickly mobilised to crush any efforts to unionise. Amazon formed a reaction team involving ten departments. According to an article by the *New York Times*,[41] eleven vice presidents of the company were alerted. One email, mistakenly sent to over a thousand people, described Mr Smalls as 'not smart, or articulate'. The company fired Smalls, saying he had violated quarantine rules by attending the walkout.

Smalls and his best friend from the warehouse, Derrick Palmer, only became more determined and began their organising efforts. They started off at the bus stop outside the warehouse, they built bonfires to warm colleagues brought homemade meals of all varieties to appeal to immigrant workers and they made TikTok videos to reach workers across the city.[42]

The union spent $120,000 overall, raised through GoFundMe; meanwhile, Amazon spent more than $4.3 million just on anti-union consultants nationwide in the same year.[43] But their big money failed. Employees cast 2,654 votes for unionisation and 2,131 against, giving the union a win by more than 10 percentage points.[44] Smalls and Palmer delivered one of the biggest wins for the trade union movement in a generation. And they haven't stopped there, inspiring organising in Amazon warehouses across the country.[45]

When I ran a trade union-backed think tank, I would see the

power of people coming together. But these things do not just happen. Like the Amazon workers, you have got to find ways to bring people together, especially as governments have legislated increasingly in favour of companies making it difficult for trade unions to take action.

Whether it is Amazon, Starbucks or any other multinational corporation, and of course the rail and postal strikes here in the UK, you can see something changing. After years of being told that the way to improve your economic lot is to lift yourself up by your bootstraps, many workers have come to realise that the best way to lift themselves up is through collective power. That is, by unionising. We need to become many Davids against Goliath. If we are going to have to work a hundred times harder than those born into privilege, we might as well work harder for each other.

We can go further still in our solidarity. Uniting our struggles and standing up for each other is critical if we are to build a movement big and strong enough to counter the vested interests that are maintaining the status quo. Looking around the world you see the formation of bottom-up movements that have successfully translated housing justice issues into the mainstream, with racial justice advocates highlighting the impact of discriminatory housing policies on the current wealth distribution. Environmental justice movements are demanding more sustainable urban policies and people are standing up for immigrants of all kinds. If you have seen the film *Pride* (2014), you will know the true story of those fighting for gay rights going to support Welsh miners, who in return came to gay rights protests. Stupidly, I watched the film on a plane and couldn't stop blubbering! Solidarity is beautiful!

## THINGS CAN CHANGE

When the financial crisis first hit in 2008, politicians and bankers ran around like headless chickens. At the time I used to walk from my flat in Whitechapel to the South Bank. The frenzy was immediately evident those mornings as the crisis unfolded. It was like an air of anxiety had drifted over the famous Square Mile. Previous long queues for breakfast bacon sarnies vanished. You could feel the tension emanating from City workers. The world reacted quickly. Billions were spent to bail out the banks, steady economies and try to mitigate the recession. We all expected a reckoning for the banking system and the bankers who had made this crisis happen, but, very quickly, UK politics and media became obsessed with talking about how the government had spent 'too much'. No, not on bailing out the banks, but on public services throughout the decade before the financial crisis. The story went that we were in trouble because we had spent too much and got into uncontrollable debt levels. Therefore, we had to pay back our debt by cutting spending in a period of austerity. The blame moved quickly from the bankers to the politicians who had invested in the NHS and education.[46]

It was very clever, but a lie. Not only had the government not spent 'too much', but by cutting spending we were going to undermine our economic recovery and hurt the generation of children currently going through our schools. It was a sneaky ploy to shrink the public sector while protecting the bankers from further scrutiny. Of course, the shadow chancellor at the time, George Osborne, had previously worked as a banker in the City.

If only I had a pound for every time I screamed at the radio or TV because of stupid comments about maxing out credit cards or not having a 'magic money tree!' There were so many economic myths spread on the airwaves between 2010 and 2017 and barely any journalists pushed back on the lies! Meanwhile, people, especially the poorest, were suffering the consequences of this lie cooked up by the Tories to protect their friends. In those years, when anyone tried to argue that there was an alternative route forward, that austerity was hurting not just our public services but our economy, that with low interest rates the country should be investing not cutting back, we were scoffed at and made to feel like we didn't understand economics.

But then something shifted in the years after 2017, and by 2019, the story completely flipped. A few months after the bruising election defeat of the 2019 election, I was doing one of my then frequent appearances on Sky talking about new budget announcements. Conservative commentators were always well prepped with messaging points from Conservative HQ and occasionally I would get a look at them. I was all ready to make my arguments about the need to borrow and invest in light of the climate crisis and years of austerity, when I looked down at the Conservative Party representatives' talking points and saw all the arguments I had been using for ten years! When he started reading them out, I started smiling. 'I think you'll find I've been saying this for ten years' – he started smiling too, he couldn't deny that, in doing a U-turn, they had lifted their arguments from progressive thinkers.

The cause of the shift in public attitudes of course isn't simply about the argument that myself and other progressives made; ultimately a lot of people could see the harm it was doing to their communities. But the fact that the ruling party eventually did make a U-turn does show that the story can change. While the disastrous but short tenure of Liz Truss brought a new wave of politicians arguing for austerity, at least there is far more pushback. We can win the argument – even against the money and connections of the superrich. At the time of writing, Chancellor Jeremy Hunt and Prime Minister Rishi Sunak are again using arguments of public spending cuts to justify their economic policies, but this time they are facing far more resistance and questioning than in 2010.

People are increasingly aware that the economic model that promised that wealth and opportunity would trickle down is a lie. The promise of a dynamic, private, consumption-orientated economy that would float all boats has been shown up, and for those that don't already recognise that now, they will as things inevitably get worse.

The 2021 UK Social Mobility Barometer found that two-fifths (39 per cent) of the public think that it is becoming more difficult for people from less advantaged backgrounds to move up in British society. Forty-six per cent of UK adults believe that where you end up in society is mainly determined by your background and who your parents are. More than half of the people in the younger age groups are likely to say the same (51 per cent of 18- to 24-year-olds and 52 per cent of 25- to 49-year-olds). People of colour are a little wiser than others, perhaps because of their experiences. While figures are based only on a small sub-sample of ethnic minority respondents, the survey suggests that over half of BME (Black and minority ethnic) respondents (54 per cent) believe that where individuals end up is mainly determined by their background and who their parents are. Additionally, only a quarter (25 per cent) of BME respondents believe that everyone has a fair chance to go as far as their talent and hard work will take them.[47]

A decade of austerity, a cost of living crisis teamed with a recession, decades of increasing housing prices and stagnant wages have stored up social immobility for the next two generations at least. It definitely feels like things are coming to a head. Recent inflation comes on top of a long-simmering affordability crisis. The price of housing is sapping budgets and forcing families to make awful decisions to keep down costs. The costs of childcare, elder care, higher education and medical care remain outrageous as well, affecting families far up the income scale, though of course those at the bottom are the most burdened. The cornucopia of consumer goods that we were told was our key to a brighter future is not going to look that appealing when (a) most of us can't afford it and (b) it is killing the planet.

The climate crisis will lead to the biggest levelling down of human opportunity ever seen. The current cost of living crisis, with ballooning food and energy prices, will be nothing in comparison to the disruption in food supply. How will we talk about opportunities for young people when millions are being forced to migrate because of famine and increasing extreme weather events? This will have an impact across the middle class – and soon. And don't think that if you're in the rich world you'll escape it. Where are you going to go on your holidays when the Maldives are under the sea? Plants and animals are at risk of losing more than half of their habitats, rising seas will sweep away large swathes of human habitat, and that won't make for a pretty view from your exclusive resort.

If this doesn't convince you that we need urgent action, then perhaps think about the way wealth concentration is leading to a concentration of power at the top. Our democracy is being undermined by the dominance of politicians from wealthy backgrounds or put there to protect the interests of the rich, and people are being made despondent by the hollow political salesmanship of these liars.

A new settlement is way overdue. We need to throw out this

idea of 'making it', of individualising success and hardship, and understand the role of society. The numbers in this book dance around the realisation that the individual is a product of society. There is nothing wrong with relying on others and drawing on collective support; indeed, the reality is that we all do it. The myth of social mobility is a form of violence and class war – trapping people instead of setting them free. If you are not the exception, rather you are the rule, you shouldn't feel bad – the system has set most of us up to fail and then blame ourselves and each other instead of those at the top who rig the game. If we don't start thinking of each other, changing our ideas of what success is, what a healthy society is, we will all fail.

## RESIST AND REBEL

Hope can be hard to hold on to in this world. I felt a lot of my hope drain away that election night in December 2019 and for a while found myself extremely angry at how our futures were being vandalised, but without a clear way to channel this anger. The way the Covid-19 pandemic was handled, the deliberate destruction of the NHS, the lack of democracy after two changes of prime minister without a public vote, the reluctance to protect people from rising inflation and interest rates, the way in which Rishi Sunak was celebrated as some sort of symbol of social mobility when he is far from it, all enraged me! There is so much we need to rebel against.

After a timeout in New York and work travel that took me around the globe, I came to realise that I don't want to escape my home – there is no escape, not while so many struggle and the institutions that supported me and my family are being systematically trashed. We need to fight for a brighter future. Persuaded to run again, I was surprised when I got so much support and won my parliamentary candidate selection in 2022. That connection I have with the people in my community is alive, it is powerful and it is a reminder that I'm part of something bigger than myself, we all are. Inspired by the policies and protest I have seen in countries I've worked with around the world, I believe and know that change can happen.[48]

*Our stories of human greatness often tell us about an individual overcoming personal adversity, but it is time we change the narrative to highlight ways of working together to overcome human adversity. From individual social mobility to community and even global advancement. We need to increase the odds of a better life for all of us. This is the only way forward if we want humanity to win.*

# ACKNOWLEDGEMENTS

Writing a book about social mobility and luck has demonstrated to me the immense gratitude I owe to so many people who have touched my life. For love, for friendship, for support, for inspiration, for teaching me, for cheering me on, for believing in me, for laughing with me, for knocking on doors to get people to vote for me, for fighting and paying for a benefits system that supported me and my family. I might not mention you all by name, but you are in my heart.

Thank you to my husband, Akin, who puts up with me working all the time and supports me unconditionally in my endless expeditions. Somehow all those childhood years of watching Bollywood movies and dreaming about a charming, funny, handsome husband like Shah Rukh Khan manifested you in real life! I am so blessed to have your love.

To my sister, Nadia. For the laughs through the hard times. A big sister's love is so powerful.

To my in-laws, Anne and Baba, who are so loving and kind, and make me feel like I still have parents. Please forgive me for not being a Man Utd supporter!

To Riffat *khala*, Veena *baji*, Gaitee *baji* and my late great Fakir uncle, who have aways been our rocks. Special thanks to my very Aussie soul sister Zobia, my gorgeous niece Marlie and nephew Tristen, and of course Akin's brother from another mother, Thierry. Whenever I need good vibes I close my eyes and think of you. To my nieces Zahra, Neeshy, Emma and Ari, who are kind enough to give me their time and teach me about Jack Harlow, SZA and TikTok trends relevant to inequality! Phool *khala* and all my family in Pakistan, I may be far away and my Urdu may not allow me to convey it, but I'm always thinking of you and love you dearly.

My friends have been so important to me and have given me so much strength and joy over the years. To all the people that love me so much that they tried to talk me out of going into politics again – Mel, Kash, Meriame, Rachel and Mihir. I know you worry, and I'm counting on you to tell me if I'm turning into a horrible person! Nida Kirmani, I'm writing your whole name so everyone who thinks they're your friend can see that you're actually mine! To the people who have consistently been there for me – Emma, Shomsia, Tamara, Cyprian, Josh, Rowan. Ernie, you always put a smile on my face! Olumide, thank you for letting me be your friend even though I'm old! To Gemma Jones and Nitisha Ramasamy – teenage friendships are intense and you helped me more than you could ever know.

Mr Mahir, you wrote in my leavers' book that you wanted a mention in my first book, so here you are! Sorry it took so long; I'm forever thankful to you. That goes also to all the teachers who made me feel capable and the impossible seem possible: Mr Osborne at Chingford C of E; Mr Reeves at Sir George Monoux College, who got me thinking about the economy; and my politics tutor at Oxford, Francisco González, who looked out for me and made a special effort because he knew I was the only working-class socialist in the room!

To all the incredible friends and experts who were kind enough to read chapters of this book, and many of whom I also tested ideas on: Maya Goodfellow, Mike Savage, Diane Reay, Fred Bauma, Raquel Jesse (you're an incredible young woman and I can't wait to read your book one day) and Milos Djordjevic (the best of humans). Thank you to Eran Cohen for working with me on the wealth statistics, for comments and for moral support. Claire, I appreciate all your advice on covers and your NYC hospitality.

To my lovely colleague and friend Paula for putting up with me moaning about writing the last few years. So many people I have met over the last couple of years – Leah Zamore at NYU; Momo in Sierra Leone; Jurist and Vivi in Indonesia; Duda in Brazil; Mehrinaz, Mona and John in Lebanon – have made me think and reflect and inevitably helped both this book and my own growth.

Karolina Sutton, thank you for taking me under your wing, and thanks to Holly Harris and all the team at Simon & Schuster for picking my book.

All those that have my back in the dark world of politics have my eternal gratitude: Helen, Mick, Sarah, Norma, Derrick, Rav, Harpreet, Miriam, Andy, Hanna, Mary, John, Sa'id, Bill, Sonia, Matt, Carys and so many others that have been willing to dedicate their free time and energy to this effort. To my Chingford and Woodford Green community – you're home and I hope I can make you proud.

Dad, do you remember how happy you were when Norman Tebbit had to give me all those academic prizes at school? When you picked me up from Oxford and told me that when you used to take exams in Fiji it would say 'University of Oxford Examinations' at the top of the pages, and that you couldn't have begun to imagine that years later your own daughter would go there? Thank you for giving me my politics and being honest in telling me from day one that I needed to work harder than anyone else around me to get anywhere. I hope I don't have to tell the next generation the same.

Mum, *ummie-jhan*, I miss you so much. Everything I ever do will be for you.

# NOTES

## PROLOGUE: TAKING ON THE MAN IN THE MANSION AND LOSING

1   Royal Society for the Prevention of Accidents (RoSPA), 'Lightning at leisure',
    https://www.rospa.com/leisure-water-safety/leisure-safety/lightning.
2   Michael Crick, *Newsnight*, BBC (18 Dec. 2002), see press release (19 Dec. 2002),
    https://www.bbc.co.uk/pressoffice/pressreleases/stories/2002/12_
    december/19/newsnight_ids_cv.shtml.

## CHAPTER 1: THE EXCEPTION THAT PROVES THE RULE

1   Author's own calculations based on ONS population data, University of
    Oxford and University of Cambridge admissions data, 2000.
2   Tony Blair, Commonwealth Heads of Government Meeting,
    Oct. 1997, in David Civil, 'Conservatives, Grammar Schools and
    the "Great Meritocracy"', Modern British Studies Birmingham
    (20 Mar. 2017), https://mbsbham.wordpress.com/2017/03/20/
    conservatives-grammar-schools-and-the-great-meritocracy/.
3   Justin Pot, 'You can't pull yourself up by your bootstraps',
    Zapier (3 Dec. 2021), https://zapier.com/blog/
    you-cant-pull-yourself-up-by-your-bootstraps/.
4   Pascal Tréguer, '"Get on Your Bike" (Exhortation to Take Action)',
    Word Histories (19 Dec. 2021), https://wordhistories.net/2021/12/19/
    get-on-your-bike/.
5   Michael Young, *The Rise of the Meritocracy, 1870–2033* (Transaction
    Publishers, 1958).
6   Michael Young, 'Down with meritocracy', *Guardian* (29 June 2001), https://
    www.theguardian.com/politics/2001/jun/29/comment.

7   Amartya Sen, 'Merit and Justice', in Kenneth Arrow, Samuel Bowles
    and Steven N. Durlauf, eds, *Meritocracy and Economic Inequality* (Princeton
    University Press, 2000).
8   Sarah Churchwell, *Behold, America: A History of America First and the American
    Dream* (2018; Bloomsbury Publishing, 2019).
9   University of Oxford admissions statistics 2000, https://gazette.web.ox.ac.
    uk/files/admissions-2000pdf.
10  Table ID KS006, Nomis, https://www.nomisweb.co.uk/census/2001/ks006,
    accessed 3 Jan. 2023.
11  Gregory Clark and Neil Cummins, 'Surnames and social mobility in
    England, 1170-2012', *Human Nature*, 25/4 (Dec. 2014), 517–37.
12  Gregory Clark, *The Son Also Rises: Surnames and the History of Social Mobility*
    (2014; Princeton University Press, 2015).
13  'A Broken Social Elevator? How to Promote Social Mobility', OECD (15 June
    2018), https://www.oecd.org/social/broken-elevator-how-to-promote-
    social-mobility-9789264301085-en.htm.
14  Haroon Siddique, 'Who's Who study sheds new light on power of old boy
    network', *Guardian* (30 Oct. 2017), https://www.theguardian.com/inequality/
    2017/oct/30/whos-who-study-sheds-new-light-on-power-of-old-boy-network.
15  Lee Elliot Major and Stephen Machin, *What Do We Know and What Should We
    Do About Social Mobility?* (SAGE, 2020).
16  See for instance, J. H. Goldthorpe, 'Understanding – and
    Misunderstanding – Social Mobility in Britain: The Entry of the Economists,
    the Confusion of Politicians and the Limits of Educational Policy', *Journal of
    Social Policy*, 42 (2013), 431–450.
17  Patrick Butler, 'Social mobility in decline in Britain, official survey finds',
    *Guardian* (21 Jan. 2020), https://www.theguardian.com/society/2020/
    jan/21/social-mobility-decline-britain-official-survey-finds.
18  The Sutton Trust, *Elitist Britain, 2019*, The Sutton Trust and Social
    Mobility Commission, 2019, https://www.suttontrust.com/wp-content/
    uploads/2020/01/Elitist-Britain-2019-Summary-Report.pdf.
19  The Sutton Trust, *Elitist Britain, 2019*.
20  The Sutton Trust, *Elitist Britain, 2019*.
21  Paul Gregg, et al., 'The Role of Education for Intergenerational Income
    Mobility: A comparison of the United States, Great Britain, and Sweden',
    *Social Forces*, 96/1 (Sept. 2017), 121–152.
22  Jo Blanden, 'Cross-country rankings in intergenerational mobility: A
    comparison of approaches from economics and sociology', *Journal of Economic
    Surveys*, 27/1 (June 2011), 38–73.
23  Richard Wilkinson, 'How economic inequality harms societies' [video],
    TED Talk (2011), https://www.ted.com/talks/richard_wilkinson_how_
    economic_inequality_harms_societies?language=en.

24 George Carlin, *Brain Droppings* (Hyperion, 1997).

25 Eric Williams, 'Cambridge welcomes record number of state school students', *Varsity* (11 Sept. 2022), https://www.varsity.co.uk/news/24187.

26 'Disadvantage', University of Oxford, https://www.ox.ac.uk/about/facts-and-figures/admissions-statistics/undergraduate-students/current/disadvantage, accessed 3 Jan. 2023.

27 *Daily Mail* reporter, 'Oxford University under fire after admitting only one black Caribbean student during academic year', *Daily Mail* (18 Oct. 2010), https://www.dailymail.co.uk/news/article-1321056/Oxford-University-admitting-black-Caribbean-student-academic-year.html.

28 Matthew Whearty, 'Oxbridge must do more to combat the North–South divide', *Oxford Student* (19 Sept. 2016), https://www.oxfordstudent.com/2016/09/19/oxbridge-must-combat-north-south-divide/.

29 Quentin Fottrell, 'This is what American teenagers want to be when they grow up (they don't want to work in offices)', MarketWatch (6 May 2017), https://www.marketwatch.com/story/american-teenagers-dont-want-to-work-in-an-office-2017-04-05.

30 Policy Evidence and Analysis Team, 'Young people's career aspirations versus reality', ONS (27 Sept. 2018), https://www.ons.gov.uk/employmentandlabourmarket/peopleinwork/employmentandemployeetypes/articles/youngpeoplescareeraspirationsversusreality/2018-09-27.

31 Poorna Bell (@poornabell), Twitter post, 2.45 p.m., 24 Oct. 2022, https://twitter.com/poornabell/status/1584541570866769921.

32 Michael Savage and Jon Ungoed-Thomas, 'Teachers and nurses face tax increase after mini-budget hands cut to bankers', *Guardian* (24 Sept. 2022), https://www.theguardian.com/uk-news/2022/sep/24/teachers-and-nurses-face-tax-increase-after-mini-budget-hands-cut-to-bankers.

33 'David Cameron', Sky History, https://www.history.co.uk/biographies/david-cameron, accessed 3 Jan. 2023.

34 For example see Rakib Ehsan, 'Why Rishi Sunak's race matters', *Telegraph* (24 Oct. 2022), https://www.telegraph.co.uk/news/2022/10/24/why-rishi-sunaks-race-matters/.

35 Rupert Neate, 'Finance, property and mining: the money behind Sunak's £460,000 leadership bid', *Guardian*, (29 Oct. 2022), https://www.theguardian.com/business/2022/oct/29/rishi-sunak-leadership-donors-liz-truss.

36 John Siddle, 'Rishi Sunak accepted cash from fossil fuel investors in campaign to become PM', *Mirror* (29 Oct. 2022), https://www.mirror.co.uk/news/politics/rishi-sunak-accepted-cash-fossil-28361452.

37 Glen Owen, 'Tories accuse Angela Rayner of Basic Instinct ploy as she 'crosses and uncrosses legs' at PMQs', *Daily Mail* (23 Apr. 2022),

https://www.dailymail.co.uk/news/article-10746873/Tories-accuse-Angela-Rayner-Basic-Instinct-ploy-crosses-uncrosses-legs-PMQs.html.

38  Justin Rowlatt, 'Elon Musk's six secrets to business success', BBC News (7 Jan. 2021), https://www.bbc.com/news/business-55554343.

39  Jeff Grubb, 'How games helped make Elon Musk the real-life Tony Stark', VentureBeat (7 Apr. 2015), https://venturebeat.com/games/how-games-helped-make-elon-musk-the-real-life-tony-stark/.

40  Jason Lalljee, 'Elon Musk is speaking out against government subsidies. Here's a list of the billions of dollars his businesses have received', *Insider* (15 Dec. 2021), https://www.businessinsider.com/elon-musk-list-government-subsidies-tesla-billions-spacex-solarcity-2021-12.

41  Julia Carrie Wong, 'Tesla factory workers reveal pain, injury and stress: "Everything feels like the future but us"', *Guardian* (18 May 2017), https://www.theguardian.com/technology/2017/may/18/tesla-workers-factory-conditions-elon-musk.

42  Jessica Taylor, 'Tesla Gigafactory workers allege wage theft, dangerous conditions' KEYE TV CBS Austin (15 Nov. 2022), https://cbsaustin.com/news/local/tesla-gigafactory-workers-allege-wage-theft-dangerous-conditions-austin-travis-county-elon-musk-workers-defense-project.

43  James Baldwin, *The Fire Next Time* (1963; Dell, 1964).

44  Ava DuVernay (@ava), Twitter post, 9.23 p.m., 27 Feb. 2015, https://twitter.com/ava/status/571420353714483200?lang=en.

45  Edelman Trust, *2023 Edelman Trust Barometer Global Report* (Jan. 2023), https://www.edelman.com/sites/g/files/aatuss191/files/2023-01/2023%20Edelman%20Trust%20Barometer%20Global%20Report_Jan19.pdf.

## CHAPTER 2: 'ASPIRATION NATION': THE POLITICS OF SOCIAL MOBILITY AND OPPORTUNITY

1  Rishi Sunak, 'PM speech on building a better future', GOV.UK (4 Jan. 2023), https://www.gov.uk/government/speeches/pm-speech-on-making-2023-the-first-year-of-a-new-and-better-future-4-january-2023.

2  Liz Truss, 'Prime Minister Liz Truss's statement', GOV.UK (6 Sept. 2022) https://www.gov.uk/government/speeches/prime-minister-liz-trusss-statement-6-september-2022.

3  PoliticsHome staff, 'Boris Johnson's speech to the 2019 Conservative Party conference', PoliticsHome (2 Oct. 2019), https://www.politicshome.com/news/article/read-in-full-boris-johnsons-speech-to-the-2019-conservative-party-conference.

4  Theresa May, 'Britain, the great meritocracy', GOV.UK (9 Sept. 2016),

https://www.gov.uk/government/speeches/britain-the-great-meritocracy-prime-ministers-speech.

5  David Cameron, 'Conservative Party Conference 2012 in Birmingham: Full transcript of David Cameron's speech', *Independent* (10 Oct. 2012), https://www.independent.co.uk/news/uk/politics/conservative-party-conference-2012-in-birmingham-full-transcript-of-david-cameron-s-speech-8205536.html.

6  Gordon Brown, 'Acceptance speech' [video], C-SPAN (24 June 2007), https://www.c-span.org/video/?199403-1/gordon-brown-acceptance-speech.

7  Tom Happold, 'Blair pledges "opportunity society"', *Guardian* (11 Oct. 2004), https://www.theguardian.com/politics/2004/oct/11/labour.uk.

8  D. Clark, 'Median disposable income in the United Kingdom 1977–2021, by quintile', Statista (28 Mar. 2022), https://www.statista.com/statistics/1133683/uk-disposable-income-by-quintile/.

9  'Distribution of individual total wealth by characteristic in Great Britain: April 2018 to March 2020', ONS (7 Jan. 2022), https://www.ons.gov.uk/peoplepopulationandcommunity/personalandhouseholdfinances/incomeandwealth/bulletins/distributionofindividualtotalwealthbycharacteristicingreatbritain/april2018tomarch2020.

10  'Distribution of individual total wealth by characteristic in Great Britain: April 2018 to March 2020', ONS.

11  Robert Chote, et al., *Public spending under Labour*, Institute for Fiscal Studies (12 Apr. 2010), https://ifs.org.uk/publications/public-spending-under-labour.

12  Jo Blanden and Stephen Machin, *Recent changes in intergenerational mobility in Britain*, The Sutton Trust (1 December 2007), https://www.suttontrust.com/our-research/recent-changes-intergenerational-mobility-britain/.

13  Pascale Bourquin, Mike Brewer and Thomas Wernham, *Trends in income and wealth inequalities*, Institute for Fiscal Studies (9 Nov. 2022), https://ifs.org.uk/publications/trends-income-and-wealth-inequalities.

14  *More For Less: What has happened to pay at the top and does it matter? – interim report*, High Pay Commission (May 2011).

15  Peter Mandelson, '[New Labour] is intensely relaxed about people getting filthy rich', speech to executives in Silicon Valley, California (Oct. 1999).

16  Bourquin, Brewer and Wernham, *Trends in income and wealth inequalities*.

17  Howard Reed, *The Impact of Planned Cuts to Public Spending over the 2015–20 Parliament*, Trade Union Congress (March 2016), https://www.tuc.org.uk/sites/default/files/Spending-cuts-Report.pdf.

18  J. Walker, et al., *The Commitment to Reducing Inequality Index 2022*, DFI and Oxfam (10 June 2019), https://oxfamilibrary.openrepository.com/bitstream/handle/10546/621419/rr-cri-2022-111022-en.pdf?sequence=33.

19  Annette Hastings, et al., *The cost of the cuts: the impact on*

*local government and poorer communities*, Joseph Rowntree
Foundation (10 Mar. 2015), https://www.jrf.org.uk/report/
cost-cuts-impact-local-government-and-poorer-communities.

20  Miles Corak, 'Inequality from generation to generation: the United States in comparison' (2012), https://milescorak.files.wordpress.com/2012/01/inequality-from-generation-to-generation-the-united-states-in-comparison-v3.pdf.

21  Robert Booth, Holly Watt and David Pegg, 'David Cameron admits he profited from father's Panama offshore trust', *Guardian* (7 Apr. 2016), https://www.theguardian.com/news/2016/apr/07/david-cameron-admits-he-profited-fathers-offshore-fund-panama-papers.

22  Claire Milne, 'How many people use food banks?', Full Fact (28 Apr. 2017), https://fullfact.org/economy/how-many-people-use-food-banks/.

23  Robert Watts, 'The Sunday Times Rich List 2017: Boom time for billionaires' *Sunday Times* (7 May 2017), https://www.thetimes.co.uk/article/the-sunday-times-rich-list-2017-boom-time-for-billionaires-pzbkrfbv2.

24  Michael Savage, 'Theresa May faces new crisis after mass walkout over social policy', *Guardian* (3 Dec. 2017), https://www.theguardian.com/politics/2017/dec/02/theresa-may-crisis-mass-walkout-social-policy-alan-milburn.

25  Alix Robertson, 'Twelve new social mobility commissioners appointed', Schools Week (31 Oct. 2018), https://schoolsweek.co.uk/twelve-new-social-mobility-commissioners-appointed.

26  *Conservative Party Manifesto 2019*, Conservatives, https://www.conservatives.com/our-plan/conservative-party-manifesto-2019.

27  Paul Swinney, 'Why free ports do not hold the answer to job creation in a post-Brexit world' Centre for Cities (12 July 2019), https://www.centreforcities.org/blog/why-free-ports-do-not-hold-the-answer-to-job-creation-in-a-post-brexit-world/.

28  'Freeports', UK in a Changing Europe (2 Mar. 2021), https://ukandeu.ac.uk/wp-content/uploads/2021/03/Freeports.pdf.

29  Sally Weale, 'Youth services suffer 70% funding cut in less than a decade', *Guardian* (20 Jan. 2020), https://www.theguardian.com/society/2020/jan/20/youth-services-suffer-70-funding-cut-in-less-than-a-decade.

30  Graham Atkins and Stuart Hoddinott, *Neighbourhood services under strain: how a decade of cuts and rising demand for social care affected local services*, Institute for Government (May 2022), https://www.instituteforgovernment.org.uk/sites/default/files/publications/neighbourhood-services-under-strain.pdf.

31  Atkins and Hoddinott, *Neighbourhood services under strain*.

32  Jon Stone, 'Priti Patel says fans have right to boo England team for "gesture politics" of taking the knee', *Independent* (14 June 2021), https://www.independent.co.uk/news/uk/politics/priti-patel-taking-knee-boo-england-b1865409.html.

33  Ninian Wilson, 'Tories vote in real terms cut to Universal Credit and pensions amid skyrocketing cost of living', *The National* (8 Feb. 2022), https://www.thenational.scot/news/19907405.tories-vote-real-terms-cut-universal-credit-pensions-amid-skyrocketing-cost-living/.

34  Jane Bradley, Selam Gebrekidan and Allison McCann, 'Waste, Negligence and Cronyism: Inside Britain's Pandemic Spending', *New York Times* (17 Dec. 2020), https://www.nytimes.com/interactive/2020/12/17/world/europe/britain-covid-contracts.html.

35  Heather Stewart, Josh Halliday and Peter Walker, 'Chaos and fury as Boris Johnson forces curbs on Greater Manchester', *Guardian* (20 Oct. 2020), https://www.theguardian.com/world/2020/oct/20/burnham-says-government-playing-with-peoples-lives-as-tier-3-covid-rules-imposed.

36  Ben van der Merwe, 'Weekly data: The problem with levelling up the UK', Investment Monitor (18 Jan. 2022), https://www.investmentmonitor.ai/analysis/weekly-data-problem-levelling-up-uk.

37  Peter Foster, Sebastian Payne and Jennifer Williams, 'UK fails to meet pledge on post-Brexit regional funding', *Financial Times* (8 Apr. 2022), https://www.ft.com/content/bf8fa303-c1c5-4307-89c5-7ae1e20f1cbb.

38  Rachel Wearmouth, 'Rishi Sunak boasted of taking money from "deprived urban areas" to help wealthy towns', *New Statesman* (5 Aug. 2022), https://www.newstatesman.com/politics/conservatives/2022/08/exclusive-rishi-sunak-taking-money-deprived-urban-areas.

39  Pippa Crerar, 'Rishi Sunak constituency bid raises fears of "levelling up" favouritism', *Guardian* (18 Jan. 2023), https://www.theguardian.com/politics/2023/jan/18/rishi-sunak-constituency-bid-raises-fears-of-levelling-up-favouritism.

40  'Fees', Eton College (2023), https://www.etoncollege.com/admissions/fees/.

41  'Financial Year 2021–22 School funding statistics', GOV.UK (27 Jan. 2022), https://explore-education-statistics.service.gov.uk/find-statistics/school-funding-statistics.

42  'Home Secretary Priti Patel updates MPs on new points-based immigration system', UK Parliament (24 Feb. 2020), https://www.parliament.uk/business/news/2020/february/statement-on-points-based-immigration-system/.

43  *Benefits Street* (series 1), Channel 4 (Jan. 2014).

44  'Osborne unveils £10bn benefits cut package', Channel 4 News (8 Oct. 2012), https://www.channel4.com/news/osborne-unveils-10bn-benefits-cut-package.

45  'Poverty in the UK is "systematic" and "tragic", says UN special rapporteur', BBC News (22 May 2019), https://www.bbc.com/news/uk-48354692.

46  'Results – Election 2015', BBC News (2015), https://www.bbc.co.uk/news/election/2015/results.

47  May Bulman, 'More than 17,000 sick and disabled people have
    died while waiting for welfare benefits, figures show', *Independent*
    (14 Jan. 2019), https://www.independent.co.uk/news/uk/home-news/
    pip-waiting-time-deaths-disabled-people-die-disability-benefits-personal-
    independence-payment-dwp-a8727296.html.

48  *Information held by the Department for Work & Pensions on deaths by suicide of benefit
    claimants*, National Audit Office (7 Feb. 2020), https://www.nao.org.uk/
    reports/information-held-by-the-department-for-work-pensions-on-deaths-
    by-suicide-of-benefit-claimants/.

49  Patrick Butler, 'Disabled man starved to death after DWP stopped
    his benefits' *Guardian* (28 Jan. 2020), https://www.theguardian.com/
    society/2020/jan/28/disabled-man-starved-to-death-after-dwp-stopped-his-
    benefits.

50  Sam Corbishley, 'Tory MP sparks fury after suggesting free school
    meals cash "goes to crack dens"', *Metro* (24 Oct. 2020), https://metro.
    co.uk/2020/10/24/tory-mp-sparks-fury-after-suggesting-free-school-meals-
    cash-goes-to-crack-dens-13473875/.

51  Haroon Siddique, 'Marcus Rashford forces Boris Johnson into second U-turn
    on child food poverty', *Guardian* (8 Nov. 2020), https://www.theguardian.
    com/education/2020/nov/08/marcus-rashford-forces-boris-johnson-into-
    second-u-turn-on-child-food-poverty.

52  Alex Homer, 'Seven out of 10 win benefits challenges at tribunal', BBC News
    (24 Sept. 2021), https://www.bbc.com/news/uk-58284613.

53  'The most common mental health problems: statistics',
    Mental Health Foundation (2022), https://www.mentalhealth.
    org.uk/explore-mental-health/mental-health-statistics/
    most-common-mental-health-problems-statistics.

54  Christine Farquharson, Imran Rasul and Luke Sibieta, 'Key workers' hourly
    wages are 8% lower on average than other employees', Institute for Fiscal
    Studies (23 Apr. 2020), https://ifs.org.uk/news/key-workers-hourly-wages-
    are-8-lower-average-other-employees.

55  PA News Agency, 'Ministers will not be "held to ransom" by unions, says
    Wallace', *Messenger* (29 Dec. 2022), https://www.messengernewspapers.co.uk/
    news/national/23218889.ministers-will-not-held-ransom-unions-says-wallace/.

56  'Peerage of the United Kingdom', Wikipedia (last edited 28 Dec. 2022),
    https://en.wikipedia.org/wiki/Peerage_of_the_United_Kingdom.

57  Caitlin, 'House of Lords Statistics in 2022', Highland Titles (28 Oct.
    2021, updated 6 June 2022), https://www.highlandtitles.com/blog/
    house-of-lords-statistics/.

58  'MPs and Lords – Lords membership – by gender', UK Parliament (2023),
    https://members.parliament.uk/parties/lords/by-gender.

59  Paul Gosling, 'The link between poor social mobility and corruption',

ACCA (1 Jan. 2019), https://www.accaglobal.com/in/en/member/member/accounting-business/2019/01/insights/social-mobility.html.

60   Tom Williams, 'Boris Johnson hands his brother a seat in the House of Lords', *Metro* (31 July 2020), https://metro.co.uk/2020/07/31/boris-johnson-hands-brother-seat-house-lords-13066631/.

61   'The companies who benefitted from the "VIP Lane" for PPE contracts', Good Law Project, https://goodlawproject.org/47-companies.

62   Bradley, Gebrekidan and McCann, 'Waste, Negligence and Cronyism'.

63   Paul Waugh, 'Grouse Shooting and Hunting Exempt from Johnson's "Rule of Six" Covid Curbs', *HuffPost UK* (14 Sept. 2020), https://www.huffingtonpost.co.uk/entry/boris-johnson-rule-of-six-hunting-shooting-exemption_uk_5f5f4ad0c5b6b4850803110f.

64   Waugh, 'Grouse Shooting and Hunting Exempt'.

65   Jim Fitzpatrick, 'Crispin Odey: How Kwarteng's ex-boss is cashing in on cost-of-living crisis', OpenDemocracy (28 Sept. 2022), https://www.opendemocracy.net/en/kwasi-kwarteng-crispin-odey-government-bonds-profit/.

66   David Burke, Those profiting from pound plummet – Tory donor who placed bet and "Truss supporters"', *Mirror* (28 Sept. 2022), https://www.mirror.co.uk/news/politics/those-profiting-pound-plummet-tory-28101558.

67   Thomas Piketty, *Capital in the Twenty-First Century* (2014; Harvard University Press, 2017).

68   Lexis (@niilexis), Twitter post, 7.39 p.m., 27 Mar. 2021, https://twitter.com/niilexis/status/1375895294378962952?lang=en.

## CHAPTER 3: THE LOTTERY OF BIRTH

1   'World Bank Country and Lending Groups', World Bank (2022), https://datahelpdesk.worldbank.org/knowledgebase/articles/906519-world-bank-country-and-lending-groups.

2   'Population, Total for High Income Countries', World Bank (27 Dec. 2022), accessed from St. Louis Fed, https://fred.stlouisfed.org/series/SPPOPTOTLHIC.

3   'As world passes 7 billion milestone, UN urges action to meet key challenges,' UN News (31 Oct. 2011), https://news.un.org/en/story/2011/10/393602.

4   'Neonatal mortality', UNICEF (Jan 2023), https://data.unicef.org/topic/child-survival/neonatal-mortality/.

5   Author's own calculations based on the UNICEF 'Neonatal mortality' data series.

6   Branko Milanovic, 'Global inequality of opportunity: how much of our income is determined by where we live?', *Review of Economics and Statistics*, 97/2 (2015), 452–460, https://doi.org/10.1162/rest_a_00432.

7  Milanovic, 'Global inequality of opportunity'.

8  'Percentage of people living outside their country of birth worldwide, 1990–2015', Statista (5 Aug. 2022), https://www.statista.com/statistics/679787/international-migrant-stock-as-a-percentage-of-world-population/, accessed 5 Jan. 2023.

9  Milanovic, 'Global inequality of opportunity'.

10  Dominique Legros, at al., 'The Evolution of Mortality Among Rwandan Refugees in Zaire Between 1994 and 1997', *Forced Migration and Mortality* (National Academies Press, 2001), https://nap.nationalacademies.org/read/10086/chapter/4.

11  Dr Benjamin Coghlan, et al., *Mortality in the Democratic Republic of Congo: An ongoing crisis*, International Rescue Committee (2007), https://www.rescue.org/sites/default/files/document/661/2006-7congomortalitysurvey.pdf.

12  'DR Congo emergency', UNHCR, UN Refugee Agency (Nov. 2022), https://www.unhcr.org/en-us/dr-congo-emergency.html.

13  'Democratic Republic of the Congo', World Food Programme (2022), https://www.wfp.org/countries/democratic-republic-congo.

14  '"A fire that is just going to keep getting bigger": What you need to know about the global cholera outbreak', Concern Worldwide US (4 Jan. 2023), https://www.concernusa.org/story/global-cholera-outbreak-explained/.

15  Siddharth Kara, *Cobalt Red: How the Blood of the Congo Powers Our Lives* (St. Martin's Press, 2023).

16  'Global Passport Power Rank 2023: Passports of the world ranked by their total mobility score', Passport Index (2023), https://www.passportindex.org/byRank.php.

17  'Life expectancy at birth, total (years) – High income', World Bank (2022), https://data.worldbank.org/indicator/SP.DYN.LE00.IN?locations=XD.

18  'Life expectancy at birth, total (years) – High income', World Bank.

19  Sarah Nzau, et al., 'Social networks and economic mobility – what the findings reveal', Brookings (9 Mar. 2021), https://www.brookings.edu/blog/how-we-rise/2021/03/09/social-networks-and-economic-mobility-what-the-findings-reveal/.

20  Pam Foley, 'Week 1: The lottery of birth', Open University (2016), https://www.open.edu/openlearn/ocw/mod/oucontent/view.php?id=21379&printable=1.

21  *The Global Social Mobility Report 2020: Equality, Opportunity and a New Economic Imperative*, World Economic Forum (Jan. 2020), https://static.poder360.com.br/2021/05/WEF-Global-Social-Mobility-Report-2020.pdf.

22  Max Roser, 'Global economic inequality: What matters most for your living conditions is not who you are, but where you are', Our World in Data (9 Dec. 2021), https://ourworldindata.org/global-economic-inequality-introduction.

23   Will Martin, 'Paradise Papers: The biggest names caught up in the leak so far', *Insider* (8 Nov. 2017), https://www.businessinsider.com/paradise-papers-biggest-celebrities-named-2017-11.

24   Milena, 'Tax evasion statistics – 2022 update', Balancing Everything (31 Jan. 2021), https://balancingeverything.com/tax-evasion-statistics.

25   Mark Bou Mansour, '\$427bn lost to tax havens every year: landmark study reveals countries' losses and worst offenders', Tax Justice Network (20 Nov. 2020), https://taxjustice.net/2020/11/20/427bn-lost-to-tax-havens-every-year-landmark-study-reveals-countries-losses-and-worst-offenders/.

26   Emma Agyemang, 'UK admits it has no idea how much tax is being evaded through offshore assets', *Financial Times* (19 May 2022), https://www.ft.com/content/a14162d0-0f65-4c63-842e-e0778516d03a.

27   Alex Cobham, et al.,'The State of Tax Justice 2020', Tax Justice Network (20 Nov. 2022), https://taxjustice.net/reports/the-state-of-tax-justice-2020.

28   Shashi Tharoor, *Inglorious Empire: What the British did to India* (2017; Penguin Classics, 2018).

29   'Sixty-four countries spend more on debt payments than health', Debt Justice (Formerly Jubilee Debt Campaign) (12 Apr. 2020), https://debtjustice.org.uk/press-release/sixty-four-countries-spend-more-on-debt-payments-than-health.

30   Jesse Griffiths, 'Low-income country debt: three key trends', ODI (n.d.), https://odi.org/en/insights/low-income-country-debt-three-key-trends/, accessed 5 Jan. 2023.

31   *The 2022 Commitment to Reducing Inequality (CRI) Index*, Oxfam International (12 Oct. 2022), https://www.oxfam.org/en/research/2022-commitment-reducing-inequality-cri-index.

32   'Devastating floods in Pakistan', UNICEF (n.d.), https://www.unicef.org/emergencies/devastating-floods-pakistan-2022, accessed 5 Jan. 2023.

33   Savin S. Chand and Kevin J. E. Walsh, 'Influence of ENSO on Tropical Cyclone Intensity in the Fiji Region', *Journal of Climate*, 24/15 (1 Aug. 2011), 4096–4108, https://doi.org/10.1175/2011jcli4178.1.

34   'UK defence and security export statistics for 2019', GOV.UK (6 Oct. 2020), https://www.gov.uk/government/statistics/uk-defence-and-security-export-statistics-for-2019/uk-defence-and-security-export-statistics-for-2019#defence-statistics.

35   Al Jazeera, 'UK approved \$1.9bn of arms sales to Saudi Arabia since ban lifted.' *Al Jazeera* (9 Feb. 2021), https://www.aljazeera.com/news/2021/2/9/uk-approved-1-4bn-of-arms-sales-to-saudi-arabia-post-export-ban.

36   David Wearing, *AngloArabia: Why Gulf Wealth Matters to Britain* (Polity Press, 2018).

37   'Yemen is experiencing largest humanitarian crisis in the history,' UNICEF Global, https://help.unicef.org/children-yemen-in-emergency?country=SG.

38 Ashley Kirk, et al., 'Canada and UK among countries with most vaccine doses ordered per person', *Guardian* (29 Jan. 2021), https://www.theguardian.com/world/2021/jan/29/canada-and-uk-among-countries-with-most-vaccine-doses-ordered-per-person.

39 Joe McDonald and Huizhong Wu, 'Top Chinese official admits vaccines have low effectiveness', Associated Press News (20 Apr. 2021), https://apnews.com/article/china-gao-fu-vaccines-offer-low-protection-coronavirus-675bcb6b5710c7329823148ffbff6ef9.

40 Georges Nzongola-Ntalaja, *The Congo from Leopold to Kabila: A People's History* (2002; Zed Books Ltd, 2013).

41 Adam Hochschild, *King Leopold's Ghost: A Story of Greed, Terror and Heroism in Colonial Africa* (Mariner Books, 1998); 'DR Congo: Chronology', Human Rights Watch (21 Aug. 2009), https://www.hrw.org/news/2009/08/21/dr-congo-chronology.

42 Nzongola-Ntalaja, *The Congo from Leopold to Kabila*.

## CHAPTER 4: WEALTH: THE SOCIAL ENGINEER

1 'Household total wealth in Great Britain: April 2018 to March 2020', ONS (7 Jan. 2022), https://www.ons.gov.uk/peoplepopulationandcommunity/personalandhouseholdfinances/incomeandwealth/bulletins/totalwealthingreatbritain/april2018tomarch2020.

2 'The Sunday Times Rich List 2022', *The Times*, https://www.thetimes.co.uk/sunday-times-rich-list, accessed 4 Jan. 2023.

3 Michael Sherraden, *Assets and the Poor: A New American Welfare Policy* (M. E. Sharpe, Inc., 1991).

4 Lisa Adkins, et al., 'Class in the 21st century: asset inflation and the new logic of inequality', *Environment and Planning A: Economy and Space* 53/3 (Sept. 2019), 548–72, https://doi.org/10.1177/0308518X19873673.

5 Samuel Stein, *Capital City: Gentrification and the Real Estate State* (Verso Books, 2019).

6 Tom Archer and Ian Cole, 'The financialisation of housing production: exploring capital flows and value extraction among major housebuilders in the UK', *Journal of Housing and the Built Environment*, 36/4 (2021), 1367–1387.

7 Oliver Wainwright, 'Fatcat developers created our housing crisis. Here's how to stop them', *Guardian* (30 Apr. 2020), https://www.theguardian.com/artanddesign/2020/apr/30/fatcat-developers-created-our-housing-crisis-heres-how-to-stop-them.

8 Martin Adeney, 'Tony Pidgley obituary', *Guardian* (1 July 2020), https://www.theguardian.com/business/2020/jul/01/tony-pidgley-obituary.

# Notes

9 Rana Foroohar, *Makers and Takers: The rise of finance and the fall of American business* (Currency, 2016).

10 Costas Lapavitsas, *Profiting Without Producing: How finance exploits us all* (2013; Verso Books, 2014).

11 Stephen Taub, 'The 20th Annual Rich List, the Definitive Ranking of What Hedge Fund Managers Earned in 2020', *Institutional Investor* (22 Feb. 2021), https://www.institutionalinvestor.com/article/b1qmsgpxhzolpt/The-20th-Annual-Rich-List-the-Definitive-Ranking-of-What-Hedge-Fund-Managers-Earned-in-2020.

12 Rebecca Jones, 'Can hedge funds ever be ethical?', Good With Money (24 Jan. 2019), https://good-with-money.com/2019/01/24/can-hedge-funds-ever-be-ethical/.

13 Simon Goodley, 'Who is the Brexit-supporting Lord Bamford of JCB fame?' *Guardian* (25 Jan. 2019), https://www.theguardian.com/business/2019/jan/25/brexit-supporting-lord-bamford-of-jcb-fame-boris-johnson-david-davis.

14 'Blacklisting Workers in the Construction Industry', Corporate Watch (20 May 2009), https://corporatewatch.org/blacklisting-workers-in-the-construction-industry/.

15 Terry Macalister, 'Blacklisted workers win £10m payout from construction firms' *Guardian* (9 May 2016), https://www.theguardian.com/business/2016/may/09/blacklisted-workers-win-10m-payout-from-construction-firms.

16 Rob Evans, '50 blacklisted trade unionists win £1.9m from building firms', *Guardian* (14 May 2019), https://www.theguardian.com/business/2019/may/14/50-blacklisted-trade-unionists-win-19m-from-building-firms.

17 Sarah Woolley, 'In Low-Wage Britain, the People Who Produce Our Food Can't Afford to Eat', *Tribune* (22 Apr. 2021), https://tribunemag.co.uk/2021/04/in-low-wage-britain-the-people-who-produce-our-food-cant-afford-to-eat.

18 Clean Clothes Campaign, https://cleanclothes.org/.

19 'State of the Industry: Lowest Wages to Living Wages', Lowest Wage Challenge, https://www.lowestwagechallenge.com/post/state-of-the-industry, accessed 4 Jan. 2023.

20 '2017 impact', Fashion Revolution, https://www.fashionrevolution.org/2017-impact/, accessed 4 Jan. 2023.

21 'The Sunday Times Rich List 2022'.

22 Hannah Westwater, 'Why the crisis in music education is a crisis for all', *Big Issue* (12 Feb. 2019), https://www.bigissue.com/culture/music/why-the-crisis-in-music-education-is-a-crisis-for-all/.

23 Brink Lindsey and Steven Michael Teles, *The Captured Economy: How the Powerful Enrich Themselves, Slow Down Growth, and Increase Inequality* (Oxford University Press, 2017).

24 Jane Bradley and Euan Ward, 'King Charles Inherits Untold Riches, and Passes

Off His Own Empire', *New York Times* (13 Sept. 2022), https://www.nytimes.com/2022/09/13/world/europe/king-charles-wealth.html.

25 Bill Chappell, 'No, King Charles III Won't Pay Any Inheritance Tax on His Massive Gain,' NPR, (15 Sept. 2022), https://www.npr.org/2022/09/15/1123151802/king-charles-iii-inheritance-tax.

26 Sophie Lewis, 'An 18-year-old will fly to space with Jeff Bezos — becoming the youngest ever to launch', CBS News (15 July 2021), https://www.cbsnews.com/news/jeff-bezos-flight-to-space-18-year-old-oliver-daemen-blue-origin/.

27 Bill Chappell, 'Blue Origin's Flight Will Include the Youngest and the Oldest Humans to Go to Space', NPR (20 July 2021), https://www.npr.org/2021/07/15/1016510564/blue-origin-space-18-year-old-bezos-oliver-daemen-netherlands.

28 Nate Jones, 'An All But Definitive Guide to the Hollywood Nepo-Verse', *Vulture* (19 Dec. 2022), https://www.vulture.com/article/hollywood-nepotism-babies-list-taxonomy.html.

29 Lindsay Lowe, 'What are "nepo babies" and why is the internet talking about them? *TODAY* (23 Dec. 2022), https://www.today.com/popculture/nepo-baby-meaning-list-rcna62963.

30 Lily Allen (@lilyallen), Twitter post, 6.18 p.m., 19 Dec. 2022, https://twitter.com/lilyallen/status/1604903982589218832.

31 Nicholas W. Papageorge and Kevin Thom, *Genes, Education, and Labor Market Outcomes: Evidence from the Health and Retirement Study*, W. E. Upjohn Institute for Employment Research (1 May 2017), https://research.upjohn.org/cgi/viewcontent.cgi?article=1291&context=up_workingpapers.

32 Simon Kuper, et al., *Power, Privilege, Parties: the shaping of modern Britain* [podcast and video], International Inequalities Institute (26 May 2022), https://www.lse.ac.uk/Events/2022/05/202205261830/power.

33 Rachel Sandler, 'The Forbes 400 Self-Made Score 2021: From Silver Spooners To Bootstrappers', *Forbes* (5 Oct. 2021), https://www.forbes.com/sites/rachelsandler/2021/10/05/the-forbes-400-self-made-score-2021-from-silver-spooners-to-bootstrappers.

34 'Noubar Afeyan', Flagship Pioneering (n.d.), https://www.flagshippioneering.com/people/noubar-afeyan.

35 Sheryl Gay Stolberg and Rebecca Robbins, 'Moderna and U.S. at Odds Over Vaccine Patent Rights', *New York Times* (9 Nov. 2021), https://www.nytimes.com/2021/11/09/us/moderna-vaccine-patent.html.

36 Amy Borrett, 'How UK house prices have soared ahead of average wages', *New Statesman* (20 May 2021), https://www.newstatesman.com/politics/2021/05/how-uk-house-prices-have-soared-ahead-average-wages.

37 Liz Lucking, 'London Property Prices Grew 86% in a Decade', Mansion Global (28 Feb. 2019), https://www.mansionglobal.com/articles/london-property-prices-grew-86-in-a-decade-123029.

38 'How much is the UK worth? – Residential Property Focus', Savills, Issue

1, 2017, https://pdf.euro.savills.co.uk/uk/residential-property-focus-uk/residential-property-focus-issue-1-2017.pdf.

39 Judith Evans, 'UK housing stock value soars to a record £6.8tn', *Financial Times* (18 Jan. 2017), https://www.ft.com/content/4906a246-dcb7-11e6-86ac-f253db7791c6.

40 Wendy Wilson, et al., *Extending home ownership: Government initiatives*, House of Commons Library, UK Parliament (30 Mar. 2021), https://commonslibrary.parliament.uk/research-briefings/sn03668.

41 Rupert Jones, 'House price growth outstrips wages in 90% of England and Wales', *Guardian* (23 Mar. 2022), https://www.theguardian.com/money/2022/mar/23/house-price-growth-outstrips-wages-england-wales.

42 'The Intergenerational Commission', https://www.intergencommission.org/publications/home-affront-housing-across-the-generations/.

43 George Hammond, 'Help to Buy has pushed up house prices in England, says report', *Financial Times* (10 Jan. 2022), https://www.ft.com/content/19236eef-abed-4401-a6b1-25c1035ab095.

44 Lucie Heath, 'Welsh government to create national construction company as part of Plaid Cymru co-operation agreement', Inside Housing (22 Nov. 2021), https://www.insidehousing.co.uk/news/news/welsh-government-to-create-national-construction-company-as-part-of-plaid-cymru-co-operation-agreement-73458.

45 '"Cut consumption or get a new higher-paid job" says Conservative Party chair', Sky News (2 Oct. 2022), https://news.sky.com/video/cut-consumption-or-get-a-new-higher-paid-job-says-conservative-party-chair-12710016.

46 Lucine Francis, et al., 'Child Poverty, Toxic Stress, and Social Determinants of Health: Screening and Care Coordination', *Online Journal of Issues in Nursing*, 2018 Sep;23(3):2. Doi: 10.3912/OJIN.Vol23No03Man02. Epub 2018 Sep 30. PMID: 31427855; PMCID: PMC6699621.

47 Greg J. Duncan and Richard J. Murnane, eds, *Whither Opportunity? Rising Inequality, Schools, and Children's Life Chances* (Russell Sage Foundation, 2011).

48 'The Effects of Poverty', Child Poverty Action Group (5 June 2017), https://cpag.org.uk/child-poverty/effects-poverty.

49 Christine Farquharson, Sandra McNally and Imran Tahir, *Education Inequalities*, IFS Review of Inequalities, Institute for Fiscal Studies (16 Aug. 2022), https://ifs.org.uk/inequality/education-inequalities/.

50 'UK poverty statistics', Joseph Rowntree Foundation, https://www.jrf.org.uk/data/workers-poverty, accessed 4 Jan. 2023.

51 'Lack of support for low-income families will see 1.3 million people pushed into absolute poverty next year' [press release], Resolution Foundation (24 Mar. 2022), https://www.resolutionfoundation.org/press-releases/33284/.

52 Grace Hetherinton, 'Large-scale study reveals scale of debt crisis among low-

income households', Joseph Rowntree Foundation (21 Oct. 2022), https://www.jrf.org.uk/press/large-scale-study-reveals-scale-debt-crisis-among-low-income-households.

53  Alex Wickham and Todd Gillespie, 'UK Sees Up to £170 Billion Excess Profits for Energy Firms', Bloomberg (30 Aug. 2022), https://www.bloomberg.com/news/articles/2022-08-30/uk-predicts-up-to-170-billion-excess-profits-for-energy-firms.

54  Jasper Jolly and Mark Sweney, 'Big oil's quarterly profits hit £50bn as UK braces for even higher energy bills' Guardian (2 Aug. 2022), https://www.theguardian.com/business/2022/aug/02/big-oil-profits-energy-bills-windfall-tax.

55  Errol Schweizer, 'How Windfall Profits Have Supercharged Food Inflation', Forbes (10 May 2022), https://www.forbes.com/sites/errolschweizer/2022/05/10/how-windfall-profits-have-supercharged-food-inflation/?sh=7352343b6672.

56  Josh Bivens, 'Corporate profits have contributed disproportionately to inflation. How should policymakers respond?' Economic Policy Institute (21 Apr. 2022), https://www.epi.org/blog/corporate-profits-have-contributed-disproportionately-to-inflation-how-should-policymakers-respond/.

57  Ashoka Mukpo, 'Did Wall Street play a role in this year's wheat price crisis?' Mongabay (27 July 2022), https://news.mongabay.com/2022/07/did-wall-street-play-a-role-in-this-years-wheat-price-crisis/.

58  Karen Braun, 'Column: Funds forge all-time bullish bets in CBOT grains and oilseeds', Reuters (25 Apr. 2022), https://www.reuters.com/markets/europe/funds-forge-all-time-bullish-bets-cbot-grains-oilseeds-2022-04-25/.

59  Alex Lawson, '"Greed and fear": How BP and Shell oil profit is boosted by own traders', Guardian (12 May 2022), https://www.theguardian.com/business/2022/may/12/trading-in-turbulent-market-helps-bp-and-shell-secure-record-profits.

60  Jane Bradley, Salem Gebrekidan and Allison McCann, 'Waste, Negligence and Cronyism'.

61  Michael Savage, 'Top lawyers warn Johnson over role of judges as constitution fears grow', Guardian (21 Dec. 2019), https://www.theguardian.com/politics/2019/dec/21/law-society-warns-boris-johnson-on-independent-judiciary.

62  Rowena Mason, 'Jacob Rees-Mogg business partner given senior ministerial role', Guardian (2 Oct. 2022), https://www.theguardian.com/politics/2022/oct/02/jacob-rees-mogg-business-partner-dominic-johnson-given-senior-minister-role.

63  Steph Brawn, 'King Charles allowed to vet proposed Rent Freeze Bill in Scotland', The National (4 Oct. 2022), https://www.thenational.scot/news/23019009.king-charles-allowed-vet-proposed-rent-freeze-bill-scotland/.

64  Bob Colenutt, The Property Lobby: The Hidden Reality Behind the Housing Crisis (Policy Press, 2020).

65  Jacob Hacker and Paul Pierson, *Winner-Take-All Politics: How Washington Made the Rich Richer—and Turned its Back on the Middle Class* (Simon & Schuster, 2010).

66  Rowena Mason, 'Rishi Sunak and wife donate over £100,000 to Winchester college', *Guardian* (5 Apr. 2022), https://www.theguardian.com/politics/2022/apr/05/rishi-sunak-and-wife-donate-over-100000-to-winchester-college.

67  Mohit Mookim, 'The World Loses Under Bill Gates' Vaccine Colonialism', *Wired* (19 May 2021), https://www.wired.com/story/opinion-the-world-loses-under-bill-gates-vaccine-colonialism/.

68  Lindsey McGoey, *No Such Thing as a Free Gift: The Gates Foundation and the Price of Philanthropy* (Verso Books, 2015).

69  Anand Giridharadas, *Winners Take All: The Elite Charade of Changing the World* (2018; Penguin, 2019).

70  'Stormzy scholarships programme expanded', University of Cambridge (28 July 2021), https://www.cam.ac.uk/news/stormzy-scholarships-programme-expanded.

71  Elizabeth Aubrey, 'Stormzy pledges his support for Jeremy Corbyn: "He is the first man in a position of power who is committed to giving the power back"', *NME* (25 Nov. 2019), https://www.nme.com/news/music/stormzy-pledges-support-jeremy-corbyn-first-man-position-power-committed-giving-power-back-2578153.

## CHAPTER 5: 'SHE CAN'T EVEN SPEAK PROPERLY': CLASS, PREJUDICE AND THE STRUGGLE

1  Adam Boulton (@adamboultonTABB), Twitter post, 10.33 a.m., 22 Oct. 2018, https://twitter.com/adamboultonTABB/status/1054304790874914816.

2  'Accents in Britain', Accent Bias Britain (n.d.), https://accentbiasbritain.org/accents-in-britain/.

3  Mark Sweney, 'Television workers twice as likely to have attended private school', *Guardian* (18 Sept. 2019), https://www.theguardian.com/media/2019/sep/18/television-workers-twice-as-likely-to-have-attended-private-school.

4  Omar Khan is now the director of Transforming Access and Student Outcomes in Higher Education (TASO).

5  'The world has become obsessed with elites', *The Economist* (15 Dec. 2016), https://www.economist.com/books-and-arts/2016/12/15/the-world-has-become-obsessed-with-elites.

6  ONS employment by industry by regions 2021, https://www.ons.gov.uk/employmentandlabourmarket/peopleinwork/employmentandemployeetypes/datasets/workforcejobsbyregionandindustryjobs05/current.

7  Raquel Jesse, 'They look down on us: Insights from the diverse working

class on race and class in Britain today', Centre for Labour and Social Studies (CLASS) (3 Aug. 2022).

8  Mike Savage, *Social Class in the 21st Century* (Penguin UK, 2015).

9  'Child poverty in working families on the rise', Child Poverty Action Group (28 Mar. 2019), https://cpag.org.uk/news-blogs/news-listings/child-poverty-working-families-rise.

10  Robert Booth and Michael Goodier, 'Soaring rents making life "unaffordable" for private UK tenants, research shows', *Guardian* (1 Dec. 2022), https://www.theguardian.com/society/2022/dec/01/soaring-rents-making-life-unaffordable-for-private-uk-tenants-research-shows.

11  *British social attitudes 33rd edition*, NatCen Social Research (n.d.) https://www.bsa.natcen.ac.uk/latest-report/british-social-attitudes-33/social-class.aspx, accessed 5 Jan. 2023.

12  Sam Friedman, Dave O'Brien and Ian McDonald, 'Deflecting Privilege: Class Identity and the Intergenerational Self', *Sociology*, 55/4 (2021), 716–733.

13  Anat Shenker-Osorio, 'Why Americans All Believe They Are "Middle Class"', *Atlantic* (1 Aug. 2013), https://www.theatlantic.com/politics/archive/2013/08/why-americans-all-believe-they-are-middle-class/278240/.

14  *Class on Class* [podcast], Episode 2, interviewed by Faiza Shaheen, https://podcasts.apple.com/gb/podcast/class-on-class/id1284525511.

15  Sam Friedman, 'Why do so many professional, middle-class Brits insist they're working class?', *Guardian* (18 Jan. 2021), https://www.theguardian.com/commentisfree/2021/jan/18/why-professional-middle-class-brits-insist-working-class.

16  E. P. Thompson influentially dates it in the 1790–1830s.

17  Tim Strangleman, 'Thatcher and the Working Class: Why History Matters' Working-Class Perspectives (23 Apr. 2013), https://workingclassstudies.wordpress.com/2013/04/23/thatcher-and-the-working-class-why-history-matters/.

18  David Goodhart, *The Road to Somewhere: The Populist Revolt and the Future of Politics* (2017; Oxford University Press, 2020).

19  Danny Dorling and Benjamin D. Hennig, 'In Focus: The EU Referendum' (Sept. 2016), https://www.dannydorling.org/wp-content/files/dannydorling_publication_id6545.pdf.

20  Lorenza Antonucci, et al., 'The malaise of the squeezed middle: Challenging the narrative of the "left behind" Brexiter', *Competition & Change*, 21/3 (2017), 211–229.

21  Robert Ford, 'Britain's new political landscape: what the voting numbers tell us', *Guardian* (15 Dec. 2019), https://www.theguardian.com/politics/2019/dec/15/britains-new-political-landscape.

22  Peter Belmi, et al., 'The social advantage of miscalibrated individuals: the relationship between social class and overconfidence and its implications for class-based inequity', *Journal of Personality and Social Psychology*, 118/2 (Feb. 2020), 254–282.

23  Peter Belmi, et al., 'The social advantage of miscalibrated individuals'.

24  The Sutton Trust, *Elitist Britain, 2019*, The Sutton Trust and Social
Mobility Commission, 2019, https://www.suttontrust.com/wp-content/
uploads/2020/01/Elitist-Britain-2019-Summary-Report.pdf.

25  Discussed in relation to politics in Simon Kuper, *Chums: How a Tiny Caste of
Oxford Tories Took Over the UK* (Profile, 2022).

26  UNICEF, 'Would you stop if you saw this little girl on the street?
[video], YouTube (uploaded 28 June 2016), https://www.youtube.com/
watch?v=MQcN5DtMT-0.

27  Sam Friedman and Daniel Laurison, *The Class Ceiling: Why it Pays to be
Privileged* (Policy Press, 2020).

28  This is classified as Class 1, i.e. higher managerial, administrative and
professional occupations, in the National Statistics Socio-Economic
Classification (NS-SEC). For more information see 'The National Statistics
Socio-Economic Classification (NS-SEC)', Office for National Statistics, https://
www.ons.gov.uk/methodology/classificationsandstandards/otherclassifications/
thenationalstatisticssocioeconomicclassificationnssecrebasedonsoc2010.

29  Friedman and Laurison, *The Class Ceiling*.

30  Dan Bulley, Jenny Edkins, and Nadine El-Enany, eds, *After Grenfell: Violence,
Resistance and Response*, (Pluto Press UK, 2019).

31  Robert Booth, 'Five surrender to police over burning effigy of Grenfell
Tower', *Guardian* (6 Nov. 2018), https://www.theguardian.com/
uk-news/2018/nov/05/police-appeal-video-mock-up-grenfell-tower-burned.

32  'One year on from the Grenfell Fire, and yet so little has changed', *Guardian*
(13 June 2018), https://www.theguardian.com/uk-news/2018/jun/13/
one-year-on-from-the-grenfell-fire-and-yet-so-little-has-changed.

33  *Phase 1 Report*, Grenfell Tower Inquiry (2019), https://www.
grenfelltowerinquiry.org.uk/phase-1-report, accessed 5 Jan. 2023.

34  Zohra Nabi, '"Shameful dereliction of duty": Tory MPs vote against Grenfell
inquiry recommendations', *Justice Gap* (9 Sept. 2020), https://www.
thejusticegap.com/shameful-dereliction-of-duty-tory-mps-vote-against-
grenfell-inquiry-recommendations/.

35  *Phase 1 Report*, Grenfell Tower Inquiry.

36  Lucy Thornton, 'Firefighters who saved lives at Grenfell Tower are diagnosed
with terminal cancer', *Mirror* (12 Jan. 2023), https://www.mirror.co.uk/
news/uk-news/multiple-firefighters-who-saved-lives-28941465.

37  For all information see http://lakanalhousefire.co.uk/.

38  Robert Booth, 'Grenfell refurbishers knew cladding would fail, inquiry told',
*Guardian* (28 Jan. 2020), https://www.theguardian.com/uk-news/2020/
jan/28/grenfell-tower-refurbishers-knew-cladding-would-fail-inquiry-told.

39  'UK Government to be legally obligated to implement Public Inquiry
recommendations' [petition], Change.org. (14 June 2021), https://www.

change.org/p/uk-government-uk-government-to-be-legally-obligated-to-implement-public-inquiry-recommendations-2.

40  'New Grenfell council leader had never been in tower block before', ITV News (12 July 2017), https://www.itv.com/news/2017-07-12/grenfell-tower-aftermath.

41  Daniel Thomas, 'PwC reveals class gap among employees', *Financial Times* (15 Sept. 2021), https://www.ft.com/content/7ab18305-84cd-4370-b23d-e849c590c00d.

42  Emma Jacobs, 'Can social class hold back your career?', *Financial Times* (17 Nov. 2021), https://www.ft.com/content/f85ba669-2602-445a-8863-90a1651dbb68.

43  Charlotte Geiger, 'Accounting for influence: how the Big Four are embedded in EU tax avoidance policy' (10 July 2018), Finance Watch, https://www.finance-watch.org/accounting-for-influence-how-the-big-four-are-embedded-in-eu-tax-avoidance-policy/.

44  Daniel Thomas, 'PwC reveals class gap among employees'.

# CHAPTER 6: RACISM

1  Andrew Sparrow, 'More than half of UK's black children live in poverty, analysis shows', *Guardian* (2 Jan. 2022), https://www.theguardian.com/world/2022/jan/02/more-than-half-of-uks-black-children-live-in-poverty-analysis-shows.

2  Vikki Boliver, 'Exploring Ethnic Inequalities in Admission to Russell Group Universities', *Sociology*, 50/2 (May 2015), 247–66, https://doi.org/10.1177/0038038515575859.

3  Reverend Nims Obunge, Oral evidence in *Young Black People and the Criminal Justice System: Second Report of Session 2006–7, Volume II*, House of Commons Home Affairs Committee , 2007, https://publications.parliament.uk/pa/cm200607/cmselect/cmhaff/181/181ii.pdf.

4  Roger Jowell and Patricia Prescott-Clarke, 'Racial Discrimination and White-Collar Workers in Britain', *Race*, 11/4 (Apr. 1970), 397–417, https://doi.org/10.1177/030639687001100401.

5  Haroon Siddique, 'Minority ethnic Britons face "shocking" job discrimination, *Guardian* (17 Jan. 2019), https://www.theguardian.com/world/2019/jan/17/minority-ethnic-britons-face-shocking-job-discrimination.

6  Chris Millward, 'White students who are left behind: The importance of place', Office for Students (26 Jan. 2021), https://www.officeforstudents.org.uk/news-blog-and-events/blog/white-students-who-are-left-behind-the-importance-of-place/.

7  *Ethnic group, local authorities in the United Kingdom: Census 2021*, ONS (29 Nov. 2022), https://www.ons.gov.uk/peoplepopulationandcommunity/

culturalidentity/ethnicity/bulletins/ethnicgroupenglandandwales/
census2021.

8 Alex Macdougall and Ruth Lupton, 'The "London Effect": Literature
Review', Inclusive Growth Analysis Unit, University of Manchester and
Joseph Rowntree Foundation (Apr. 2018), https://documents.manchester.
ac.uk/display.aspx?DocID=37617.

9 'Child poverty and education outcomes by ethnicity', ONS (25 Feb. 2020), https://
www.ons.gov.uk/economy/nationalaccounts/uksectoraccounts/compendium/
economicreview/february2020/childpovertyandeducationoutcomesbyethnicity.

10 'Child poverty by ethnicity', ONS, (25 Feb. 2020),
https://www.ons.gov.uk/economy/nationalaccounts/
uksectoraccounts/compendium/economicreview/february2020/
childpovertyandeducationoutcomesbyethnicity#child-poverty-and-ethnicity.

11 Department for Education, 'Permanent exclusions and suspensions in England:
2020 to 2021', GOV.UK (28 July 2022), https://www.gov.uk/government/
statistics/permanent-exclusions-and-suspensions-in-england-2020-to-2021.

12 Department for Education, 'Revised A Level and other 16–18 results in
England 2018/19', GOV.UK (23 Jan. 2020), https://assets.publishing.
service.gov.uk/government/uploads/system/uploads/attachment_data/
file/859515/2019_revised_A-Level_and_other_16_to_18_results_in_
England.pdf.

13 Department for Education, 'Provisional A Level and other 16–18 results
in England 2018/19', GOV.UK, (17 Oct. 2019) https://assets.publishing.
service.gov.uk/government/uploads/system/uploads/attachment_data/
file/840413/2019_provisional_A_level_and_other16-18_results_in_
Englandv2.pdf.

14 Vikki Boliver, 'Why are British Ethnic Minorities Less Likely to be Offered
Places at Highly Selective Universities?', in Claire Alexander and Jason Ardy
(eds), *Aiming Higher: Race, Inequality and Diversity in the Academy* (Runnymede
Trust, 2015), https://assets.website-files.com/61488f992b58e687f1108c7c/
617bcf1cd124685da56a014c_Aiming%20Higher.pdf.

15 Rebecca Montacute, *Access to advantage*, The Sutton Trust (Dec. 2018), https://
www.suttontrust.com/wp-content/uploads/2019/12/AccesstoAdvantage-
2018.pdf.

16 Sawdah Bhaimiya, 'Black and South Asian women take nearly 2 months
longer than their white peers to land their first job, research suggests', *Insider*
(28 June 2022), https://www.businessinsider.com/black-south-asian-women-
wait-longer-land-jobs-white-peers-2022-6. The 'White British (non-private
school)' statistic here refers to all of the white group, as separate data for
state and privately educated white students was not available.

17 Georgina Bowyer and Morag Henderson, *Race Inequality in the Workforce*,
Carnegie UK Trust, UCL Centre for Longitudinal Studies and Operation

Black Vote (2020), https://cls.ucl.ac.uk/wp-content/uploads/2017/02/Race-Inequality-in-the-Workforce-Final.pdf. This is controlling for gender, social class background, housing tenure during adolescence, equivalised household income during adolescence, GCSE attainment and degree attainment. 'White British (non-private school)' here refers to all of the white group as above.

18  'UK Unemployment Rate by Ethnicity 2022', Statista (Nov. 2022), https://www.statista.com/statistics/1123370/unemployment-rate-in-the-united-kingdom-uk/. 'White British (non-private school)' here refers to all of the white group as above.

19  Simon Burgess and Ellen Greaves, 'Test Scores, Subjective Assessment, and Stereotyping of Ethnic Minorities, *Journal of Labor Economics*, 31/3 (July 2013), 535–576.

20  Caroline Finkel, *Osman's Dream: The Story of the Ottoman Empire 1300–1923* (John Murray, 2005).

21  Marlon Brando, 'That Unfinished Oscar Speech', *New York Times* (30 Mar. 1973), https://archive.nytimes.com/www.nytimes.com/packages/html/movies/bestpictures/godfather-ar3.html.

22  Arthur Martin, 'Duggan "was one of Britain's most violent gangsters": Inquest hears he was linked to ten shootings and two murders' *Daily Mail* (23 Sept. 2013), https://www.dailymail.co.uk/news/article-2430081/Mark-Duggan-Britains-violent-gangsters-Inquest-hears-linked-shootings.html.

23  Moustafa Bayoumi, 'They are "civilised" and "look like us": the racist coverage of Ukraine', *Guardian* (2 Mar. 2022), https://www.theguardian.com/commentisfree/2022/mar/02/civilised-european-look-like-us-racist-coverage-ukraine.

24  'Girls' Education', World Bank (10 Feb. 2022), https://www.worldbank.org/en/topic/girlseducation, accessed 6 Jan. 2023.

25  Jessica Elgot, 'Tories under pressure to suspend councillors over anti-Islam tweets', *Guardian* (30 May 2019), https://www.theguardian.com/news/2019/may/30/tories-under-pressure-to-suspend-councillors-over-anti-islam-tweets.

26  'Fox News in Ofcom breach for Birmingham "Muslim only" claim', BBC News (21. Sept 2015), https://www.bbc.com/news/uk-england-birmingham-34317107.

27  Brian Reed and Hamza Syed, *The Trojan Horse Affair* [podcast], Serial Productions, *New York Times* (Feb. 2022).

28  Samira Shackle, 'Trojan Horse: the real story behind the fake "Islamic plot" to take over schools', *Guardian* (1 Sept. 2017), https://www.theguardian.com/world/2017/sep/01/trojan-horse-the-real-story-behind-the-fake-islamic-plot-to-take-over-schools.

29  Brian Reed and Hamza Syed, *The Trojan Horse Affair*.

30  *The Week* staff, 'A history of the Trojan Horse scandal', *The Week* (17 Feb. 2022), https://www.theweek.co.uk/news/uk-news/955783/history-of-trojan-horse-scandal-true-story.

31 Sonia Sodha, 'The Trojan Horse Affair: how Serial podcast got it so wrong', *Guardian* (20 Feb. 2022), https://www.theguardian.com/commentisfree/2022/feb/20/the-trojan-horse-affair-how-serial-podcast-got-it-so-wrong.

32 Karla Hoff and Priyanka Pandey, 'Making up people – the effect of identity on preferences and performance in a modernizing society', Policy Research Working Paper Series, No. 6223 , The World Bank (2012).

33 Ilan Dar-Nimrod and Steven Heine, 'Exposure to Scientific Theories Affects Women's Math Performance', *Science*, (20 Oct 2006) 435.

34 Charlton McIlwain, 'Of course technology perpetuates racism. It was designed that way.', *MIT Technology Review* (3 June 2020), https://www.technologyreview.com/2020/06/03/1002589/technology-perpetuates-racism-by-design-simulmatics-charlton-mcilwain/.

35 George Joseph and Kenneth Lipp, 'IBM used NYPD surveillance footage to develop technology that lets police search by skin color', *The Intercept* (6 Sept. 2018), https://theintercept.com/2018/09/06/nypd-surveillance-camera-skin-tone-search/.

36 Kavitha Surana, 'How racial profiling goes unchecked in immigration enforcement', ProPublica (8 June 2018), https://www.propublica.org/article/racial-profiling-ice-immigration-enforcement-pennsylvania/.

37 Aaron Glantz and Emmanuel Martinez, 'For people of color, banks are shutting the door to homeownership', *Reveal* (15 Feb. 2018), https://revealnews.org/article/for-people-of-color-banks-are-shutting-the-door-to-homeownership/.

38 Kevin Rawlinson, 'Toby Young faces fresh calls for his sacking in misogyny row', *Guardian* (7 Jan. 2018), https://www.theguardian.com/media/2018/jan/07/toby-young-faces-fresh-calls-for-his-sacking-in-misogyny-row.

39 Martin Belam, 'Toby Young quotes on breasts, eugenics and working-class people', *Guardian* (3 Jan. 2018), https://www.theguardian.com/media/2018/jan/03/toby-young-quotes-on-breasts-eugenics-and-working-class-people.

40 Simon Kuper, *Chums: How a Tiny Caste of Oxford Tories Took Over the UK* (Profile, 2022).

41 Kristen Vogt Veggeberg, 'The History of the American Eugenics Movement', Illinois Science Council (3 Aug. 2020), https://www.illinoisscience.org/2020/08/the-history-of-the-american-eugenics-movement/.

42 Linda Villarosa, 'The Long Shadow of Eugenics in America', *New York Times Magazine* (8 June 2022), https://www.nytimes.com/2022/06/08/magazine/eugenics-movement-america.html.

43 Gavin Evans, 'The Unwelcome Revival of "Race Science"' *Guardian* (2 Mar. 2018), https://www.theguardian.com/news/2018/mar/02/the-unwelcome-revival-of-race-science.

44 Hannah Summers, 'Black women in the UK four times more likely to die in pregnancy or childbirth', *Guardian* (15 Jan. 2021), https://www.theguardian.

com/global-development/2021/jan/15/black-women-in-the-uk-four-times-more-likely-to-die-in-pregnancy-or-childbirth.

45  Kelly M. Hoffman, et al., 'Racial bias in pain assessment and treatment recommendations, and false beliefs about biological differences between blacks and whites' *PNAS*, 113/16 (4 Apr. 2016), https://www.pnas.org/doi/abs/10.1073/pnas.1516047113.

46  Zoe Williams, 'Want to go to Oxbridge but not terribly bright? Let Boris and Toby be your guides...' *Guardian* (13 Mar. 2019), https://www.theguardian.com/education/shortcuts/2019/mar/13/us-admissions-scandal-oxbridge.

47  Claire Phipps, Kevin Rawlinson and Rowena Mason, 'Toby Young resigns from the Office for Students after backlash', *Guardian* (9 Jan. 2018), https://www.theguardian.com/media/2018/jan/09/toby-young-resigns-office-for-students.

48  'Stop and search', Ethnicity facts and figures, GOV.UK, https://www.ethnicity-facts-figures.service.gov.uk/crime-justice-and-the-law/policing/stop-and-search/latest.

49  Nadine White, 'Black people 12 times more likely to be prosecuted for cannabis, new analysis shows', *Independent* (28 May 2021), https://www.independent.co.uk/news/uk/politics/black-people-cannabis-prosecutions-b1853669.html.

50  White, 'Black people 12 times more likely to be prosecuted for cannabis, new analysis shows'.

51  Nick Sommerlad, 'Tories blasted for links to medical cannabis industry despite UK ban on "life-saving" drug', *Mirror* (13 June 2018), https://www.mirror.co.uk/news/politics/tories-blasted-links-medical-cannabis-12701871.

52  *Reduction in Sentence for a Guilty Plea: Definitive Guideline*, Sentencing Council (Jan. 2017), https://www.sentencingcouncil.org.uk/wp-content/uploads/Reduction-in-Sentence-for-Guilty-Plea-definitive-guideline-SC-Web.pdf.

53  *The Lammy Review: an independent review into the treatment of, and outcomes for, Black, Asian and Minority Ethnic individuals in the Criminal Justice System* (8 Sept. 2017).

54  Rachel Makinson, 'LASPO: How A Near-Decade of Legal Aid Cuts Has Affected Britain's Most Vulnerable', *Lawyer Monthly* (26 Aug. 2021), https://www.lawyer-monthly.com/2021/08/laspo-how-a-near-decade-of-legal-aid-cuts-has-affected-britains-most-vulnerable/.

55  Nicola Harris, Roxanna Dehaghani and Daniel Newman, 'Vulnerability, the future of the criminal defence profession, and the implications for teaching and learning' *The Law Teacher*, 55/1 (2021), 57–67, https://doi.org/10.1080/03069400.2021.1872872.

56  'Inequality within Britain's legal aid funding system', BoltBurdonKemp (n.d.), https://www.boltburdonkemp.co.uk/campaigns/inequality-in-britains-legal-aid-funding-system/.

57  'High Court to decide whether victims of domestic violence should have access to Legal Aid – 12 December 2014', Rights of Women (12 Dec. 2014),

https://rightsofwomen.org.uk/media/high-court-decide-whether-victims-domestic-violence-access-legal-aid-12-december-2014/.

58  'Cuts to Legal Aid have "decimated access to justice" for thousands of the most vulnerable', Amnesty International UK (10 Oct. 2016), https://www.amnesty.org.uk/press-releases/cuts-legal-aid-have-decimated-access-justice-thousands-most-vulnerable.

59  Claire Burrows, 'The prison industrial complex, racism and immigration', Centre for Crime and Justice Studies (5 Aug. 2020), https://www.crimeandjustice.org.uk/resources/prison-industrial-complex-racism-and-immigration.

60  Sam Dean, 'Is this the end of private prisons?' *Telegraph* (18 Feb. 2017), https://www.telegraph.co.uk/business/2017/02/18/end-private-prisons/.

61  Jamie Grierson and Pamela Duncan, 'Private jails more violent than public ones, data analysis shows', *Guardian* (13 May 2019), https://www.theguardian.com/society/2019/may/13/private-jails-more-violent-than-public-prisons-england-wales-data-analysis.

62  'Privatising prisons is a disaster', We Own It (6 Aug. 2012), https://weownit.org.uk/public-ownership/prisons.

63  Gregmar Galinato and Ryne Rohla, 'Do privately-owned prisons increase incarceration rates?', *Labour Economics*, 67 (2020), https://doi.org/10.1016/j.labeco.2020.101908.

64  Galinato and Rohla, 'Do privately-owned prisons increase incarceration rates?'.

65  Sonia Rothwell, 'Public sector outsourcing: The political connections', *Channel 4 News* (29 Aug. 2012), https://www.channel4.com/news/public-sector-outsourcing-the-political-connections.

66  Press Association, 'Serco fined £22.9m over electronic tagging scandal', *Guardian* (3 July 2019), https://www.theguardian.com/business/2019/jul/03/serco-fined-229m-over-electronic-tagging-scandal.

67  Peter Geoghegan, Russell Scott and Caroline Molloy, 'Revealed: "Failing" Serco won another £57m COVID contract without competition', Open Democracy (16 Oct. 2020), https://www.opendemocracy.net/en/dark-money-investigations/revealed-failing-serco-won-another-57m-covid-contract-without-competition/.

68  'Ethnicity and the Criminal Justice System, 2020', Ministry of Justice, GOV.UK (2 Dec. 2021), https://www.gov.uk/government/statistics/ethnicity-and-the-criminal-justice-system-statistics-2020/ethnicity-and-the-criminal-justice-system-2020.

69  Ibram X. Kendi, *How to Be an Antiracist* (Oneworld, 2019).

70  Eric Williams, *Capitalism and Slavery* [doctoral dissertation], published in 1944.

71  Charisse Burden-Stelly, 'Modern U.S. Racial Capitalism.' *Monthly*

*Review* (1 July 2020), https://monthlyreview.org/2020/07/01/ modern-u-s-racial-capitalism/.

72 *Alone Together*, British Business Bank (21 Oct. 2020), https://www.british-business-bank.co.uk/research-alone-together.

73 *Alone Together*, British Business Bank.

74 Omar Khan, *The Colour of Money*, Runnymede Trust (2020), https://www.runnymedetrust.org/publications/the-colour-of-money.

75 Khan, *The Colour of Money*.

76 Edward Malnick, 'Museums told to stop pulling down statues or risk funding cuts', *Telegraph* (26 Sept. 2020), https://www.telegraph.co.uk/news/2020/09/26/museums-told-stop-pulling-statues-risk-funding-cuts/.

77 Ned Simons, 'Priti Patel Accuses England Football Team of "Gesture Politics" for Taking the Knee', *HuffPost UK* (14 June 2021), https://www.huffingtonpost.co.uk/entry/priti-patel-england-knee_uk_60c748ffe4b0c1abbe6ae0ee.

78 Nadine White and Ashley Cowburn, '"Institutional racism doesn't exist," government's race commission suggests in landmark report', *Independent* (31 Mar. 2021), https://www.independent.co.uk/news/uk/politics/race-commission-report-institutional-racism-b1824605.html.

79 Maya Goodfellow, *Hostile Environment: How Immigrant Became Scapegoats* (Verso Books, 2019).

80 2021 Census, ONS.

81 Emily Badger, et al., 'Extensive data shows punishing reach of racism for black boys', *New York Times* (19 Mar. 2018), https://www.nytimes.com/interactive/2018/03/19/upshot/race-class-white-and-black-men.html.

82 Gillian B. White, 'Black Workers Really Do Need to Be Twice as Good', *The Atlantic* (7 Oct. 2015), https://www.theatlantic.com/business/archive/2015/10/why-black-workers-really-do-need-to-be-twice-as-good/409276/.

83 'Will Britain ever have a Black Prime Minister? The probability model', BBC, https://www.bbc.co.uk/programmes/articles/3PzrtXmfxlVQWpkVb7D615X/will-britain-ever-see-a-black-prime-minister-the-probability-model.

## CHAPTER 7: EDUCATION: THE GREAT UN-EQUALISER

1 Sadiyah Zaman, 'State, Private and Grammar School; What's the Difference?', Tutor House (4 Aug. 2022), https://tutorhouse.co.uk/blog/state-private-and-grammar-school-whats-the-difference.

2 Laurie Long Kwan Ho, et al., 'Impact of Poverty on Parent–Child Relationships, Parental Stress, and Parenting Practices', *Frontiers in Public Health*, 10 (2022), https://doi.org/10.3389/fpubh.2022.849408.

3 Leonard Lopoo and Andrew London, 'How Does Household

Crowding Affect Education Outcomes?', Housing Matters (7 Mar.
2018), https://housingmatters.urban.org/research-summary/
how-does-household-crowding-affect-education-outcomes.

4   Kitty Stewart and Mary Reader, 'Prioritise early years to reduce childhood
    inequalities', LSE (10 May 2021), https://blogs.lse.ac.uk/covid19/2021/05/10/
    prioritise-early-years-to-reduce-childhood-inequalities/.

5   David Rubinstein and Colin Stoneman (eds), *Education for
    Democracy* (Penguin, 1970).

6   See Rethinking Economics, https://www.rethinkeconomics.org/.

7   Ann Pettifor, *The Coming First World Debt Drisis* (Palgrave Macmillan, 2006).

8   Janelle Mansfield, 'Harvard walks out of Econ 10', *The Tech* (2011, November
    15), https://thetech.com/2011/11/15/occupyharvard-v131-n52.

9   'Full text of Tony Blair's speech on education', *Guardian* (23 May 2001),
    https://www.theguardian.com/politics/2001/may/23/labour.tonyblair.

10  Jack Britton, Christine Farquharson and Luke Sibieta, *2019 annual report on
    education spending in England*, Institute for Fiscal Studies (19 Sept. 2019), https://
    ifs.org.uk/publications/2019-annual-report-education-spending-england.

11  Heather Stewart and Richard Adams, 'English schools to get three-year
    £14bn funding boost', *Guardian* (31 Aug. 2019), https://www.theguardian.
    com/education/2019/aug/30/english-schools-to-get-three-year-14bn-
    funding-boost.

12  Richard Adams, 'Education spending fall from 2010 to now was worst since
    1970s – IFS', *Guardian* (19 Sept. 2019), https://www.theguardian.com/education/
    2019/sep/19/education-spending-fall-from-2010-to-now-was-worst-since-1970s-
    ifs.

13  Adams, 'Education spending fall from 2010 to now was worst since 1970s – IFS'.

14  Harrison Jones, 'Gap between rich and poor university student numbers
    grows', *Metro* (30 July 2020), https://metro.co.uk/2020/07/30/
    gap-rich-poor-university-students-grows-13061711/.

15  See Figure 1, *Universities and Social Mobility: Summary Report*, The Sutton Trust
    (Nov. 2021), https://www.suttontrust.com/wp-content/uploads/2021/11/
    Universities-and-social-mobility-final-summary.pdf.

16  Diane Reay, *Miseducation: Inequality, education and the working classes* (Policy
    Press, 2017).

17  *A World Ready to Learn: Prioritizing Quality Early Childhood Education*, UNICEF
    (Apr. 2019), https://www.unicef.org/reports/a-world-ready-to-learn-2019.

18  J. Stiles and T. L. Jernigan, 'The Basics of Brain Development',
    *Neuropsychology Review*, 20 (2010), 327–348, http://dx.doi.org/10.1007/
    s11065-010-9148-4.

19  Kitty Stewart and Mary Reader, 'Prioritise early years to reduce childhood
    inequalities', LSE (10 May 2021), https://blogs.lse.ac.uk/covid19/2021/05/10/
    prioritise-early-years-to-reduce-childhood-inequalities/.

20 Portia Miller, et al., 'Wealth and child development: Differences in associations by family income and developmental stage', *RSF: The Russell Sage Foundation Journal of the Social Sciences*, 7/3 (2021), 154–174.

21 Imran Tahir, 'The UK education system preserves inequality – new report', The Conversation (18 Aug. 2022), https://theconversation.com/the-uk-education-system-preserves-inequality-new-report-188761.

22 Carl Cullinane and Rebecca Montacute, *Covid-19 and social mobility Impact Brief 1: School closures*, The Sutton Trust (2020), https://www.suttontrust.com/our-research/covid-19-and-social-mobility-impact-brief/.

23 Eleanor Busby, 'One in eight schools do not have library and poorer children more likely to miss out, study finds', *Independent* (16 Oct. 2019), https://www.independent.co.uk/news/education/education-news/school-library-reading-poorer-children-books-funding-cuts-austerity-study-a9158601.html.

24 'Pay Campaign', National Education Union (NEU) (2022), https://neu.org.uk/pay/pay-campaign.

25 *TALIS – The OECD Teaching and Learning International Survey 2018*, https://www.oecd.org/education/talis/.

26 Diane Reay, *Miseducation*.

27 Yekaterina Chzhen, et al., *An Unfair Start*, UNICEF (2018), https://www.unicef.org.uk/wp-content/uploads/2018/10/UN0245008.pdf.

28 Sol Gamsu, *Why are some children worth more than others? The private–state school funding gap in England*, Common Wealth (9 June 2021), https://www.common-wealth.co.uk/reports/why-are-some-children-worth-more-than-others.

29 *Programme for International Student Assessment (PISA) Results from PISA 2018: United Kingdom – Country Note*, OECD, 2018, https://www.oecd.org/pisa/publications/PISA2018_CN_GBR.pdf.

30 Yekaterina Chzhen, et al., *An Unfair Start*.

31 Robert De Vries, *Earning By Degrees*, The Sutton Trust (17 Dec. 2014), https://www.suttontrust.com/our-research/earning-by-degrees-salary-subject-university/.

32 Chris Belfield, et al., *The impact of undergraduate degrees on early-career earnings*, Institute for Fiscal Studies (27 Nov. 2018), https://ifs.org.uk/publications/impact-undergraduate-degrees-early-career-earnings

33 Source: Christine Farquharson, et al., *Education Inequalities*, Institute for Fiscal Studies (16 Aug. 2022), https://ifs.org.uk/inequality/education-inequalities/. Author's own calculations using: H. Espinoza, et al., 'Post-18 education – who is taking the different routes and how much do they earn?', Centre for Vocational Education Research, Briefing Note 013 (Sept. 2020). Reproduced with permission from authors.

34 Department for Education A-Level results data, 2018, 2019, https://www.gov.uk/government/statistics/a-level-and-other-16-to-18-results-2018-to-2019-revised.

35  Stuart Nicholson, 'How austerity policies are killing music education', *Jazzwise* (23 July 2019), https://www.jazzwise.com/opinion/article/how-austerity-policies-are-killing-music-education.

36  Lucy Dyer, 'Impact of austerity leaves schoolchildren at risk of missing out on music', *South West Londoner* (9 Nov. 2017), https://www.swlondoner.co.uk/life/09112017-impact-austerity-leaves-children-risk-missing-music.

37  *Consultation on recurrent funding for 2021–22*, Office for Students (26 Mar. 2021), https://www.officeforstudents.org.uk/publications/consultation-on-recurrent-funding-for-2021-22/.

38  Alan Smithers, *The Ins and Outs of Selective Secondary Schools*, (Civitas, 2015), https://alansmithers.com/reports/InsAndOuts.pdf.

39  'Apprenticeships and traineeships, Academic Year 2021/22', ONS (27 Jan. 2022), https://explore-education-statistics.service.gov.uk/find-statistics/apprenticeships-and-traineeships/2021-22.

40  'Skilled trades have "golden foundations" in Germany', Deutsch Centre International (22 July 2020), https://deutschcentre.com/skilled-trades-have-golden-foundations-in-germany/.

41  John Ydstie, 'Robust Apprenticeship Program Key to Germany's Manufacturing Might', NPR (4 Jan. 2018), https://www.npr.org/2018/01/04/575114570/robust-apprenticeship-program-key-to-germanys-manufacturing-might.

42  'Which electricians make the most money?', Payaca (21 Oct. 2022), https://www.payaca.com/post/which-electricians-make-the-most-money.

43  Ian Goldin, *Employment Transitions*, NYU Center on International Cooperation (14 Sept. 2021), https://cic.nyu.edu/resources/employment-transitions/.

44  Chris Rock, *Total Blackout: The Tamborine Extended Cut* (2021), Netflix special.

45  Raj Chetty, 'Social capital II: Determinants of economic connectedness', *Nature*, 608/7921 (2022), 122–134, https://doi.org/10.1038/s41586-022-04997-3.

46  Cathleen Stasz and Christian van Stalk, *The Use of Lottery Systems in School Admissions, Working Paper*, RAND (Jan. 2007), https://www.rand.org/content/dam/rand/pubs/working_papers/2007/RAND_WR460.pdf.

47  Stewart and Reader, 'Prioritise early years to reduce childhood inequalities'.

48  Trevor Male, 'The rise and rise of academy trusts: continuing changes to the state-funded school system in England', *School Leadership & Management*, 42/4 (2022), 313–333.

49  Bronagh Munro, 'Profits before Pupils? The Academies Scandal', BBC *Panorama* (15 Sept. 2018), https://www.bbc.co.uk/programmes/b0bk5q99.

50  'Save our Children's education! Allow failed academies to return to Local Authority', Change.org (2018), https://www.change.org/p/save-our-children-s-education-allow-failed-academies-to-return-to-local-authority-takebackourschools.

## CHAPTER 8: WHEN WORK KEEPS YOU
## IN YOUR PLACE

1   *Variety,* 'Kim Kardashian's Business Advice: "Get Your F**king Ass Up and Work"' [video], YouTube (uploaded 9 Mar. 2022), https://www.youtube.com/watch?v=XX2izzshRmI.

2   Cole Delbyck, 'Kim Kardashian Says "Get Your F**king Ass Up and Work" Remark Was "Taken Out Of Context"', *HuffPost* (28 Mar. 2022), https://www.huffpost.com/entry/kim-kardashian-says-get-your-fking-ass-up-and-work-remark-was-taken-out-of-context_n_6241be6ee4b0e340f6a6b9db.

3   Trevor Noah, *The Daily Show*, Comedy Central, 'Kim Kardashian Under Fire For Career Advice To Women' [video], YouTube (uploaded 11 Mar. 2022), https://www.youtube.com/watch?v=fcqKoMmKDEg.

4   Emma Munbodh, 'Dubai-based billionaires behind P&O Ferries as it axes 800 jobs amid living crisis', *Mirror* (17 Mar. 2022), https://www.mirror.co.uk/money/dubai-based-billionaires-behind-po-26494175.

5   Agencies, 'P&O Ferries will not face criminal proceedings for mass sacking of staff', *Guardian* (20 Aug. 2022), https://www.theguardian.com/business/2022/aug/20/po-wont-face-criminal-proceedings-for-mass-sacking.

6   David Cameron, *Live Lounge* interview, BBC Radio 1, April 2015.

7   'UK set for "worst real wage squeeze" in the G7', TUC (15 July 2022), https://www.tuc.org.uk/news/uk-set-worst-real-wage-squeeze-g7.

8   Claire Milne, 'Is wage growth at the same level as during the Napoleonic wars?', Full Fact (10 Nov. 2017), https://fullfact.org/economy/wage-growth-napoleonic-wars/.

9   'UK set for "worst real wage squeeze" in the G7', TUC.

10  Anna Cooban, 'UK workers suffer biggest hit to their wages since records began', CNN (16 Aug. 2022), https://www.cnn.com/2022/08/16/economy/uk-real-wages-biggest-drop-on-record.

11  Ethan Ilzetzki, 'If the UK is high tech, why is productivity growth slow? Economists weigh in', LSE (7 Mar. 2020), https://blogs.lse.ac.uk/businessreview/2020/03/07/if-the-uk-is-high-tech-why-is-productivity-growth-slow-economists-weigh-in/.

12  Alexander Guschanski and Özlem Onaran, 'The decline in the wage share: falling bargaining power of labour or technological progress? Industry-level evidence from the OECD', *Socio-Economic Review*, 20/3 (Mar. 2021), 1091–1124, https://doi.org/10.1093/ser/mwaa031.

13  Jack Copley, *Governing Financialization: The Tangled Politics of Financial Liberalization in Britain* (Oxford University Press, 2021).

14  Asher Schechter, 'The Rise of Market Power and the Decline of

Labor's Share', Pro Market (14 Aug. 2017), https://www.promarket.org/2017/08/14/rise-market-power-decline-labors-share/.

15 Thomas Piketty, *Capital in the Twenty-First Century* (2014; Harvard University Press, 2017).

16 Richard Partington, 'Four million British workers live in poverty, charity says', *Guardian* (4 Dec. 2018), https://www.theguardian.com/business/2018/dec/04/four-million-british-workers-live-in-poverty-charity-says.

17 'Benefits: Who Gets Them and How Much Do They Cost?' BBC News (5 Oct. 2022), https://www.bbc.co.uk/news/explainers-63129705.

18 Spencer Thompson and Izzy Hatfield, *Employee Progression in European Labour Markets*, IPPR (Feb. 2015), https://www.ippr.org/files/publications/pdf/employee-progression-EU-labour-markets_Feb2015.pdf.

19 'Executive pay at FTSE 100 firms recovers to pre-pandemic levels', PricewaterhouseCoopers (7 Nov. 2022), https://www.pwc.co.uk/press-room/press-releases/executive-pay-at-ftse-100-firms-recovers-to-pre-pandemic-levels.html.

20 See High Pay Centre, https://highpaycentre.org/.

21 David Milliken, 'UK CEO pay rebounds, gap widens with workers, report says', Reuters (23 May 2022), https://www.reuters.com/world/uk/uk-ceo-pay-rebounds-gap-widens-with-workers-report-2022-05-23/.

22 Cristobal Young, 'If you tax the rich, they won't leave: US data contradicts millionaires' threats', *Guardian* (20 Nov. 2017), https://www.theguardian.com/inequality/2017/nov/20/if-you-tax-the-rich-they-wont-leave-us-data-contradicts-millionaires-threats.

23 Dan Ariely, et al., 'Large stakes and big mistakes', *Review of Economic Studies*, 76 (2009) 451–469.

24 Theo Francis, 'Best-Paid CEOs Run Some of Worst-Performing Companies, *Wall Street Journal* (25 July 2016), https://www.wsj.com/articles/best-paid-ceos-run-some-of-worst-performing-companies-1469419262.

25 Wai Kwen Chan, 'UK economic outlook worsens as income inequality rises', *Financial Times* (25 May 2022), https://www.ft.com/content/073b0504-7cbc-4a40-b9cc-09a1d74956ea.

26 D. Clark, 'Average annual wages and salaries per household in the UK, by decile group 2020', Statista (28 Mar. 2022), https://www.statista.com/statistics/811418/average-annual-wages-and-salaries-per-household-uk/.

27 Laura Gardiner and Adam Corlett, *Looking through the hourglass – Hollowing out of the UK jobs market pre- and post-crisis*, Resolution Foundation (Mar. 2015), https://www.resolutionfoundation.org/app/uploads/2015/03/Polarisation-full-slide-pack.pdf.

28 Daniel Markovits, 'How McKinsey Destroyed the Middle Class, *The Atlantic* (3 Feb. 2020), https://www.theatlantic.com/ideas/archive/2020/02/how-mckinsey-destroyed-middle-class/605878/.

29 Yanitsa Petkova, 'Contracts that do not guarantee a minimum number of hours: April 2018', ONS (22 Apr. 2018), https://www.ons.gov.uk/ employmentandlabourmarket/peopleinwork/earningsandworkinghours/ articles/contractsthatdonotguaranteeaminimumnumberofhours/april2018.

30 Faiza Shaheen and Raquel Jesse, *Coronavirus and the Workers Emergency: Labour Market Realities 2020*, Centre for Labour and Social Studies (2020), http://classonline.org.uk/docs/Report_LMR2020_Workers_Emergency_ FinalAmends2.pdf.

31 'uberization' Wiktionary, https://en.wiktionary.org/wiki/uberisation, accessed 5 Jan. 2023.

32 Brian M. Carney, 'Let's uberize the entire economy', *Forbes* (27 Oct. 2014), https://www.forbes.com/sites/realspin/2014/10/27/ lets-uberize-the-entire-economy/?sh=e4c3d8b4c600.

33 Niamh McIntyre and Rosie Bradbury, 'The Eyes of Amazon: How the Tech Giant Secretly Watches Employees' Every Move From Afar', *The Defender* – Children's Health Defense (1 Dec. 2022), https://childrenshealthdefense.org/ defender/amazon-employee-surveillance/.

34 Business, Energy and Industrial Strategy Committee, *Working practices at Sports Direct inquiry*, UK Parliament (22 July 2016), https://old. parliament.uk/business/committees/committees-a-z/commons- select/business-innovation-and-skills/inquiries/parliament-2015/ working-practices-at-sports-direct-inquiry-16-17/.

35 Sara O'Brien, 'Uber's UK drivers to get paid vacation, pensions following Supreme Court ruling', CNN (16 Mar. 2021), https://www.cnn. com/2021/03/16/tech/uber-uk-vacation-pensions-drivers/index.html.

36 'The Fawcett Society announces date of Equal Pay Day 2021', The Fawcett Society (2021), https://www.fawcettsociety.org.uk/News/ the-fawcett-society-announces-date-of-equal-pay-day-2021?mc_ cid=479b2b7eba&mc_eid=9f173efeb8.

37 Asaf Levanon, Paula England and Paul Allison, 'Occupational Feminization and Pay: Assessing Causal Dynamics Using 1950–2000 U.S. Census Data', *Social Forces*, 88/2 (Dec. 2009), 865–891, https://doi.org/10.1353/sof.0.0264.

38 'Non-disabled workers paid 17% more than disabled peers – TUC', TUC (7 Nov. 2022), https://www.tuc.org.uk/news/ non-disabled-workers-paid-17-more-disabled-peers-tuc.

39 'One in eight young people without degrees work in graduate jobs', ONS (18 Sept. 2018), https://www.ons.gov.uk/employmentandlabourmarket/ peopleinwork/employmentandemployeetypes/articles/ oneineightyoungpeoplewithoutdegreesworkingraduatejobs/2018-09-18.

40 'One in eight young people without degrees work in graduate jobs', ONS.

41 'Growing proportion of UK graduates ending up in low-skilled jobs, where they experience lower levels of job and life satisfaction',

CIPD (4 Nov. 2022), https://www.cipd.co.uk/about/media/
press/041122-graduate-overqualification-cipd-report#gref.

42 *The National Minimum Wage: The Evidence of its Impact on Jobs and Inequality*,
   CEP (Sept. 2008), https://cep.lse.ac.uk/_new/publications/abstract.
   asp?index=3022.

43 Jonathan Cribb, et al., *The impact of the National Living Wage
   on wages, employment and household incomes*, Institute for Fiscal
   Studies (9 Dec. 2021), https://ifs.org.uk/publications/
   impact-national-living-wage-wages-employment-and-household-incomes.

44 Jasmine Urquhart, 'Third of workers living payday to payday, survey finds',
   *People Management* (28 June 2022), https://www.peoplemanagement.co.uk/
   article/1791426/third-workers-living-payday-payday-survey-finds.

45 Pippa Crerar, 'Leaked audio reveals Liz Truss said British
   workers needed "more graft"', *Guardian* (16 Aug. 2022),
   https://www.theguardian.com/politics/2022/aug/16/
   leaked-audio-reveals-liz-truss-said-british-workers-needed-more-graft.

46 'International comparisons of UK productivity (ICP), final estimates:
   2020', ONS (20 Jan. 2022), https://www.ons.gov.uk/economy/
   economicoutputandproductivity/productivitymeasures/bulletins/
   internationalcomparisonsofproductivityfinalestimates/2020.

47 Dominic Price, 'It's time to stop measuring productivity', *Work Life*
   (29 June 2022), https://www.atlassian.com/blog/productivity/
   the-problem-with-productivity-metrics.

48 Price, 'It's time to stop measuring productivity'.

49 Dr Issam Samiri and Prof. Stephen Millard, 'Why is UK Productivity Low
   and How Can It Improve?', NIESR (26 Sept. 2022), https://www.niesr.
   ac.uk/blog/why-uk-productivity-low-and-how-can-it-improve.

50 Clement Bellet, Jan-Emmanuel De Neve and George Ward, 'Does Employee
   Happiness have an Impact on Productivity?' Saïd Business School WP 2019–
   13 (14 Oct. 2019), https://doi.org/10.2139/ssrn.3470734.

51 Oscar Wilde, *The Picture of Dorian Gray*, (1891; Bernhard Tauchnitz, 1908).

52 Eilís Lawlor, Helen Kersley, Susan Steed, S. *A Bit Rich: Calculating the real
   value to society of different professions*, New Economics Foundation (14 Dec.
   2009), https://neweconomics.org/2009/12/a-bit-rich.

53 Committee on Communications, 'Children, Adolescents, and Advertising',
   *Pediatrics*, 118/6 (Dec. 2006), 2563–2569, https://publications.aap.org/
   pediatrics/article/118/6/2563/69735/Children-Adolescents-and-Advertising.

54 'Two-thirds of the public now support nurse strike, poll shows, as Royal
   College of Nursing announces increased strike payments for members',
   Royal College of Nursing (2 Sept. 2022), https://www.rcn.org.uk/
   news-and-events/Press-Releases/public-polling-story.

55 Sarah Cliffe and Ian Goldin, 'Our "soldiers" are not only in the

military – key workers face risks for us too', *Guardian* (8 May, 2021), https://www.theguardian.com/commentisfree/2021/mar/08/ soldiers-key-workers-protections-pay-pensions-risk-society.

56 'Rose Schneidermann in Ohio', *Life and Labor*, National Women's Trade Union League (Sept. 1912), https://babel.hathitrust.org/cgi/ pt?id=wu.89058506775.

57 Simply Sayo (@Simply_Sayo), TikTok post, 3 Apr. 2022, https://www.tiktok.com/@simply_sayo/video/7082420373060324614?is_from_ webapp=v1&item_id=7082420373060324614.

58 Precious Mayowa Agbabiaka, 'Why you're probably using "soft life" wrong', *i* (18 Aug. 2022), https://inews.co.uk/opinion/ why-youre-probably-using-soft-life-wrong-1800779.

59 David Graeber, *Bullshit Jobs: A Theory*, (2018; Simon & Schuster, 2019).

60 Will Stronge and Aidan Harper (eds), *The Shorter Working Week: A Radical and Pragmatic Proposal*, Autonomy (2019), https://autonomy.work/wp-content/ uploads/2019/02/Shorter-working-week-docV5.pdf.

61 Robert Booth, 'Is this the age of the four-day week?', *Guardian* (13 Mar. 2019), https://www.theguardian.com/world/2019/mar/13/ age-of-four-day-week-workers-productivity.

62 Jasper Jolly, 'A hundred UK companies sign up for four-day week with no loss of pay', *Guardian* (27 Nov. 2022), https://www.theguardian.com/ business/2022/nov/27/a-hundred-uk-companies-sign-up-for-four-day-week- with-no-loss-of-pay.

## CHAPTER 9: CHANGING OUR STORY OF SUCCESS

1 Gil Scott-Heron, TV interview, PBS, 1991.

2 Robert H. Frank, 'Why Luck Matters More Than You May Think', *The Atlantic* (May 2016), https://www.theatlantic.com/magazine/ archive/2016/05/why-luck-matters-more-than-you-might-think/476394/.

3 Mark Fisher, *Capitalist Realism: Is there no alternative?* (John Hunt Publishing, 2009).

4 'Just 8 men own same wealth as half the world', Oxfam International (16 Jan. 2017), https://www.oxfam.org/en/press-releases/ just-8-men-own-same-wealth-half-world.

5 Sarah O'Connor, 'Left behind: can anyone save the towns the UK economy forgot?', *Financial Times* (16 Nov. 2017), https://www.ft.com/blackpool.

6 Rosemary Rizq, 'States of Abjection in Managed Care' in John Lees, ed., *The Future of Psychological Therapy: From Managed Care to Transformational Practice* (Routledge, 2016).

7 Dan Ioan Dascălu, 'Individualism and mass communication in the context of

globalization', *Procedia – Social and Behavioral Sciences*, 163 (Dec. 2014), 1–6, https://doi.org/10.1016/j.sbspro.2014.12.278

8 Hamid Dabashi, 'Hollywood Orientalism is not about the Arab world', Al Jazeera (10 Nov. 2021), https://www.aljazeera.com/opinions/2021/11/10/hollywood-orientalism-is-not-about-the-arab-world.

9 Eunji Kim, 'Entertaining Beliefs in Economic Mobility', *American Journal of Political Science*, 67/1 (Jan. 2023), 39–54, https://doi.org/10.1111/ajps.12702.

10 Melanie C. Green, et al., 'Understanding Media Enjoyment: The Role of Transportation Into Narrative Worlds, *Communication Theory*, 14/4 (Nov. 2004), 311–327, https://psycnet.apa.org/doi/10.1111/j.1468-2885.2004.tb00317.x.

11 For instance, see Harold D. Lasswell, *Politics: Who Gets What, When, How* (1936; Pickle Partners Publishing, 2018).

12 John Berger, *Ways of Seeing* (1972; Penguin UK, 2008).

13 Xander Richards, 'BBC slammed for portraying Rishi Sunak as Superman', *The National* (31 July 2020), https://www.thenational.scot/news/18620765.bbc-slammed-portraying-rishi-sunak-superman/.

14 Jack Peat, 'Sunak ignores pleas for an Emergency Budget as he jets off to Santa Monica', *The London Economic* (4 Apr. 2022), https://www.thelondoneconomic.com/politics/sunak-ignores-pleas-for-an-emergency-budget-as-he-jets-off-to-santa-monica-318326/.

15 Matthew Parris, 'Wealth envy shouldn't bar Rishi Sunak from No 10', *The Times* (8 Apr. 2022), https://www.thetimes.co.uk/article/wealth-envy-shouldnt-bar-rishi-sunak-from-no-10-pkn23505w

16 Dr Lindsay Richards, 'Can we ever return to the Golden Age of social mobility?', The British Academy (15 Mar. 2016), https://www.thebritishacademy.ac.uk/blog/can-we-ever-return-golden-age-social-mobility/.

17 Roger Middleton, *The British Economy Since 1945.* (Palgrave Macmillan, 2000).

18 Stephen A. Marglin and Juliet B. Schor, *The Golden Age of Capitalism: Reinterpreting the Postwar Experience* (Oxford University Press, 1992).

19 *A New Generational Contract: The final report of the Intergenerational Commission*, Resolution Foundation (8 May 2018), https://www.resolutionfoundation.org/advanced/a-new-generational-contract/.

20 Derek Fraser, *The Beveridge Report: Blueprint for the Welfare State* (1st ed.), (Routledge, 2022), https://doi.org/10.4324/978100316740.2.

21 Social Mobility Commission, *Social Mobility Barometer 2019: Public views on social mobility*, GOV.UK (21 Jan. 2020), https://www.gov.uk/government/news/social-mobility-barometer-poll-results-for-2019#:~:text=The%20Social%20Mobility%20Commission's%202019,east%20and%2078%25%20of%20Londoners.

22 *Living longer: changes in housing tenure over time*, ONS (10 Feb. 2020), https://www.ons.gov.uk/peoplepopulationandcommunity/birthsdeathsandmarriages/ageing/articles/livinglonger/

changesinhousingtenureovertime#what-would-be-the-implications-of-an-
increase-in-older-people-renting-privately.

23  *England: Age and financing distribution homeowners 2022* (n.d.), Statista, https://
www.statista.com/statistics/321097/distribution-of-home-owners-in-england-
uk-by-type-of-home-financing-and-age/, accessed 4 Jan. 2023.

24  Dawn Foster, 'Right to buy: a history of Margaret Thatcher's controversial
policy', *Guardian* (7 Dec. 2015), https://www.theguardian.com/housing-
network/2015/dec/07/housing-right-to-buy-margaret-thatcher-data.

25  Guardian News, 'Suella Braverman blames "Guardian-reading, tofu-eating
wokerati" for disruptive protests #shorts' [video], YouTube (uploaded
19 Oct. 2022), https://www.youtube.com/watch?v=gTfo1Dm-oBA.

26  Raquel Jesse, *The Divide and Rule Playbook*, Centre for Labour and Social
Studies (CLASS) (6 Sept. 2022), http://classonline.org.uk/pubs/item/
the-divide-and-rule-playbook.

27  Isabel Wilkerson, *Caste: The Origins of Our Discontents* (Random House, 2020).

28  Moustafa Bayoumi, 'They are "civilised" and "look like us": the racist
coverage of Ukraine', *Guardian* (2 Mar. 2022), https://www.theguardian.
com/commentisfree/2022/mar/02/civilised-european-look-like-us-racist-
coverage-ukraine.

29  J. G. A. Pocock, 'The Classical Theory of Deference', *The American Historical
Review*, 81/3 (June 1976), 516, https://doi.org/10.2307/1852422.

30  'Boris Johnson did write that "blue collar" men are likely to be drunk,
criminal, aimless, feckless and hopeless', Full Fact (27 Feb. 2020), https://
fullfact.org/online/Boris-Johnson-working-men/.

31  Catherine Marshall, *Political Deference in a Democratic Age: British Politics and the
Constitution from the Eighteenth Century to Brexit* (Palgrave Macmillan, 2021).

32  Marshall, *Political Deference in a Democratic Age*.

33  These are the types of messages that were found to work in the UK: see
Raquel Jesse, *The UK race class narrative report*, CLASS (17 May 2022), http://
classonline.org.uk/pubs/item/the-uk-race-class-narrative-report.

34  Duncan Green, 'What can we learn from 200 case studies of "emergent
agency in a time of Covid"?' From Poverty to Power [blog] (17 Mar. 2021),
https://oxfamapps.org/fp2p/what-can-we-learn-from-200-case-studies-of-
emergent-agency-in-a-time-of-covid/, accessed 4 Jan. 2023.

35  Maria Fernandes-Jesus, et al., 'More than a COVID-19 Response: Sustaining
Mutual Aid Groups During and Beyond the Pandemic', *Frontiers in Psychology*,
12 (2021).

36  *Coronavirus and the Impact on UK households and businesses: 2020*, ONS (19
April 2021), https://www.ons.gov.uk/economy/nationalaccounts/
uksectoraccounts/articles/coronavirusandtheimpactonukhouseholds
andbusinesses/2020.

37  Guanlan Mao, 'How participation in Covid-19 mutual aid groups affects

subjective well-being and how political identity moderates these effects',
*Analyses of Social Issues and Public Policy*, 21/1 (2021), 1082–1112.

38  Ibn Khaldūn, *The Muqaddimah: An Introduction to History - Abridged Edition*
(written 1377; Princeton University Press, 2020).

39  Annie M (@teaceeme), Twitter post, 15.35, 9 Oct. 2021, 'Years ago a
teacher asked us to rank a list of professions in order of importance. Most
put medics at the top and bin men at the bottom until she carefully explained
how one prevents disease, the other treats it and we need both. A lesson I
never forgot.' Account has been deleted.

## CHAPTER 10: A LAND OF OPPORTUNITIES

1   John Rawls, *The Law of Peoples* (Harvard University Press, 1971).

2   Matt Padley, et al., *A Minimum Income Standard for the UK in 2022*, Joseph
Rowntree Foundation (2 Sept 2022), https://www.jrf.org.uk/report/
minimum-income-standard-uk-2022.

3   Padley, et al., *A Minimum Income Standard for the UK in 2022*.

4   Matthew Yglesias, 'The case for a maximum wage', *Vox* (6 Aug. 2014),
https://www.vox.com/2014/8/6/5964369/maximum-wage.

5   Rachel Kay and Luke Hildyard, *Pay Ratios and the FTSE 350: An analysis of
the first disclosures*, High Pay Centre (2020), https://highpaycentre.org/
pay-ratios-and-the-ftse-350-an-analysis-of-the-first-disclosures/.

6   *English Housing Survey, Private Rented Sector 2019–20*, Ministry of Housing,
Communities & Local Government, and National Statistics (2021), https://
assets.publishing.service.gov.uk/government/uploads/system/uploads/
attachment_data/file/1000052/EHS_19-20_PRS_report.pdf.

7   Carol Lewis, 'Average UK property costs seven times the typical
wage,' *The Times* (3 Oct. 2022), https://www.thetimes.co.uk/article/
average-uk-property-costs-seven-times-the-typical-wage-5qgj526q3.

8   Martin Williams, 'A quarter of Tory MPs are private landlords',
OpenDemocracy (22 July 2021), https://www.opendemocracy.net/en/
dark-money-investigations/quarter-tory-mps-are-private-landlords/.

9   Benjamín Nahoum and Raúl Vallés, 'The Uruguayan Experience: 50 years of
housing cooperatives' in Manuel Martín Hernández and Vicente Díaz García,
eds, *Visiones del Hábitat en América Latina: participación, autogestión, habitabilidad*
(Editorial Reverté, 2018).

10  Anna Ford, 'Mums doing lion's share of childcare and home-learning during
lockdown – even when both parents work', University of Sussex (21 June
2020), https://www.sussex.ac.uk/broadcast/read/52267.

11  Sean Fleming, 'These countries have the most expensive childcare', World
Economic Forum (23 Apr. 2019), https://bit.ly/3mOCzcH.

12  *Creating a Caring Economy: A Call to Action*, Women's Budget Group, https://wbg.org.uk/wp-content/uploads/2020/09/WBG-Report-v8-ES-1.pdf.

13  'Average childcare costs', Money Helper (n.d.), https://www.moneyhelper.org.uk/en/family-and-care/becoming-a-parent/childcare-costs.

14  Lester Coleman, Sam Shorto and Dalia Ben-Galim, *Childcare Survey 2022*, Coram Family and Childcare (2022), https://www.coram.org.uk/sites/default/files/resource_files/Coram%20Childcare%20Survey%20-%202022.pdf.

15  *LMF1.2. Maternal employment rates*, OECD Family Database (2020), https://www.oecd.org/els/family/LMF1_2_Maternal_Employment.pdf.

16  Gabrielle Meagher and Marta Szebehely, 'Equality in the social service state: Nordic childcare models in comparative perspective' in Jon Kvist, et al. (eds), *Changing Social Equality: The Nordic Welfare Model in the 21st Century* (Policy Press Scholarship Online 2012), https://doi.org/10.1332/policypress/9781847426604.003.0005.

17  Carmina Ravanera and Anjum Sultana, *A Feminist Economic Recovery Plan for Canada*, Gender and the Economy (July 2020), https://www.gendereconomy.org/a-feminist-economic-recovery-plan-for-canada/.

18  Cornelia Heintze, *On the Highroad – The Scandinavian Path to a Care System for Today: A Comparison between Five Nordic Countries and Germany*, WISO Diskurs, *Studies and Publications on Economic and Social Policy*, Politics and Society Forum and Friedrich-Ebert-Stiftung (Nov. 2013), https://library.fes.de/pdf-files/id/10333.pdf.

19  *Creating a Caring Economy: A Call to Action*, Women's Budget Group.

20  *Renewable Energy and Jobs – Annual Review 2020*, International Renewable Energy Agency (IRENA) (Sept. 2020), https://www.irena.org/publications/2020/Sep/Renewable-Energy-and-Jobs-Annual-Review-2020.

21  'A European Green Deal,' European Commission, https://ec.europa.eu/info/strategy/priorities-2019-2024/european-green-deal_en.

22  Renewable Energy Prospects: Germany, REmap 2030 analysis, International Renewable Energy Agency (IRENA), https://www.irena.org/-/media/Files/IRENA/Agency/Publication/2015/IRENA_REmap_Germany_summary_2015_EN.PDF.

23  Frank Martela, et al., 'The Nordic Exceptionalism: What Explains Why the Nordic Countries Are Constantly Among the Happiest in the World', *The World Happiness Report* (20 Mar. 2020), https://worldhappiness.report/ed/2020/the-nordic-exceptionalism-what-explains-why-the-nordic-countries-are-constantly-among-the-happiest-in-the-world/.

24  Nick Smith, 'North Sea oil: A tale of two countries', *E&T* (20 Jan. 2021), https://eandt.theiet.org/content/articles/2021/01/north-sea-oil-a-tale-of-two-countries/.

25  'How much money does the UK make from North Sea oil?', Viaro Energy https://www.viaro.co.uk/how-much-money-does-the-uk-make-from-north-sea-oil/.

26  *Who owns the wind, owns the future. Why we need public ownership of offshore wind in the UK*, Labour Energy Forum (Sept. 2017), https://transitioneconomics. net/wp-content/uploads/2022/02/who-owns-the-wind.pdf.

27  'Ultra-Millionaire Tax', Elizabeth Warren.com, https://elizabethwarren. com/plans/ultra-millionaire-tax, accessed 5 Jan. 2023.

28  'Poll shows 70% support raising taxes on rich, Patriotic Millionaires UK (21 Sept. 2022), https://www.patrioticmillionaires.uk/media/ release-poll-shows-70-support-raising-taxes-on-rich.

29  Attiya Waris, 'Solidarity Taxes in the Context of Economic Recovery Following the COVID-19 Pandemic,' NYU Center on International Cooperation (2021), https://cic.nyu.edu/publications/ solidarity-taxes-context-economic-recovery-following-covid-19-pandemic.

30  Chris Giles, 'IMF proposes "solidarity" tax on pandemic winners and wealthy', *Financial Times* (7 Apr. 2021), https://www.ft.com/ content/5dad2390-8a32-4908-8c96-6d23cd037c38.

31  Attiya Waris, 'Solidarity Taxes'.

32  Ben Tippet, Rafael Wildauer and Özlem Onaran, *The case for a progressive annual wealth tax in the UK, University of Greenwich* (2021), https://gala.gre.ac.uk/id/ eprint/33819/20/33819%20TIPPET_The_Case_for_a_Progressive_Annual_ Wealth_Tax_%282021%29_v2.pdf.

33  Ben Quinn, et al. 'Tory MP Neil Parish faces investigation over claims of watching pornography in Commons', *Guardian* (29 Apr. 2022), https:// www.theguardian.com/politics/2022/apr/29/tory-mp-neil-parish-faces- investigation-over-claims-of-watching-pornography-in-commons.

34  Graeme Demianyk, 'Neil Parish MP Discussed "Watching Porn" Allegation On TV Before Being Named', *HuffPost UK*, (29 Apr. 2022), https://www.huffingtonpost.co.uk/entry/ neil-parish-porn-commons-gb-news_uk_626c01cce4b04a9ff89b8de7.

35  Esther Webber, 'UK parliament dogged by misconduct claims as two more MPs suspended', *POLITICO* (8 Dec. 2022), https://www.politico.eu/article/ uk-parliament-misconduct-claims-julian-knight-conor-mcginn-mp-suspended- tory-labour/.

36  Sabrina Johnson, 'Sexist of the year prize "handed out at No 10 lockdown- breaking Christmas party"', *Metro* (2 May 2022), https://metro.co.uk/2022/05/02/ sexist-of-the-year-prize-handed-out-at-no-10-christmas-party-16568545/.

37  Darren McGarvey, *The Social Distance Between Us: How Remote Politics Wrecked Britain* (Ebury Press, 2022).

38  Celina Tebor, 'Feds have "concerns," but no punishment, for Amazon after deadly warehouse collapse in tornado', *USA TODAY* (26 Apr. 2022), https://www.usatoday.com/story/news/nation/2022/04/26/ amazon-illinois-warehouse-collapse-osha-punishment/9545707002/.

39  Annie Palmer, 'Amazon drivers sought safety at warehouse as tornado hit but

found only death and destruction', CNBC (20 Dec. 2021), https://www.cnbc.
com/2021/12/20/amazon-warehouse-in-illinois-hit-by-tornado-killing-6.html.

40 '"Thank Jeff Bezos for Space Trips": Amazon Labour Union Founder Has an
Iconic Message', News18 (2 Apr. 2022), https://www.news18.com/news/
buzz/thank-jeff-bezos-for-space-trips-amazon-labour-union-founder-has-an-
iconic-message-4935590.html.

41 Jodi Kantor and Karen Weise, 'How two best friends beat Amazon', New
York Times (14 Apr. 2022), https://www.nytimes.com/2022/04/02/business/
amazon-union-christian-smalls.html.

42 Amazon Labour Union (@amazonlabourunion), TikTok post, 2022, https://
www.tiktok.com/@amazonlaborunion/video/7080216176004992299.

43 Dave Jamieson, 'Amazon Spent $4.3 Million on Anti-Union Consultants
Last Year', HuffPost (31 Mar. 2022), https://www.huffpost.com/entry/
amazon-anti-union-consultants_n_62449258e4b0742dfa5a74fb.

44 K. Weise and N. Scheiber, 'Amazon Workers on Staten Island Vote
to Unionize', New York Times, (1 Apr. 2022), https://www.nytimes.
com/2022/04/01/technology/amazon-union-staten-island.html.

45 Gloria Oladipo, '"The revolution is here": Chris Smalls' union win
sparks a movement at other Amazon warehouses', Guardian (6 Apr.
2022), https://www.theguardian.com/technology/2022/apr/06/
chris-smalls-amazon-union-warehouses.

46 Carys Afoko and Daniel Vockins, Framing the economy: The austerity story, New
Economics Foundation (11 Sept. 2013), https://neweconomics.org/2013/09/
framing-the-economy.

47 Social Mobility Commission, Social Mobility Barometer – public attitudes
to social mobility in the UK, GOV.UK (11 Mar. 2021), https://www.
gov.uk/government/publications/social-mobility-barometer-2021/
social-mobility-barometer-public-attitudes-to-social-mobility-in-the-uk.

48 Faiza Shaheen, et al., From Rhetoric to Action: Delivering Equality & Inclusion,
NYU Centre on International Cooperation (Sept. 2021), https://www.sdg16.
plus/delivering-equality-and-inclusion.

# INDEX